THE SHORT STORIES OF THOMAS HARDY

THE SHORT STORIES
OF THOMAS HARDY

Kristin Brady

St. Martin's Press   New York

© Kristin Brady 1982

All rights reserved. For information, write:
St. Martin's Press, Inc., 175 Fifth Avenue,
New York, NY 10010
Printed in Hong Kong
First published in the United States of America in 1982

ISBN 0–312–72219–2

Library of Congress Cataloging in Publication Data

Brady, Kristin, 1949–
 The short stories of Thomas Hardy.

 1. Hardy, Thomas, 1840–1928—Criticism and
 interpretation. I. Title.
PR4754.B58   1981   823'.8   81–5665
ISBN 0–312–72219–2   AACR2

To my parents

Contents

Preface   ix

Acknowledgements   xi

Textual Note   xii

1 *Wessex Tales*: Pastoral Histories   1

2 *A Group of Noble Dames*: Ambivalent Exempla   51

3 *Life's Little Ironies*: Tragedies of Circumstance   95

4 Miscellaneous Stories: Reflections on a Career   157

Notes   203

A Selected Bibliography   219

Index   227

Preface

Thomas Hardy's novels have long been the subject of critical ◆ scrutiny and his poetry has recently begun to receive the recognition he always wanted it to have. His short stories, however, have never been seriously studied, except as an adjunct to his larger fictional canon. Generally, he has been considered a short-story writer manqué, a novelist writing in an unfamiliar genre. Yet some of Hardy's first attempts in fiction were short stories, and his productivity in the form increased as he felt more free to write what he pleased – after he had established himself, professionally and financially, as a novelist. Many of the best stories are products of his maturity and the careful organization of the short-story volumes especially demonstrates Hardy's own awareness of the themes and techniques that draw together his otherwise different narratives. The collections are themselves single fictional works. The aim of this study is to examine Hardy's short fiction in close detail in an attempt to understand his developing conception of the short story as a literary form. In many instances, the novels and poems are invoked in order to illuminate an aspect of a story or collection, but my chief concern is to study the short stories in isolation, as works of literature distinct from, though not utterly unlike, Hardy's other achievements in prose and verse. My focus is primarily on the narratives collected in *Wessex Tales*, *A Group of Noble Dames*, and *Life's Little Ironies* – not only because these are the works which Hardy freely chose to reprint, but also because they are artistic wholes in their own right and exemplify three distinct kinds of story in his fictional canon. Because *A Changed Man* was never considered by Hardy as a coherent fictional unit, my treatment of the stories in that volume is confined to a retrospective survey in the concluding chapter of all Hardy's short stories, collected and uncollected. This is not in itself a judgment on the quality of *A Changed Man* – though Hardy himself thought it inferior – but rather a decision to focus on those stories which Hardy considered his best, and which he collected into carefully ordered volumes.

Hardy's status as a writer of short fiction can be measured by the quality of his entire corpus, by its variety, and by his artistry in its individual forms. In each of the first three collections, there is discernible not only a particular kind of subject matter but also a correspondingly distinct narrative perspective which gives to the volume its own coherence and integrity. I have coined three descriptive terms to designate the forms that emerge from these different narrative perspectives: a specifically regional voice informs the 'pastoral histories' of *Wessex Tales*; the narrowly subjective view of the Wessex Field and Antiquarian Club makes it possible to think of their stories in *A Group of Noble Dames* as 'ambivalent exempla'; and the ironic stance of the voice in *Life's Little Ironies* turns ostensibly farcical situations into 'tragedies of circumstance'. My concern in making these distinctions is to argue not for generic differences between the collections but rather for variations, with some overlapping, in the prevailing mode of each. The stories are discussed individually and in the order of their arrangement in the volumes, but attention is also paid to the juxtapositions and thematic relationships among them. Stories which seem especially important are treated at greater length than others, with some reference to their sources and textual histories. The emphasis, however, is on the shape of the volumes as a whole and on the unique forms of their stories – evidence of Hardy's originality as a writer of the short story and his consciousness of what he called 'beauty of shape' and a 'well-knit interdependence of parts' in fiction. By discussing the short stories in terms of the organization Hardy chose to give them, I hope to provide a better understanding of the narratives themselves, and of the volumes in which they were collected.

Acknowledgements

I would like to acknowledge the financial aid of the Social Sciences and Humanities Research Council of Canada which made the work on this book possible. I am also grateful to the Trustees of the late F. E. Dugdale for allowing me to quote material from unpublished Hardy manuscripts and notebooks and to the Trustees of the Leslie Stephen Estate for permitting the publication of part of Stephen's 1880 letter to Hardy. A version of my discussion of 'On the Western Circuit' appeared in the *Journal of the Eighteen Nineties Society*, and the editor has kindly allowed me to reprint it here. My thanks are also due to Mr Roger Peers, Curator of the Dorset County Museum, who granted me access to the Museum's collection of unpublished Hardy materials.

It gives me pleasure to thank several friends and scholars who aided me in the composition and revision of this book. Professor Jane Millgate first inspired my interest in Victorian fiction, Dr Marjorie Garson offered many useful insights during the early stages of writing, and Avrum Fenson read a completed draft of the book with a sharp eye for problems in clarity and style. Dr Judith Williams brought her valuable editorial skills to the manuscript in the final stages of revision, and Rea Wilmshurst added to expert typing services her own high standards in proofreading. I am also indebted to readings of the manuscript by Professors Henry Auster, W. J. Keith, and Dale Kramer. My greatest debt, however, is to Professor Michael Millgate – for the generosity with which he made available the results of his own researches, for the cogency of his criticism and advice, and for the encouragement of his scholarly example.

Textual Note

Except where otherwise indicated, page references both in the notes and the text are to the Macmillan Wessex Edition as the source for Hardy's prose fiction, drama, and prefaces. For purposes of quotation, I have used printings of the Wessex edition (listed below) which include the revisions supplied by Hardy to Macmillan in 1919. Where the context does not indicate a source, parenthetical page references will include the following abbreviations:

A Changed Man	CM
Far from the Madding Crowd	FMC
A Group of Noble Dames	GND
Jude the Obscure	J
Life's Little Ironies	LLI
The Mayor of Casterbridge	TMC
Poems of the Past and the Present	PPP
The Return of the Native	RN
Tess of the d'Urbervilles	T
The Trumpet-Major	TTM
Two on a Tower	TT
Under the Greenwood Tree	UGT
Wessex Tales	WT
The Woodlanders	TW

Also included within parentheses in the text are page references to the following:

The Complete Poems of Thomas Hardy, ed. James Gibson (London: Macmillan, 1976)   CP

Florence Emily Hardy, *The Early Life of Thomas Hardy, 1840–1891* (London: Macmillan, 1928)   EL

——, *The Later Years of Thomas Hardy, 1892–1928* (London: Macmillan, 1930)   LY

1 *Wessex Tales*: Pastoral Histories

Until recently, Thomas Hardy's short stories have been ignored by critics and readers alike. Yet the tales occupy an important place in Hardy's career and an interesting, if minor, one in the development of narrative form. They were written between 1865 and 1900, a longer period than he devoted to novel writing and a time when the genre of the short story was only beginning to be accepted in England. Hardy himself used the terms story, tale, and novel interchangeably, and appears to have made no strict theoretical distinction between the novel and short story as literary genres. For him, a story *'worth the telling'* (*LY*, 158) was the single criterion for good fiction, and form was more a matter of 'shape'[1] than of length. In practice, however, he was forced to distinguish between short stories and novels because the two genres were differently perceived by the British public. When he began to write in the 1860s, the three-volume novel, preceded by magazine serialization, was the standard and most lucrative form of publication, while publishers were in general more reluctant than in America or on the Continent to print serious short fiction.[2] George Saintsbury reports that the story 'was very *un*popular' in the Victorian era 'and library customers would refuse collections of them with something like indignation or disgust'.[3] Probably for this reason, Hardy devoted most of his energy at the beginning of his career to novel writing and did not begin to write short fiction with any regularity until the 1880s. Even then, Hardy only published the occasional story in periodicals and did not collect any stories in volume form until the appearance of *Wessex Tales* in 1888. Yet *Wessex Tales* is the product of a writer with a sophisticated and confident sense of both the short story and the short-story collection as fictional genres. Hardy chose for it five of his best short stories ('A Tradition of Eighteen Hundred and Four' and 'The Melancholy Hussar of the German Legion' were added in 1912) and organized them into a book that is itself an artistic whole. The stories are all firmly grounded in Dorset life and folklore during the mid-nineteenth century and are drawn together by a unique narrative perspective, the pastoral voice.

The stories in *Wessex Tales* were written at a time when Hardy was frequently shifting his residence between rural Dorset and 'the contrasting world of London'.[4] This moving 'Between Town and Country'[5] gave him a clear sense of how Dorset's landscape and culture could be misunderstood by an outsider and contributed to his complaint in 'The Dorsetshire Labourer' (1883) that the 'dull, unvarying, joyless' caricature commonly called Hodge had begun to be taken as a typical representative of country life.[6] In *Wessex Tales* as in the other 'Novels of Character and Environment', Hardy counters this stereotypical image by presenting a scrupulously observed picture of the rural world based on the actual particularities of his native Dorset. Each story embodies Hardy's personal understanding of his local past, and communicates that vision by a narrative technique that makes it accessible to the non-native. Hodge becomes for the reader, as he is for Hardy, 'disintegrated into a number of dissimilar fellow-creatures, men of many minds, infinite in difference'.[7]

Wessex Tales reflects in its narrative details the social, economic, and cultural diversity of Dorset life. Within a narrow range (no aristocrats or gentry are presented), a complex hierarchy is portrayed, from the shepherds and artisans of 'The Three Strangers' to the relatively wealthy tradesmen of 'Fellow-Townsmen' and 'Interlopers at the Knap'. Most places described in the volume have factual counterparts in Dorset. The sheltered cove in 'A Tradition of Eighteen Hundred and Four' is probably Lulworth; the village in 'The Melancholy Hussar of the German Legion' is Bincombe, near Weymouth; the pond at which Gertrude Lodge stops on her way to Casterbridge is Rushy-Pond, located near Hardy's birthplace at Bockhampton; Port-Bredy of 'Fellow-Townsmen' is Bridport, the centre for a prospering flax and twine industry during the early nineteenth century, and one of the few manufacturing towns in Dorset at that time; the Knap of 'Interlopers' is based on the ancestral home of Hardy's mother's family at Towns End, Melbury Osmond; and Nether-Moynton of 'The Distracted Preacher' is Owermoigne, an isolated hamlet near the Dorset coast.

These and other details in *Wessex Tales* serve to establish the traditional and local character of the volume as a whole. References are often made to the present state of sites on which significant events occurred and to living persons who had known the principal characters, and although not all of the stories have first-person narrators, each to some degree is told as though it were taken from oral tradition. Much of the traditional material in *Wessex Tales* is, in fact, an amalgam of written and oral sources. Combined with stories Hardy heard from old people is the evidence – and inspiration – he gleaned from the 'casual relics' (*TTM*, vii) of the past that dotted the Dorset landscape, and from such documentary sources as newspapers and parish records. In the composition of 'The Melancholy Hussar', for example, Hardy drew upon all of these: he had talked with old people who had known the 'original' of Phyllis Grove, he knew where the two hussars were buried,[8] he examined old newspapers and church registers to find accounts of the execution and burials.[9] The story of 'The Withered Arm' came more exclusively from oral tradition,[10] but the details about smuggling in 'The Distracted Preacher' were variously gathered from verbal reports,[11] from information included in the 'Trumpet-Major Notebook',[12] and from a contemporary newspaper account of a trial which took place in 1830.[13]

As a group, the stories in *Wessex Tales* span more than four decades and take place at least thirty-five years before they were written. The two Napoleonic stories are the earliest in dating; 'The Three Strangers', 'The Withered Arm', and 'The Distracted Preacher' are set during the agricultural unrest of the 1820s and 1830s; and 'Fellow-Townsmen' takes place around 1845. It is harder to fix the date of 'Interlopers', but the fact that one of its characters, Mr Darton, is mentioned in *The Mayor of Casterbridge* would suggest that it too can be placed somewhere in the middle of the nineteenth century. Significantly, all of the stories are set a few decades before, or less than a decade after, Hardy's birth. This time-perspective allows Hardy – here and in the Wessex novels – to isolate the fictional world from his own while also seeing connections between them. Distant yet accessible, alien yet familiar, Dorset becomes an image of a world that is past but still remembered. An object of memory, it occupies a place in the imagination and acquires a firmness and wholeness that is impossible to find in any image of the fluid present. This is not to suggest that Hardy's image of Dorset is static, but to point to its integrity as a fictional place – its status, in short, as a microcosm. Dorset becomes Wessex.

Seen as a whole, *Wessex Tales* represents Hardy's most comprehensive single depiction of the fictional world that he called Wessex. The very discontinuity and disjointedness of the short-story volume – its varied settings, unchronological sequence, diversity of style and subject matter, and seeming haphazardness of arrangement – make it, when considered as a unit, a more complete portrayal of Wessex life than one novel could be. In miniature, it represents the effect of all the Wessex novels when seen together – documenting several levels of the Wessex past and filling in empty spaces on the Wessex map. It also depicts a variety of the ways of life that contribute to the economy and culture of Wessex and exemplifies the abundance of local modes of storytelling. Less coherent internally than any of the Wessex novels, its mosaic-like unity is all the more suggestive of the wide range of human experience that Wessex history comprises.

Underlying Hardy's comprehensive picture of country life is his deeper concern to present Wessex as a symbol. This strategy of subordinating realistic details to a symbolic pattern places *Wessex Tales* firmly in the tradition of pastoral. Numerous critics have noted that the use of pastoral as a literary technique is not confined to the conventions of its classical forms but rather is based upon 'the metaphorical and ironic relationship between the world created by the poet and the real world'.[14] Conventionally, the actual world and the poet's world have been compared in terms of the contrast between 'real' and 'ideal', but as William Empson makes clear, the pastoral contrast more precisely involves the 'process of putting the complex into the simple'.[15] The opposition of simple and complex leads to other contrasts: rural versus urban, regional versus non-regional, past versus present. Such pairings, in which there are bound to be some overlapping elements, force the reader to see his own world by comparing it not to an ideal place but to another fully realized world, one as fraught with suffering and difficulty as his own.

In *Wessex Tales*, Hardy exploits the tension in the discrepancy between historical Dorset and the reader's presumed simplistic image of it. This is done by satisfying the reader's nostalgic impulse for a glimpse of the rural past while presenting this image from a perspective he had not expected to have. His yearning for a simple world is undermined and replaced by his immediate emotional engagement in the events of the stories themselves. He thus becomes familiar with Wessex not as a focus for a retreat from his own world but as a point of comparison with it. By this process of comparison the reader achieves the conventional pastoral 'return' to the present. What was intended to be a withdrawal from the complexities of the moment becomes instead an act of identification with the deeply human dimension of historical Wessex, and this exercise of the sympathetic imagination in turn restores the reader to the present. In Shakespeare's pastoral dramas, the characters retreat temporarily from the court, come to a recognition about themselves in the wood, and return finally to their own world, seeing it with a new eye. In Hardy's pastoral histories, it is the reader who makes this journey of the self.

This 'journey' is made possible because the image of Wessex is so dense and self-contained that the reader begins to view it in terms of something outside itself. As John Lynen has noted, the regional world is 'at once particular in the extreme and, by virtue of this very particularity, a world of archetypes, or ideas'.[16] Lynen describes pastoral in terms that illuminate Hardy's phrase 'Character and Environment': 'The locality, we assume, shapes the man, and the more the poet dwells upon its distinctly local aspects, both as these appear in the landscape and are reflected in the human character, the closer he comes to seeing the life-process itself.'[17] The reader's perception of Wessex as a living organism, sustained by the relationship between its human characters and its locality or 'Environment', causes him to re-examine the 'life-process' of his own time in terms of the universals that unite Wessex and the present. In a small way Hardy's experience when visiting Venice illustrates this method: 'here to this visionary place I solidly bring in my person Dorchester and Wessex life; and they may well ask why I do it. . . . Yet there is a connection. The bell of the Campanile of S. Marco strikes the hour, and its sound has exactly that tin-tray *timbre* given out by the bells of Longpuddle and Weatherbury, showing that they are of precisely the same-proportioned alloy.' (*EL*, 252–3) The reader of Hardy's pastoral histories learns to discover the 'same-proportioned alloy' that connects Wessex with his own world.

'The Three Strangers' – a pastoral history in setting, subject matter, and narrative point of view – is a fitting introduction to *Wessex Tales*. Two of its chief characters are a shepherd and shepherdess, and its action takes place in an isolated 'pastoral dwelling' (7).* In the opening paragraphs, the situation of Shepherd Fennel and his family is presented in terms of how it would be misconstrued 'by dwellers on low ground'. Any 'commiseration for the shepherd' is 'misplaced', the reader is told, because this cottage is 'as cosy and comfortable a nook as could be wished for in boisterous weather' (4). Here Hardy is summarily educating the reader, disabusing him of misconceptions before he has a chance to use them. Similarly, many of the story's details are designed to instruct an outsider in precisely how the shepherd and his friends manage to derive a living from their environment. The tale reads almost like a set of stage directions, where each visual detail, gesture, and word contributes to the unravelling of a single mystery. This use of dramatic irony is linked to Hardy's interest, evident throughout his fiction, in the way experience is visualized and interpreted by the spectator. In 'The Three Strangers', the reader's act of puzzling out the scene is especially important because it depends on his ability to construe meaning in profuse regional detail.[18] The narrative is on one level a mystery story. On another, it uses the quasi-theatrical conventions of that genre – which force the reader to see details with an especially keen eye – to present scenes from rural life with the depth that can only be given them by someone who knows the subject from the inside.

*In this chapter only, page references to *Wessex Tales* appear without identifying initials.

To join dramatic plot and narrative point of view in this way is an essential aspect of Hardy's pastoral technique. Lynen observes that pastoral

> is always potentially dramatic, for it depends upon a perspective of sharp contrasts. It portrays the town in terms of the country, the rich in terms of the poor, the complex in terms of the simple, and thus it works through a sense of conflict, through opposed points of view, through the ironic difference between people and classes. The very subject matter of pastoral produces the tensions suitable for drama.[19]

In 'The Three Strangers', the plot is worked out entirely in terms of dramatic conflicts. Set against the universal conflict between man and Nature is that between Shepherd Fennel's generosity and his wife's frugality, and – more fundamentally – that between the rural man's sense of justice and the urban man's sense of law. All of these levels of opposition are presented by a narrative voice consistently aware of the reader's own possibly erroneous preconceptions about rural life.

The opening paragraphs of the story, especially, attempt to give the reader a balanced view of the pastoral scene. Images of a pastoral ideal and realistic details are placed side by side. The pastoral image is not so much refuted by this juxtaposition as it is modified and extended in order to assimilate the harshness as well as the beauties of rural life. The downs, desolate 'during the long inimical seasons', are pleasing to artists and thinkers 'in fair weather' (3); the rainy night is fierce, but the shepherd's cottage is warm and cosy. Nature is a capricious force, sometimes over-generous and sometimes niggardly in its gifts:

> For at Higher Crowstairs, as at all such elevated domiciles, the grand difficulty of housekeeping was an insufficiency of water; and a casual rainfall was utilized by turning out, as catchers, every utensil that the house contained. Some queer stories might be told of the contrivances for economy in suds and dish-waters that are absolutely necessitated in upland habitations during the droughts of summer. But at

this season there were no such exigencies; a mere acceptance of what the skies bestowed was sufficient for an
abundant store.   (8–9)

Though this passage appears merely as informative local
colour, it expresses a truth about rural life that is reiterated
throughout the story: Nature's excesses must be controlled
and put to use in her sparing moments. This logic applies to
children and to mead as well as to rainwater. A birth is a 'glad
cause' for celebration, but one that 'a man could hardly
wish . . . to happen more than once a year' (10). The 'old
mead of those days' is delightful, but its supply is always
limited, since it is 'brewed of the purest first-year or maiden
honey' (14).

The conflict between Shepherd and Shepherdess Fennel
represents two complementary ways in which the countryman
can regard Nature. The shepherd is willing to be generous
with his hospitality and to take life as it comes, while his wife
insists on preparing for what the future may bring. He
celebrates the present christening (their second), while she
anticipates more of them. This is not the crazed hoarding of
the second Mrs Day in *Under the Greenwood Tree*, but the
prudence of one who must conserve her guineas 'till they
should be required for ministering to the needs of a coming
family' (5–6). In her careful housewifery, the shepherdess
counterbalances her husband's utter confidence in Nature's
beneficence, and as a kind of caricature of rural frugality
lends a comic aspect to the christening scene. At a deeper
level, however, she personifies an important principle of rural
life, the need to think of famine even while feasting.

The contrast between the shepherd and his wife serves to
highlight the more important contrast between the first two
strangers, the man who is sentenced to be hanged, and the
man who is designated by law to perform the execution.
Timothy Summers and the hangman provide the most
dramatic opposition in the story between the rural and the
urban worlds. Every action of each is emblematic of his
understanding of rural life and his position in its social,
economic, and moral structure. From the moment that
Summers arrives at the crossing outside the cottage, his
movements bespeak desperation, quick wit, and a resource-

fulness dependent upon his thorough knowledge of the countryman's way of life. In order not to betray his thirst, he drinks 'a copious draught' (9) of rainwater before entering the cottage. He quickly anticipates what questions will be asked him as a stranger at such a social gathering, and answers them with adept care – explaining away his ill-fitting shoes, fending off with flattery the shepherdess's inquiries about his native place, and offering the information that he is a wheelwright by trade. Without divulging his identity, Summers provides answers to the questions asked of a stranger in the rural world: 'But what is the man's calling, and where is he one of?' (15)

It is with the arrival of the second stranger that Summers's actions become curious, for what had earlier seemed the manner merely of 'a careless and candid man' (10) becomes that of one who, on the face of things at least, is overstepping the bounds of rural hospitality. It is permissible for him to take a place by the fire and to ask for a pipe and tobacco but, as the frugal shepherdess is quick to note, it is beyond the limits of a guest's rights to offer a second guest the family mug. Only at the story's conclusion does the reader realize that Summers's apparently presumptuous gestures are in fact those of a man intent on seeming to any subsequent arrivals a familiar at the christening feast.

The manners of the hangman are at first glance similar to those of Summers. But the same behaviour which in Summers betokens his desperate position and profound understanding of country ways is in the hangman a manifestation of personal arrogance and his position as an urban outsider. The initial description of the second stranger contrasts him with the first, and emphasizes his identity as a city person:

This individual was one of a type radically different from the first. There was more of the commonplace in his manner, and a certain jovial cosmopolitanism sat upon his features. He was several years older than the first arrival, his hair being slightly frosted, his eyebrows bristly, and his whiskers cut back from his cheeks. His face was rather full and flabby, and yet it was not altogether a face without power. A few grog-blossoms marked the neighbourhood of his nose. He flung back his long drab greatcoat, revealing that beneath it he wore a suit of cinder-gray shade throughout, large heavy seals, of some metal or other that would take a polish, dangling from his fob as his only personal ornament. (12)

The sensuality apparent in this physical description is also reflected in the hangman's actions, and his disregard for the mead's preciousness shows an insensitivity to the rhythms of rural life. The inappropriateness and callousness of the joke that he loves old mead 'as I love to go to church o' Sundays, or to relieve the needy any day of the week' (14) is obvious even at the point when it is told – only Summers laughs because in his precarious position he 'could not or would not refrain from this slight testimony to his comrade's humour' (14) – and the comment seems even more tasteless when Summers's crime is finally seen to have been impelled by desperate need.

It is necessity, indeed, which defines the distinction between the first and second strangers. Both overstep the bounds of hospitality and tell riddles about themselves, but from utterly different impulses. Summers's actions are deceitful and misrepresent his real character, but they are designed to enable him to escape the unjust consequences of a crime he committed out of need and without guile. His moral position in the story is bolstered by his trade. As a watchmaker, he is a member of the class of village craftsmen which Hardy praised in 'The Dorsetshire Labourer' as 'the backbone of the village life'.[20] Written in the same year as 'The Three Strangers', the essay laments that this class in particular, more 'interesting and better-informed' than that of the agricultural labourer, was being forced to move to cities by landowners who were tearing down cottages when life-leases ran out.[21] Such circumstances, familiar to the guests at Shepherd Fennel's feast whose sympathy is with 'the poor clock-maker we heard of' (18), would be of little interest to the hangman, who as an outsider would see all in the local community as 'a uniform collection of concrete Hodges'.[22]

That the hangman does regard the guests of the christening feast in just this way is made clear in his extemporaneous song addressed to 'Simple shepherds all' (19) and in his more callous expression of the same sentiment – note that 'simple' becomes 'simple-minded' – when he is speaking to Summers alone: 'These shepherd-people are used to it – simple-minded souls, you know, stirred up to anything in a moment' (23). The hangman's insensitivity to the complex nature of the persons he is dealing with and the difficult conditions under which they live is one of the story's central ironies, intensified when his powerful position in the legal structure of their society is revealed. The mention of his 'cinder-gray' suit has a sinister tone, and the imagery associated with him is distinctly demonic:

> Instinctively they withdrew further and further from the grim gentleman in their midst, whom some of them seemed to take for the Prince of Darkness himself, till they formed a remote circle, an empty space of floor being left between them and him –
> '... *circulus, cujus centrum diabolus.'* (19–20)

The Latin quotation could refer to the ability of a conjuror to call up the devil and to contain his power by drawing a chalk circle around him. In any case, it is clear that the rural community instinctively rejects the hangman, not indigenous to its locality or way of life, as an instrument of justice.

The hangman was a potent figure in the rural imagination, and this was especially true before 1832, when a man could still be hanged – as in the time of the *Second Shepherd's Play* – for stealing sheep (2 & 3 Wm IV, c. 62). Ruth Firor has noted that an 'almost universal contempt for the hangman was as great in Hardy's Wessex as ever it was in Elizabethan times',[23] but it is also true, as Hardy's preface to *Wessex Tales* indicates, that the rural mind held the hangman in peculiar esteem. A man whom Hardy knew as a boy consoled himself for not achieving the office by dwelling 'upon striking episodes in the lives of those happier ones who had held it with success and renown' (vii), and Hardy asserts that, as a child, he never questioned the 'nobleness' (viii) of the man's ambition. 'The Three Strangers', however, examines the position of the hangman in rural society from a more mature point of view. Implicit in the story's conclusion, where an unspoken law of the countryside protects Summers, is a judgment on the nature and the extent of the delegated power of this 'man of the baleful trade' (24). The community's decision to ally itself with Summers is not, however, conscious or intellectual, as the

farcical scenes with the constable indicate. A reliance on the
staff as a symbol of his authority from the king demonstrates
the constable's unquestioning belief in the power of law, but
his confusion about what authority to invoke when making an
arrest testifies to his acceptance of other forms of power as
well. After rejecting the challenge of the thief – 'Your money
or your life!' (24) – he instinctively invokes the name of God
before realizing that it is the king's authority he is exercising:
'Prisoner at the bar, surrender, in the name of the Father –
the Crown, I mane!' (25) Like the altercations between the
shepherd and shepherdess over the mead, this comic scene
has a serious underside in the questions it raises about legal
authority.

The story's judgment about the hangman can fairly be
made because it is part of a more comprehensive presentation
of a distinct society with its own laws and values, in which
Timothy Summers, who steals only to survive and who escapes
death by cajoling the man who is to hang him, can be seen as a
folk hero.[24] Only by understanding and absorbing the local
point of view can the reader see Summers as such a figure. It is
interesting that in the year that 'The Three Strangers' was
published Hardy mentioned his admiration of Mark Twain's
Life on the Mississippi,[25] for this work, though utterly different
in style, subject matter, and structure from anything Hardy
wrote, is based on an important premise that governs the
shaping of 'The Three Strangers' and underlies the pastoral
mode of its narrative voice: that a thorough, practical knowledge of a single way of life can by its very specificity suggest
general truths about human experience. As Hardy wrote in a
notebook, 'I am convinced that it is better for a writer to know
a little bit of the world remarkably well than to know a great
part of the world remarkably little.'[26] In 'The Three Strangers', as in all of Hardy's Wessex novels and stories, the social,
economic, and moral intricacies of life in a particular locality
form an essential aspect of the narrative's meaning.

Like 'The Three Strangers', 'A Tradition of Eighteen
Hundred and Four' is on one level an exercise for the reader
in learning to construe rightly what he encounters in the rural
world. But while a proper understanding of 'The Three
Strangers' depends on the reader's acceptance of the attitude
of the narrative voice, the correct interpretation of this second

story requires a recognition that its narrator is not reliable. Told by a garrulous old man and at the same time based on an accumulation of supportive details, 'A Tradition' incorporates into its narrative technique an ambiguity and tension derived from the natural tendency to romanticize the past. In 1919 Hardy considered this technique quite self-critically:

> A curious question arose in Hardy's mind at this date on whether a romancer was morally justified in going to extreme lengths of assurance – after the manner of Defoe – in respect of a tale he knew to be absolutely false. Thirty-seven years earlier, when much pressed to produce something of the nature of a fireside yarn, he had invented a picturesque account of a stealthy nocturnal visit to England by Napoleon in 1804, during the war, to spy out a good spot for invasion. Being struck with the extreme improbability of such a story, he added a circumstantial framework describing it as an old local tradition to blind the reader to the hoax. (*LY*, 194–5)

Hardy's 'case of conscience' emerged when his invented story itself became the source of a tradition, and he worried that he had been 'too natural in the art he could practise so well' (*LY*, 195). But it is difficult to accept Hardy's bald admission that the story is a 'hoax' (perhaps by 1919 he had forgotten the full complexity of his original intentions), for to see its details as aimed only to deceive is to ignore those other dimensions of the plot that undermine the foundations of its 'circumstantial framework', and direct the reader toward the tale's central subject – not the episode itself, but the process of storymaking and storytelling that makes a narrative part of a local tradition. A tendency to elaborate on an experience, and in so doing to be believed, would especially have contributed to the traditions associated with the Napoleonic era – the most exceptional and romantic period of recent Wessex history. Seen in this light, the very particulars used to disguise the story's falseness as an actual tradition have more interest and substance than the events of the plot.

The key to a correct interpretation of 'A Tradition of Eighteen Hundred and Four' lies in Hardy's sustained use – unusual in his fiction – of the first-person narrator. The story is told by someone who heard it at the fireside of an inn more than a decade earlier from Solomon Selby, who himself had witnessed the events as a young child. Most of the narrative is told in Solomon's own words, but they are framed at the beginning and end by the remarks of the unnamed narrator, whose presence reminds the reader that the story was originally directed toward a particular captive audience. The fireside setting in the midst of a rainstorm and Solomon's use of such phrases as 'as you mid know' (33) and 'as you mid suppose' (39) are ways of drawing this audience into believing what is known, Solomon says, neither to any 'maker of newspapers or printer of books', nor to any 'gentry who only believe what they see in printed lines' (36). And the audience's unquestioning acceptance of Solomon's tale is demonstrated by the narrator's reference to the old man's convincing 'manner of narrating the adventure' (41).

The reader's task is to separate himself both from Solomon and from his audience, and to consider the story as spoken by an unreliable narrator whose evidence must be scrutinized closely. Despite the slighting reference to 'the incredulity of the age' (40), such scepticism is necessary to bring out the full richness of this 'Tradition' – perhaps more appropriately named in its periodical publication, 'A Legend of the Year Eighteen Hundred and Four'.[27] So regarded, even the story's first sentence sheds some doubt on the tale's absolute truth: 'The widely discussed possibility of an invasion of England through a Channel tunnel has more than once recalled old Solomon Selby's story to my mind' (33). The narrator is reminded of the tale by the fears of invasion current in the 1880s, just as the tradition itself emerged from the fears of a previous generation. Details within Solomon's narration confirm the reader's suspicion that the story is the product of a frightened and fascinated imagination. Uncle Job's drinking, his own tendency to tell tall tales, and his obvious enjoyment in impressing his young nephew, combined with Solomon's youthful romanticism and utter belief in his uncle's stories, make it questionable that the boy could have seen events with a clear eye. This is most transparent in the passage which introduces the reputed visit by Napoleon:

While we lay there Uncle Job amused me by telling me

strange stories of the wars he had served in and the wounds he had got. He had already fought the French in the Low Countries, and hoped to fight 'em again. His stories lasted so long that at last I was hardly sure that I was not a soldier myself, and had seen such service as he told of. The wonders of his tales quite bewildered my mind, till I fell asleep and dreamed of battle, smoke, and flying soldiers, all of a kind with the doings he had been bringing up to me. (37)

Here young Solomon identifies almost completely with his uncle's glamorous exploits, and immediately after he has wakened from his romantic dreams he sees the two men whom he takes to be Napoleon and one of his officers. It is quite possible, therefore, either that he is still dreaming or that his fantasies have influenced the way he regards the newcomers.

A number of details cast further doubt on Solomon's interpretation of what he so vividly thinks he saw. His description of Napoleon seems more influenced by portraits he has seen 'a hundred times' (39) than by his memory of what he witnessed during a brief interval by lamplight, and there is a small inconsistency in his account of what he heard the men saying. He remarks first that they 'spoke in a tongue that was not ours – in French, as I afterward found' (38), while his report of the dialogue with his uncle suggests that he immediately recognized the foreign language as French. But what makes Solomon seem most unreliable as a narrator is his utter lack of irony regarding his past self, demonstrated by the seriousness with which he reports Uncle Job's hilarious reaction (possibly a performance for the child's benefit): 'O that I had got but my new-flinted firelock, that there man should die! But I haven't got my new-flinted firelock, and that there man must live.' (39)

It is impossible to say whether Hardy intended his reader to follow the example of the narrator and accept Solomon's improbable story – thus making it truly a hoax – or whether he purposely planted these seeds of doubt in the tale. One possible way of making sense of 'A Tradition' would be to consider the two references to smuggling operations in the area as a clue to what Solomon actually witnessed. It is perfectly conceivable that the men he saw were engaged either in the smuggling itself, or, as their uniforms suggest, in its detection. It is also possible that the men were members of the · King's German Legion stationed nearby, and speaking German rather than French – a theory supported by the fact that the 'boat-cloaks, cocked hats, and swords' (38) that Solomon saw bear a noticeable resemblance to the British uniform of the time.[28] Such interpretations allow the reader to discount the romantic elaborations of fact by an impressionable young boy without rejecting the convincing circumstantial details of his story.

To look at the events of 'A Tradition of Eighteen Hundred and Four' in this way not only elucidates the story's plot but also leads the reader to a consideration of its proper subject matter. If the story is a hoax, then its victim is not the discerning reader, but rather Solomon and his fireside audience who have allowed their own romantic predispositions to colour their interpretations of what they see and hear. Regarded in this way, 'A Tradition' is a depiction of the possible falseness of the oral tale, which depends so heavily not only on the honesty but also on the clearheadedness of its sources. Whether or not the story can be believed, moreover, it has, when one considers its place in *Wessex Tales*, an underlying truth. By presenting a speaker and an audience so accepting of such a story Hardy brings to life for the reader the continuing vitality, even in the 1880s, of the Napoleonic era in the communal imagination of Wessex.

To an even greater degree than 'A Tradition of Eighteen Hundred and Four', 'The Melancholy Hussar of the German Legion' draws the reader into a place and time foreign to his own experience. Here the reader's task is not to doubt the narrator's veracity, but rather to absorb his judgments in order to share his vivid understanding of Phyllis Grove's story. Hardy immediately establishes the credibility of this narrator, who is forty-seven and who heard the story at the age of fifteen from its heroine – a close correlation with Hardy's reported account that he learned of it from an old woman in 1855.[29] Unlike Solomon, this speaker is not concerned to tell his own story, but rather to narrate the correct version of a tale that has been mistold countless times before. If he has a bias, it lies in his sympathy for Phyllis, but this in turn is balanced by his posture of mature distance. He is old enough to have discounted the romantic illusions of his youth, but not yet aged enough to return to them with the old person's propensity and authority to embellish. He is therefore selective in the stories he chooses to repeat: 'Is it necessary to add that the echoes of many characteristic tales, dating from that picturesque time, still linger about here in more or less fragmentary form, to be caught by the attentive ear? Some of them I have repeated; most of them I have forgotten; one I have never repeated, and assuredly can never forget.' (46) The single fact that this narrator has forgotten other stories, while waiting twenty years after Phyllis's death to right the 'injustice' inflicted 'upon her memory' (46), suggests that he is, unlike Solomon, a man of caution and circumspection.

This narrator is an especially useful device for creating a pastoral tale based on a contrast between past and present. Himself too young to have witnessed these events, he shares the reader's interest in what actually happened, while possessing a more profound sense of the historical and cultural background which created the story. Details are seen not through the distorting lens of a nostalgic memory like Solomon's, but through the clarifying lens of intelligent historical investigation, which reconciles remembered particulars of oral tradition with the written chronicles of the time and, finally, with a firm imaginative grasp of the human situation underlying the story. Hardy's reason for creating such a compassionate narrator may have been that, as he said in his 1896 preface to *Life's Little Ironies*, 'The Melancholy Hussar' had

such a hold upon myself for the technically inadmissible reasons that the old people who gave me their recollections of its incidents did so in circumstances that linger pathetically in the memory; that she who, at the age of ninety, pointed out the unmarked resting-place of the two soldiers of the tale, was probably the last remaining eyewitness of their death and interment; that the extract from the register of burials is literal, to be read any day in the original by the curious who recognize the village.[30]

Like Hardy, the narrator is aware of gaps in the reader's

knowledge, and his storytelling technique involves a careful explanation not only of what happened, but – more essentially – of how these events must have been perceived by the characters themselves. In the first paragraph, his repeated use of the present tense and of the word 'here' impresses upon the reader the close relationship in his mind between past and present. The 'unchanged' quality of the downs, with their 'distinct traces' of the regimental camp, makes it 'impossible' (45) for him to avoid hearing and seeing the York Hussars in their tents. By this process of meditation on the events of the past, the narrator conjures up the story of Phyllis's romance with the melancholy hussar.

In a tale with a particular historical setting, one of the pastoral narrator's intentions is to educate his reader in the social and cultural assumptions of the time. This aim is evident in the description of the hussars, presented specifically as they were regarded by their contemporaries: 'Soldiers were monumental objects then. A divinity still hedged kings here and there; and war was considered a glorious thing.' (45) In a similar manner, the narrator makes a point of explaining to the 'present generation' (49) the extent of the 'solitude in country places ... in those old days' (47), and the social magnitude of Phyllis's engagement to Humphrey Gould: 'In those days unequal marriages were regarded rather as a violation of the laws of nature than as a mere infringement of convention, the more modern view, and hence when Phyllis, of the watering-place *bourgeoisie*, was chosen by such a gentlemanly fellow, it was as if she were going to be taken to heaven' (48). All of these instructive asides show the reader that Phyllis's romantic attachments are a reflection of her limited experience. She accepts Gould's marriage proposal because it is a good match from a social point of view, and falls in love with Matthäus Tina because he represents the 'golden radiance' of the York Hussars which 'flashed in upon the lives of people here, and charged all youthful thought with emotional interest' (49).

But these reactions in Phyllis can be linked as much to her alienation from the local culture as to her assimilation of its conventional attitudes, and again it is the narrator's analysis of her position which makes this fact comprehensible to the reader. Phyllis is presented as an isolated and deracinated figure, forced by her father into a life which has no roots either in urban or in rural culture. Dr Grove is the kind of character, often found in Hawthorne and Faulkner, whose propensity for introspection and abstraction separates him from any human considerations. His move to the country, like that of Fitzpiers in *The Woodlanders*, is a perverse expression of a sentimental impulse. He abandons his medical practice in order to indulge his 'taste for lonely meditation over metaphysical questions', and retreats to a country garden where he stays 'the greater part of the day, growing more and more irritable with the lapse of time, and the increasing perception that he [has] wasted his life in the pursuit of illusions' (47). The effect on Phyllis of her father's withdrawal from the world is that her life is wasted even before she has the chance, as he had had, to pursue youthful illusions. In this, her situation (though not her character) is similar to Eustacia Vye's: originally from Budmouth, she is not 'a native of the village, like all the joyous girls around her' (56).

This feeling of inadequacy causes Phyllis to value her suitors for those things she finds wanting in herself. Humphrey Gould, whom she admires for the 'methodical and dogged way in which he sometimes [takes] his pleasure' (48) and for 'his knowledge of what the Court [is] doing' (48–9), appeals to her by his self-confidence and urbanity. At the same time, she is drawn to Tina out of a need for love, both parental and sexual. Lacking these things herself, she is 'infected' with the hussar's 'own passionate longing for his country, and mother, and home' (56). Phyllis and Tina see each other as romantic images. He first perceives her as a vision against the sky, 'her white raiment ... showing conspicuously in the bright sunlight' (50), while she views him as 'almost an ideal being ... with none of the appurtenances of an ordinary house-dweller; one who had descended she knew not whence, and would disappear she knew not whither; the subject of a fascinating dream – no more' (54). Phyllis finally turns away from Gould – as solid as the metal his surname brings to mind – in favour of the illusory 'radiance' of her foreign hussar, an 'unrealistic person' (55) who presents her with a marriage proposal that is 'wild', 'vague', and 'venturesome' (59).

Out of a naive sense of honour, however, Phyllis then

betrays Tina and stays behind in Wessex to 'preserve her self-respect' and thus to let 'esteem . . . take the place of love' (60). It is obviously this point about Phyllis's essential un-selfishness which finally impels the narrator to do for her what she herself 'never attempted' – 'to excuse her conduct' (57). He emphasizes an intricacy in the plot that may have led Hardy to collect the story first in *Life's Little Ironies*. Phyllis's decision to stay behind is based both on a coincidental twist of fate (the arrival of Gould's coach just as she is waiting for her lover) and upon what Mary Caroline Richards calls 'an irony of mistaken action from ignorance of facts'[31] – of the fact, in particular, that Gould is married to another woman. The 'handsome looking-glass in a frame of *repoussé* silverwork' (61) is an appropriate image to focus this irony in the story's plot, for it is actually an emblem of Gould's falseness to Phyllis. He presents it to her as a sop 'to propitiate 'ee' (62) and as a bribe to impel her, not to act honourably, but to join in his deception of his father.

Without the presence of the story's narrator, this irony of real versus illusory, and of false versus true suitors, would appear as a superficial theme, dependent merely on an ingeniously contrived plot. But the narrator's profound understanding of Phyllis's story, achieved by his informed empathy for her isolated position in rural society, finally gives her an important place in local oral tradition and in the visual hieroglyphics of the Wessex landscape. In the story's tragic conclusion, she becomes a truer and more visible inhabitant of Wessex than the girls who formerly were more 'pre-cisely . . . of the village' (49) than she. At the same time, through this experience of suffering, Phyllis for the first time develops a feeling of association with her own local landscape. She cherishes both the place 'at the bottom of the garden where she had been accustomed to climb the wall to meet Matthäus' (63), and his grave, which she tends and points out to later generations. In this way, she makes the hussars too a part of local history. Buried far from their respective home-lands, they now belong to the oral tradition of the alien soil in which they lie.

It is through the first-person narrator of 'The Melancholy Hussar' – a native who can translate his local knowledge into a form that is comprehensible to the outsider – that the story achieves its profound pathos. His mature and informed vantage point makes him the perfect spokesman for the 'older villagers' of the locality 'who know of the episode from their parents', and who 'still recollect the place where the soldiers lie' (66). In many of Hardy's other pastoral histories, as in 'The Three Strangers', no storyteller is ever identified, but this actual narrator resembles the implicit narrators of those stories in the qualities which make his tale both convincing and compelling – his compassion, his concern for historical accuracy, and his insistence upon portraying the rural world in such a way that its values can be understood by those who live outside it.

In 'A Tradition' and 'The Melancholy Hussar' a cultural milieu is presented through a speaker whose relationship to the facts is quite specifically defined, but 'The Withered Arm' has a form closer to that of a real folk tale. There is an oral quality to its prose style, but it has no actual narrator with a personal motive for telling his story. The tale seems, indeed, to have survived a whole line of tellers who have, while leaving it intact, refined and updated its content. This accounts for the occasional references which betray the story's relative modernity. The mention of 'those days, when men were executed for horse-stealing, arson, and burglary' (95), suggests a time markedly different from the present, while the references to photography and galvanism clearly address themselves to a Victorian audience. The third-person narration also contributes to the story's neutrality toward its less credible facts: the impartial distance from events in this narrative voice allows the story to establish its own credence. It would be difficult to explain away the coincidence of the time of Rhoda's dream with the noises her son heard and with the moment that the pain shot through the arm of Gertrude Lodge, or to doubt entirely the authority of the conjuror, who rightly perceives the nature of Gertrude's ailment, and whose white magic does show her the face of her maligner. Nor is it easy to challenge the direct statement that '"the turn of the blood," predicted by the conjuror, had taken place' (106). Even with the story's references to new developments in science, it remains consistent as a folk tale.

The few equivocating remarks about supernatural phenomena were inserted into 'The Withered Arm' only after its original periodical publication. The most striking change occurs in the sentence introducing Rhoda's vision. The first edition reads, 'Rhoda Brook dreamed, since her assertion that she really saw, before falling asleep, was not to be believed', but in the *Blackwood's* version the conclusive 'since' is a speculative 'if'.[32] This alteration and others were probably inspired by the criticism of Leslie Stephen, in a letter written a few days after 'The Withered Arm' first appeared, maintaining that the tale is weakened by the lack of a material explanation for its less believable aspects:

> I don't think that you have exactly hit off the right line of belief. Either I would accept the superstition altogether and make the wizard a genuine performer – with possibly some hint that you tell the story as somebody told it; or I would leave some opening as to the withering of the arm, so that a possibility of explanation might be suggested, though, of course, not too much obtruded. Something, *e.g.* might have happened to impress the sufferer's imagination, so that the marks would be like the stigmata of papists.
>
> As it is, I don't know where I am. I begin as a believer and end up as a sceptic.[33]

Considering the specificity and extensiveness of Stephen's suggestions, the changes Hardy made are quite minor: he took no steps toward presenting the story as a superstition told by an unreliable narrator, and the phrases of equivocation which he did add in no way undermine one's belief in the withering of the arm, the powers of the conjuror, or the turning of the blood, but merely add a few late nineteenth-century scientific speculations about those otherwise unquestioned events. These small concessions are consistent with the remarks Hardy later made that 'a story dealing with the supernatural should never be explained away in the unfortunate manner of Mrs. Radcliffe', and that the letter from Stephen represented 'a dull and unimaginative example of gratuitous criticism'.[34] Hardy's sticking so firmly to his convictions in the face of suggestions from a critic he regarded highly reveals his own artistic purpose in presenting the story as a believed folk tale, demanding of its reader the same degree of respect and acceptance that it would receive from a local audience. The reader must learn that the story's less plausible details give it a particular psychological truth: the power of Rhoda's mind over her rival is so strong that it can only be expressed in an image which challenges belief. The story as a whole, in other words, creates its own extravagant ambiance.

The superstitions in 'The Withered Arm' already existed both in the Dorset culture that Hardy knew and in more universal forms of folklore. Freud called overlooking (a term for consciously or unconsciously causing evil to happen to another person) one of 'the most uncanny and wide-spread forms of superstition'[35] and it is possible that Hardy derived the idea of the withered limb from Shakespeare's Richard III, who thinks he has been overlooked by his brother's wife and Jane Shore, his brother's former mistress:

> Look how I am bewitch'd; behold mine arm
> Is, like a blasted sapling, wither'd up.
> And this is Edward's wife, that monstrous witch,
> Consorted with that harlot strumpet Shore,
> That by their witchcraft thus have marked me.
> (*Richard III*, III.iv.68–72)

Hardy's private notebooks (*EL*, 220–1, 268–9)[36] and published works,[37] as well as numerous Dorset records abound with anecdotes about conjuring and overlooking[38] and grisly tales of hangings. Hardy may have been attempting to give a special authority to the conjuror's powers by calling him 'Trendle', a form of the Anglo-Saxon word meaning circle – a mystical symbol in magic and religion. 'Trendle' is also the name of a hill near Cerne Abbas displaying a primitive human figure of huge dimensions connected even during Hardy's lifetime with fertility rituals.[39] This would suggest a link between Trendle's powers and the pre-Christian ones that reputedly still survived in the giant of Trendle Hill and in the numerous primitive rings that dotted the Dorset landscape.

Despite its superstitious content, however, the method of description in 'The Withered Arm' is more realistic than fantastical, and supernatural occurrences are consistently presented in terms of the historical, social, and even physical circumstances which surround and create them. The description of the hanging, for example, accurately reflects the atmosphere surrounding such events in early nineteenth-century Dorchester. It is carefully maintained that Conjuror Trendle is also 'a dealer in furze, turf, "sharp sand," and other local products' (88), while Hangman Davies is a 'jobbing gardener' (102). Insistently realistic details make vivid the cottages of Rhoda, the conjuror, and the hangman – as well as the dairy, with its 'large, red, rectangular animals' (69). The narrator's repeated comparisons between past and present, involving references to Enclosure Acts and the changing terrain of Wessex, also give the story a realistic framework. These particulars give credence to the less probable aspects of the narrative, while also placing it on a different footing altogether from the conventional story of the supernatural. The reader is compelled not only to suspend his disbelief – as with the reading of a ghost or fairy story – but also to immerse his sensibility in the actual circumstances which give life to the beliefs the story embodies.

This mixture of the historical with the imaginative groundwork of the story, a function of its pastoralism, is established in the opening description of the 'eighty-cow dairy' on which Rhoda works – much like Talbothays Dairy of *Tess* in its size and capitalist structure, whereby a dairyman rents cows from a landowning farmer, and in which certain workers are only 'supernumerary' (69).[40] But the dairy is actually a mixture of new and old, of entrepreneurial and feudal values, for the labourers continue to wear the traditional 'wropper' of the milkman and to hang their pails on the 'many-forked stand made as usual of the peeled limb of an oak-tree, set upright in the earth, and resembling a colossal antlered horn' (70). The 'as usual' of this sentence was added in 1912 – an effort, it would seem, to emphasize the stand's traditional shape and use. The dairy is thus an emblem of its transitional time, exemplifying the beginnings of modern agricultural organization and management in its status as a rented farm, but continuing to appear 'old-style' in its appurtenances and in the garb of its workers – as well as in their superstitious beliefs.

The initial depiction of this setting is dependent more on vivid dialogue than on description. In a pair of conversations – one among the dairy labourers, the other between Rhoda and her son – the reader is led to infer, from a carefully arranged accumulation of linked facts, Rhoda's entire situation: her past with Farmer Lodge, her present employment on one of his outlying farms, her distanced relationship with her neighbours and fellow workers, her impoverished circumstances, her feelings of fascination and envy for Lodge's pretty wife, and her boy's somewhat reckless nature. The questions Rhoda puts to the boy about Gertrude directly invoke the conventions of the ballad or folk tale. She asks repeatedly, not only about her rival's colouring and stature, but 'if her hands be white' (71)[41] and if she is 'ladylike' (74). Rhoda is interested, of course, in Gertrude's social standing, but her preoccupation with the young wife's hands, dress, and manners serves to sharpen the differences between the two women and to underline their opposing physical, social, and moral attributes: dark and fair, tall and short, strong and weak, poor and wealthy, rejected and beloved, guiltily vengeful and innocently victimized. Such a persistent contrasting of the two female characters points toward a symbolic interpretation of the forces at work in the tale. The powers of the civilized 'Lodge' are pitted against those of the rustic 'Brook'.

But in a deeper sense the two women can be seen as similar or complementary, even while they are dramatically opposed. While Rhoda's name means 'rose', Gertrude's face is 'soft and evanescent, like the light under a heap of rose-petals' (72). They are like different views of one image – Rhoda its tangible, actual aspect, and Gertrude its illusory and 'evanescent' part. This pairing is given a psychological dimension by the immediate attraction felt between the two women, inspired by the very physical features that make them appear so dissimilar:

> Rhoda said she was well enough; and, indeed, though the paler of the two, there was more of the strength that endures in her well-defined features and large frame than in the soft-cheeked young woman before her. The conversation became quite confidential as regarded their powers and weaknesses. (80)

Between the two women is a complex interplay of the 'powers

and weaknesses' drawing them together. The rejected one is the stronger, while the favoured one is weak; and the wronged woman comes eventually to be linked with witchcraft, while the triumphant one becomes the victim. There are two spells cast in the story: one unwittingly worked by Rhoda on Gertrude in her nightmare, and the other, equally without conscious source, by Gertrude, who through an indefinable force of fascination comes to inhabit Rhoda's mind. The two women continually fluctuate between affection and hostility toward each other. While Rhoda's feelings toward her sexual rival gradually soften, Gertrude is transformed from a benevolent handmaiden of mercy to a frantically self-absorbed woman. Finally, in the hanging scene at Caster-bridge, they are both utterly caught up in their own private feelings of grievance. Gertrude is so desperate for a cure that she wishes against the possibility of a reprieve for the convicted arsonist and refers to him as 'it' (103) even before he is a corpse, while Rhoda, stripped to the elemental level of her psyche which had emerged in the dream, sees Gertrude as a 'Hussy' (106) who is shattering this single moment of unity with her lover and child.

But just at this point, when the two women finally enact the physical struggle of Rhoda's dream, the narrator shifts the reader's attention to the real victim of the story: the boy who earlier had been pitifully attracted to Gertrude and her position of elegance in the parish. The child's overwhelming solitariness is the result of his unnatural relationship with his parents. His mother puts a clean shirt on him for church, but never, either by word or gesture, demonstrates affection for him; his father is indifferently irked by his presence, but never acknowledges his existence. The boy is made to live by his wits – his mother encourages his poaching – and the reckless-ness early demonstrated by his 'cutting a notch with his pocket-knife in the beech-backed chair' (71) is the predictable outcome of his neglected state. All of these facts about the nameless boy take on added significance when connected with the pathetic image of the 'body of a young man, wearing the smockfrock of a rustic, and fustian breeches' (106). Suddenly this child of conflicting impulses – so hard in his nature, yet so vulnerable when in the presence of affection and beauty – is given an important symbolic position in the tale.[42] This manipulation of the story's symbolism implicates the reader himself in the negligence which has led to the boy's death. Particulars about the boy's character have been dropped here and there, but attention has never been centred on him, except as the symbol of Rhoda's union with Lodge. In a sense, he has been neglected by the story itself, as well as by its characters. The final recognition scene thus involves everyone – Rhoda, Gertrude, Lodge, the reader, and society in general – in the shared guilt of having allowed the boy to come to such an end, and consequently draws the reader into the rural world he had originally seen only from the outside. He becomes not only a believer but also a participant in the story.

The remarkable extent to which 'The Withered Arm' challenges the reader's judgment and prods his conscience may bear some relation to Hardy's own emotional involvement with its events. As with 'The Melancholy Hussar', he claims to have known persons who were acquainted with some of the principal figures of the story and to have based it on actual incidents in local tradition, but here he includes in addition some of his own most deeply felt memories. Gertrude's view of the gallows from Rushy-Pond, with its focus on the 'white flat façade' (99) of the jail, recalls Hardy's recollection of a hanging he witnessed with the aid of a telescope from the same site: 'The sun behind his back shone straight on the white stone façade of the gaol, the gallows upon it, and the form of the murderer in white fustian, the executioner and officials in dark clothing and the crowd below being invisible at this distance of nearly three miles' (*EL*, 37). The Hangman's Cottage, pictured in the frontispiece of the 1912 *Wessex Tales*, was still inhabited by the executioner during the mid-nineteenth century, and Henry Nevinson reports that Hardy showed him 'the railings he used to climb as a boy to watch the hangman having his tea at a cottage in a hollow below on the evening before an execution, and wonder how the man could eat anything so soon before his terrible task'.[43] Hardy may have been thinking of his own youthful self when mentioning that Gertrude found the Hangman's Cottage with the help of 'a boy' (101).

Because it adds moral judgment to childish fascination, the most significant detail from Hardy's memory is the correspondence between the hanging of Rhoda's eighteen-year-old son merely because he was 'present by chance' (102) when a rick was fired, and an execution Hardy's father had described to him. He told Newman Flower:

> My father saw four men hung for *being with* some others who had set fire to a rick. Among them was a stripling of a boy of eighteen. Skinny. Half-starved. So frail, so underfed, that they had to put weights on his feet to break his neck. He had not fired the rick. But with a youth's excitement he had rushed to the scene to see the blaze. . . . Nothing my father ever said to me drove the tragedy of Life so deeply into my mind.[44]

These remarks, in which Hardy reveals just how closely the events of 'The Withered Arm' were based on personal memories and preoccupations, indirectly describe the impact of the story on the reader. Like Hardy, he comes to a sudden perception of the 'tragedy of Life'; like Lodge, he leaves the story 'chastened and thoughtful' (107).[45] This end is achieved because the story portrays with such density of reference the specific tragedy that emerged from a definite place and time in the history of Wessex, while at the same time drawing the reader into itself to such an extent that these boundaries are extended and transcended. This grounding of the general in the particular is an important aspect of pastoralism, which, by defining differences between past and present and between rural and urban, points to the essential sameness in all human experience.

The rural-urban contrast implicit in the earlier stories is expanded in 'Fellow-Townsmen', a pastoral history set in a small provincial town. In this it has interesting links with *The Mayor of Casterbridge*, published six years later, which also portrays the complex relationship between town and country in a place where they are contiguous and interconnected. In Casterbridge bees and butterflies can travel unimpeded down High Street while flying from the 'cornfields at the top of the town . . . to the meads at the bottom' (*TMC*, 65), while in Port-Bredy the 'shepherd on the east hill [can] shout out lambing intelligence to the shepherd on the west hill, over the intervening town chimneys' (111). Just as in *The Mayor of*

Casterbridge he had recorded the arrival of the railway in Dorchester, so Hardy includes in the chronology of 'Fellow-Townsmen' the same event in Bridport history.[46] In Port-Bredy, however, there is more conflict between rural and urban than in Casterbridge, which is 'the complement of the rural life around; not its urban opposite' (*TMC*, 65). In this town nature and man stand in silent opposition. The hills look 'lovely above the old roofs', but make 'every low-chimneyed house in the town as smoky as Tophet'; the rope-walks are 'overhung by apple-trees and bushes, and intruded on by cows and calves, as if trade [has] established itself there at considerable inconvenience to Nature' (126); and what appears to be a natural harbour has resisted for ten centuries all 'human industry to finish it and make it famous' (132).

This setting reflects a corresponding conflict within the personality of the story's main character, Mr Barnet – a man born to the profits, and the burdens, of his town's industry. His story is the antithesis of a traditional tale. While previous stories have demonstrated how people (even outsiders) can become part of local tradition, 'Fellow-Townsmen' deals with a contrasting set of circumstances: how a man whose family has been in a town for two hundred years can be forgotten within one generation. Having no work, no children, and no wife with local ties of her own, Barnet uproots himself from his town just as definitely as he abandons the house his grandfather had built and bequeathed to him. When Barnet returns to 'the town of his fathers' (162) after twenty-one years, he is forgotten by everyone but Lucy Savile and Charlson. Like his surname, which was dropped from the titles of local firms, his memory is erased from town history, and the house he built – the only remaining visible emblem of himself – is assumed to be the ancestral seat of its later occupants. Barnet's fate is different even from that of Farmer Lodge, who also comes from an old local family and ends his days in exile. Lodge goes to Port-Bredy to escape the memory of his past actions;[47] Barnet leaves the same place because of a failure to act.

Like Phyllis Grove, Barnet is presented not as a natural inhabitant of the place in which he lives but rather as a figure alienated from it. His position is defined mainly in terms of his inherited state of privileged unemployment: 'He was probably the first of his line who had ever passed a day without toil, and perhaps something like an inherited instinct disqualifies such men for a life of pleasant inaction, such as lies in the power of those whose leisure is not a personal accident, but a vast historical accretion which has become part of their natures' (147). Where the narrator describes the community of Port-Bredy, it appears as a contrast to Barnet, rather than as a context for him. His surname is 'used allusively by small rising tradesmen as a recommendation' (117), but he can identify neither with the self-employed shopmen nor with their hired help. The only relationship he can maintain with these people is to sign his name on their small deposits of money in the Town Savings Bank. Barnet is caught between two worlds: descended from a self-made man, he has inherited the status but not the temperament of an independent gentleman.

This bleak picture of Barnet's place in the professional and cultural sphere is paralleled by his ineptitude in his personal life, presented chiefly in his friendship with Charles Downe and his romantic attachment to Lucy. The contrast between the lives of Downe and Barnet is carefully worked out.[48] Downe has 'a plump, cheery, rather self-indulgent face' (111), possesses limited means, and is happily married with three daughters; Barnet is 'of pale and refined appearance' (111), has considerable wealth, and, childless, would be satisfied merely to maintain peace with his cold and arrogant wife. As Downe's trite and 'second-class' (145) mourning for his drowned wife illustrates,[49] he is certainly a less sensitive man than Barnet, but his very simplicity and self-indulgence serve finally to underscore an important irony – that while Downe does eventually overcome his grief to return to the responsibilities of his life, Barnet himself becomes more permanently guilty of the fault for which he has rebuked his friend: sacrificing the present and future to the memory of the past. He is guilty of this offence even at the outset when he indulges his nostalgic impulse to visit Lucy Savile, his romantic image of a lost possibility for happiness.

Later in the story, Barnet is guilty of hesitancy rather than impulsiveness. Almost simultaneously, he hears the news of his wife's death and of Downe's imminent marriage to Lucy. As Roy Morrell has noted, he does have time to stop the marriage,⁵⁰ but chooses instead to indulge his own capacity for misery by attending the wedding with a stoic smile. The full extent of his self-destructive and self-dramatizing aspect emerges when he says to Downe and Lucy, 'I'll stand back and see you pass out, and observe the effect of the spectacle upon myself as one of the public' (159). This withdrawal from life and emotion characterizes the remainder of Barnet's life, beginning with the scene in which he helps to tread in a grave while forming the 'design' (160) of his future – thus symbolically burying his past self – and continuing in his years of exile, during which he fails ever to make any fresh start in life.

It may be argued that Barnet's movements after the boat accident show that he is capable of definitive action when a situation demands it. We are told that 'Barnet had acted as if devotion to his wife were the dominant passion of his existence' (134), and for the first time he is described as more active than the local workmen he formerly, in his enforced leisure, had envied:

At what a tearing pace he had driven up that road, through the yellow evening sunlight, the shadows flapping irksomely into his eyes as each wayside object rushed past between him and the west! Tired workmen with their baskets at their backs had turned on their homeward journey to wonder at his speed. (134)

The same points can be used, however, to show that Barnet is able to act so effectively precisely because he does not feel any passion for the woman whose life he is saving. His decision to resuscitate his wife is unquestionably the only moral thing to do, but the description of his 'mechanical' efforts to save her (138) suggests that these are actions which bear no relation to his emotions. Significantly, Barnet's 'condition' while walking to Lucy's wedding is also described as 'mechanical' (158). The point, it seems, is that Barnet can allow his body to do useful and even laudable things, but only when such actions will satisfy his self-destructive tendency and feed his unhappiness. This represents a serious imbalance in Barnet's personality: his ability to find fulfilment is outweighed by his 'rich capacity for misery' (157).

The final section of the story presents Barnet's last attempt to return to his native town and to marry Lucy. Here all the signs point to the urgency of his mission. The conversation among the 'middle-aged farmers and dairymen' in the Black-Bull Hotel is about the shortening of the days as winter approaches, and Château Ringdale has acquired 'a respectable mellowness, with ivy, Virginia creepers, lichens, damp patches, and even constitutional infirmities of its own like its elder fellows' (162). But the house, like the middle-aged Lucy who is nevertheless still 'girlish' (168), projects the sense that it can be brought back to a youthful state: 'There was a stagnation in the dwelling; it seemed to be waiting. Could it really be waiting for him?' (167) Barnet fails again, however, to act in his own interest, by retreating entirely at Lucy's initial rejections. *Early Life* quotes a letter from Mrs Procter about the conclusion of 'Fellow-Townsmen': 'You are cruel. Why not let him come home again and marry his first love? But I see you are right. He should not have deserted her.' (178) This combination of reactions – frustration at Barnet's fate followed by disapproval of his actions – perfectly reflects the relationship between the story's carefully elaborated plot and its treatment of Barnet's character. The cards seem stacked against him when his wife is saved while Mrs Downe is drowned and when Mrs Barnet's death precedes Lucy's wedding by so short a space of time. But the reader's exasperation at the tricks of fate becomes eventually, after Barnet retreats so readily and inexorably when both he and Lucy are free to marry, an even greater annoyance at his submission to them. Earlier, he could be defended by the logic that circumstances were working against him, but this final section legitimizes the reader's previous uneasiness about Barnet's character, and makes explicit what was implicit all along: that even when chance is working in his favour, he is incapable of acting on his own behalf.

The dependence in the plot of 'Fellow-Townsmen' on coincidence and ironic comparison suggests that it could qualify, as Ernest Baker has noted, as a *Life's Little Ironies* story.[51] But its presence in *Wessex Tales* gives the volume a broader and more profound frame of reference by presenting a character who incorporates within his person some of the private crises which can exist even within such a small and integrated world as Wessex. The detailed portrayal of Port-

Bredy as both a source and an image of Barnet's inner conflict gives 'Fellow-Townsmen' a specifically regional context, making it a pastoral history in a special but legitimate sense: the faults in Barnet's character are firmly grounded in his relationship with his local community, and can only be fully understood when seen in this Wessex context.

'Fellow-Townsmen' and 'Interlopers at the Knap' form a thematic unit in *Wessex Tales*. Both are accounts of alienation, and their chief male characters, in failing to make proper marriage choices, demonstrate an inability to know themselves or to participate in the living culture of Wessex. Of both Darton and Barnet – their names seem hollow echoes of each other – we are told their prosperity and positions in the community were 'none of [their] own making' (178, 112). Descendants of enterprising tradesmen, both men have inherited a financial and professional but not a cultural legacy.

Darton's alienation is presented in terms of his failure to enter fully into the family life of the 'Knap' – the grail at the end of his 'pilgrimage' (179) through a 'monotonous' and difficult terrain:

> Unapprized wayfarers who are too old, or too young, or in other respects too weak for the distance to be traversed, but who, nevertheless, have to walk it, say, as they look wistfully ahead, 'Once at the top of that hill, and I must surely see the end of Long-Ash Lane!' But they reach the hilltop, and Long-Ash Lane stretches in front as mercilessly as before. (177)

Physical details – the gradual thickening of darkness and 'blurring of the air' in the misty night, the brambles along the side of the road which 'scratched their hats and hooked their whiskers as they passed' (179) and 'the ironical directing-post . . . holding out its blank arms to the raw breeze' (182) – all contribute to the sense that this is actually a metaphysical journey and that Darton, like Bunyan's Christian or Browning's Childe Roland, is about to undergo a spiritual trial. The journey is also presented as a travelling backwards in time: the 'neglected' road they are following 'had been a highway to Queen Elizabeth's subjects and the cavalcades of the past', and they are moving toward an 'old-fashioned village' 'in a

direction that was enlivened by no modern current of traffic'
(179). The reference to Skrymir the Giant implies, too, that
Darton's quest for a wife has a mythical dimension, and that he
may, like Thor of the Norse story about Skrymir, meet with
capricious powers during his journey.

These suggestions of pilgrimage and spiritual trial, conventionally images from heroic romance, are made part of the
story's pastoral frame of reference by the presentation of
Darton's character – the most serious obstacle to his successful
journey – in terms of his regional background. As a result of
his father's 'commercial subtlety', Darton is heir to a farm
whose profits and diversity make it a substantial capitalistic
enterprise: 'His turnover, as it is called, was probably thirty
thousand pounds a year. He had a great many draught horses,
a great many milch cows, and of sheep a multitude.' As the
Biblical phrasing and cadence of this passage suggest,
Darton's property gives him a patriarchal position in the
community. But unlike most patriarchal figures, he has an
'unambitious, unstrategic character' (178) that prevents him
both from trying to expand the profits of his farm and from
choosing a wife to bear his descendants. Sally's Christian
name – that of Abraham's wife, mother of the chosen
people – would suggest that she is the ideal wife for Darton,
but his own reasons for wanting to marry her reflect rather his
habitual avoidance of conflict than an appreciation of her
qualities. His failed courtship of Helena (the Homeric source
for her name suggests her potential capacity to divide a
household) makes him wary of women with social prestige:

> I have had experience enough in looking above me. 'No
> more superior women for me' said I – you know when. Sally
> is a comely, independent, simple character, with no make-
> up about her, who'll think me as much a superior to her as I
> used to think – you know who I mean – was to me.   (180)

Darton's fault is not merely that he misconstrues Sally as
simple, but also that his courtship of her is a defensive action
rather than an assertion of love. He also has a grim attitude
toward marriage, demonstrated by his gift to Sally of a gown
'rather serviceable than showy'. When he asks, 'why should a
woman dress up like a rope-dancer because she's going to do

the most solemn deed of her life except dying?' Japheth's response, in the cadence almost of a Shakespearean clown, expresses the lively and whimsical fondness for women that Darton lacks: 'Faith why? But she will, because she will, I suppose.' Darton can think only of the 'winter weather' (180) of married life, but Japheth is accepting of its festive side as well.

Jean R. Brooks has criticized the complicated plot of 'Interlopers', but, as in 'Fellow-Townsmen', what is admittedly a 'crowded synopsis' of events[52] can also be seen as a means for allowing plot to illuminate character. Darton's reactions to coincidence bring into focus his propensity for submitting to fate – or rather, what he considers to be his fate. When he unexpectedly discovers his old lover in the dress he had purchased as a wedding gift for his new one, Darton, instead of ascertaining the reason for this strange event, falls into a trance-like state of fascination, 'looking at Helena's dress and outline, and listening to her voice like a man in a dream' (193). He had earlier told Japheth that 'Hanging and wiving go by destiny' (179), and he applies the old proverb to his own life with superstitious resignation: 'He seemed to feel that fate had impishly changed his *vis-à-vis* in the lover's jig he was about to foot; that while the gown had been expected to enclose a Sally, a Helena's face looked out from the bodice; that some long-lost hand met his own from the sleeves'. (195) It is this passive fascination with his fate, rather than any strong renewal of love for Helena, that leads Darton into a marriage with her.

If Darton passively allows superstition to govern his life too fully, then Sally represents the opposite extreme: her self-reliance causes her to act too quickly and decisively in working out her destiny. While Sally is awaiting Darton's arrival, her confidence is revealed repeatedly to be a mask for her essential vulnerability. Her independent posture is evidence of an admirable determination not to be subdued by life, but after Sally has come upon Darton and Helena clasping hands in the barton, her attempt to put on a brave face becomes more self-defeating than defensive. Whereas Darton sees Helena as a vision, never seeking an explanation for the apparition, Sally immediately draws too many conclusions, and her readiness to renounce Darton reflects a fear of confronting her own jealousy. In every sense, the marriage of Darton and Helena is arranged by Sally. She impels him by her 'passionate, almost angry demeanour' (199) to leave on the night of Philip's death. She refuses to set a new date for her marriage, and she later forces Helena to meet Darton alone. Even after Helena's death, Sally continues in the role of self-reliance in which she has cast herself. Her mixture of sarcasm and cordiality toward Darton is another self-protective device, and in her final declaration to him she divulges more of her true motives than she intends: 'I don't altogether despise you. I don't think you quite such a hero as I once did – that's all' (213). This confession to a past infatuation and to a continuing adherence to romantic notions makes Sally's renunciation – not of Darton but of marriage in general – another strategy of self-defence, rather than a declaration of independence. She never learns the lesson to which Bathsheba and Elizabeth-Jane finally come: that marriage is the 'good fellowship – *camaraderie*' of 'tried friends' (*FMC*, 456), and not the conjunction of hero and heroine. Beneath Sally's renunciation lies her disappointment.

This is not to say, of course, that Darton, whose malleability and passivity are a poor match for her high-spirited qualities, is the right mate for Sally. But in her rejection of Japheth Johns, Sally's independence has become recalcitrance. Several qualities recommend Japheth as a husband. He admires her more deeply than does Darton, and possesses a wit and enthusiasm for life which makes him an appropriate spiritual partner. Like Sally, he has local roots and, with his moderately sized dairy only four miles away, is on an even social and economic footing with her – neither would be 'superior' to the other. Most important, he possesses the 'wisdom' which he accuses Darton of lacking, that of knowing Sally is 'a woman worth having if ever woman was' (203). Even his name recommends him as a worthy mate: Japheth was the son of Noah and received his father's blessing on his descendants (Gen. 9:18–29).

Despite this rigid element in Sally's character, however, she remains an attractive figure whose resilience and independence are consistently contrasted with the personal weaknesses of Charles Darton. Though she refuses to make of the 'Knap' the family 'homestead' (183) it appears destined to be, still she improves her position there by hiring new milkers, and can declare frankly of herself, 'I am happy enough as I am' (213). Sally possesses the very quality that Darton lacks: a predisposition to make the best of less-than-perfect circumstances. This trait would be especially desirable in a man such as Darton, whose economic success is dependent upon a combination of careful management and prudent initiative.

Like 'Fellow-Townsmen', 'Interlopers at the Knap' depicts a character whose personal faults are presented in terms not only of his private life but also of his function within his regional society. Despite their positions of wealth and respectability, Barnet and Darton are ineffective both as suitors and as professional men, and these stories present the two kinds of weakness as aspects of the same problem. A perception of the link between the personal and social would, of course, form part of any serious analysis of character, but here the relationship of character to environment is especially close, and is based on a detailed portrayal of a particular regional way of life. It is this dimension in both narratives which gives them a place in a volume of 'pastoral histories'.

'The Distracted Preacher', the concluding story of *Wessex Tales*, repeats the structure of 'The Three Strangers', in which the differences between regional and non-regional are dramatized by the intrusion of an uninitiated outsider into the insular world of the countryside. Both stories suggest that there is a discrepancy between the king's 'law' and true 'justice' and show the village community defending its own values against Dogberrian avatars of royal authority. Still, the two stories are significantly different. 'The Three Strangers' portrays the solidarity of the rural community in a tone that, despite light and even farcical moments, remains gravely sombre, while the mood of 'The Distracted Preacher' is predominantly humorous, and the serious consequences of the smuggling operations are carefully excluded until the story's concluding episodes. Instead, the reader is led to concentrate on the more positive aspects of smuggling: the ways in which it represented for coastal village culture not only a means of livelihood but also an occasion for excitement, a warm camaraderie, and, most important, an inherited way of life.

The light tone of 'The Distracted Preacher' derives most obviously from the character of its non-regional outsider. The callous arrogance of the hangman is replaced by the 'innocent ignorance' (223) of the minister, Richard Stockdale, whose much-delayed recognition of Lizzy Newberry's participation in the smuggling operations reflects a naivety not only about human nature but, more significantly, about the culture of the village in which he has come to live. Irving Howe was certainly right to say that Hardy aims 'a sly thrust at Victorian convention' by his portrayal of Stockdale,[53] but at the same time the story is only mildly satirical in its description of this impressionable minister who finds himself torn 'between conscience and love' (263). Compared to Randolph Twycott of 'The Son's Veto' or Percival Cope of 'For Conscience' Sake', this pre-Victorian clergyman is, despite the conventionality of his values, rather a likeable figure – perhaps on account of his healthy sexual instincts. In some ways, Stockdale is like the reader: coming to Nether-Moynton with no knowledge of its culture and equipped only with conventional morals about justice and law, he finds himself simultaneously attracted to, and disapproving of, its unreflective vitality.

The story is basically a love plot which also raises general moral issues. Even in their initial flirtations, Stockdale and Lizzy approach each other in ways that reflect their respective moral outlooks. She is calculating and confident of her own motives, while he, although equally calculating, perceives a tension between his sexual desires and his role as a minister. As Stockdale learns more of Lizzy, her sexual attractiveness and the contraband liquor become inextricably and paradoxically linked in his mind. He disapproves of her cooperation with the smugglers, but accepts the rum she siphons off to cure his cold; he hesitates to propose to her because he is disturbed by her mysterious disappearances and sleeping habits, but is drawn to her because these same activities stir 'his admiration in spite of himself' (255). While Stockdale is consistent in his arguments but not in his actions, Lizzy is firm in her own illogical convictions, but cannot see any inconsistencies in them. Like the other 'trimmers' (218) in her village, she embraces two creeds at once, and does not worry about any contradictions between them. Her defences of herself to Stockdale that she is 'only partly in man's clothes' and that she only smuggles 'in winter-time when 'tis new moon' (249) beautifully illustrate the vigorous absurdity of her reasoning.

The moral deadlock between Stockdale and Lizzy provides the narrative focus for the story's contrasting of different regional attitudes. In his arguments with Lizzy, it becomes clear that Stockdale's censuring of the smuggling is as much a part of his personal heritage as involvement in it is part of hers. Nonconformity has 'been in the Stockdale blood for some generations' (268), and the biblical story of Caesar's tribute-money is a forceful part of his cultural legacy. Lizzy, by the same token, cannot comprehend Stockdale's objections because her values, just as naturally, are based on those of her father and grandfather and 'almost everybody in Nether-Moynton'. When Stockdale asks her if she will not 'think it worth while to give up this wild business and live for me alone' (251), he does not realize that he is requiring her to overthrow her heritage – to become, in effect, a different person.

Stockdale's background also accounts for his simultaneous disapproval of, and collusion with, Lizzy's smuggling. The narrator repeatedly uses the word 'inland' to describe both the location of Stockdale's native county and the place to which the liquor is going – thus subtly emphasizing that the smuggling operations are successful only because the people of the inland areas are willing to buy contraband liquor. Though the smugglers are most openly disobeying the law, the illicit activities extend beyond the boundaries of Nether-Moynton even to Stockdale's own birthplace. This, of course, is an irony which never occurs to Stockdale or Lizzy, but it is important that the reader perceive this essential link of corruption between the smuggling villages and the areas to which the liquor is sent. In the dispute between the two lovers, neither position is fully justified, but their respective attitudes accurately represent both the economic interests and the moral values of their native regions. Seen in this way, even the personal aspects of the love plot contribute to the pastoral perspective of 'The Distracted Preacher'.

Such a reading, however, makes the story's conclusion – where Lizzy finally surrenders to Stockdale, joins him in the Midlands, and repudiates her past – a disconcerting way of reconciling the two lovers, not only because Owlett seems a better mate for Lizzy, but also because the action seems utterly inconsistent with her character. Her deepest instincts are enjoyment of life and fidelity to her local heritage, and she abandons both of these by marrying the fastidious Richard Stockdale. But it is supremely right that the story should end, despite its predominantly humorous mode, with a recognition of the sombre contingencies that were always a possible result of the smuggling. Even Hardy's preferred but unwritten conclusion, in which Lizzy 'much to her credit in the author's opinion' (287) marries her cousin, retains Owlett's emigration as part of the story's dénouement. Justified or not, the activities were illegal, and by depicting both their farcical and their serious aspects the story preserves its basic historical authenticity.[54]

The detailed topography presented in 'The Distracted Preacher' creates for the reader a vivid sense of place. Enough particulars about Nether-Moynton and its environs are offered to form a sharp image not only of the area's physical characteristics but also of its complex mode of life. This effect is produced by the precise naming and locating of the important geographical places along the coast, by the ingenious listing of all the places and objects – from 'Hollow trees' to 'Back-door gutters' (265) – searched by the preventive-men, and by the device of placing the conspirators in the church tower, where they can see 'the village lying like a map' (268) at their feet. Described in careful detail, too, are the methods of carrying and hiding the barrels, as well as the financial transactions surrounding their purchase and sale. This attention to local knowledge, reinforced by the occasional use of dialect, enables Hardy to expand and clarify his image of Wessex as a region and a frame of historical reference by depicting a locality which creates as well as encloses the characters who inhabit it. 'The Distracted Preacher' is a fitting conclusion to *Wessex Tales*, a collection of pastoral histories which, though different from each other, can only be understood within the context of their complex regional framework.

A prominent pastoral theme in *Wessex Tales* is the significance of marriage, the family, and the community as institutions which sustain country life. The unhappiness of Phyllis Grove, Rhoda Brook, Darton, and Barnet is defined in terms of their social and emotional alienation, while the attractiveness of Timothy Summers and Lizzy Newberry is based on their unambiguous closeness to the local way of life. Often, imagery associated with human dwellings is used to portray either the fulfilment or the perversion of rural values. In 'Fellow-Townsmen', for example, houses are emblems of the peaceful coexistence of man and nature. Lucy's cottage stands in a garden of 'old-fashioned flowers' (131) where time is measured by the seasonal changes from snowdrop to crocus to daffodil, while even the vulgar Château Ringdale eventually develops an association with its surrounding landscape. In fact, Château Ringdale is finally an image not of Mrs Barnet's ambition but rather of her husband's failure to make the mansion his family homestead. He formulates a distinction central to the story's meaning when he says to Downe, 'You must be happy if any man is. I would give a hundred such houses as my new one to have a home like yours.' (114) For Barnet the potential for such a 'home' lies in Lucy, and the most compelling image connected with her is the 'curl of smoke' (136) rising out of the chimney of her newly kindled hearth. After Barnet has begun to take an interest in Château Ringdale he is seen 'looking at the grain of a floor-board, and meditating where it grew, or picturing under what circumstances the last fire would be kindled in the at present sootless chimneys' (147). He is actually meditating upon the status of his house as a human dwelling, with a position in Nature and a future as a haven of family life.

Other images in 'Fellow-Townsmen' extend from the house motif. Standing as a negative counterpart to it is the elaborate tombstone which Downe plans to erect in memory of his dead wife: while a house absorbs memories into its constantly changing structure, a tombstone petrifies them, and keeps them separate from life. Lucy's house, too, though it appears to Barnet as an image of natural harmony and domestic warmth, is actually an 'enclosure' (131) surrounded by a white picket fence. A more elaborate enclosure is found in 'The Melancholy Hussar', where Phyllis's fenced rural retreat is rather a perverse *hortus conclusus* than a place of freedom. The dark 'Grove' in which she lives is not the conventional dreamlike forest of sexual abandon, but a 'twilight' of 'seclusion' (47); her home, 'on the highest point of ground to which the lane ascended' (50), is a tower prison; like Thisbe, she must meet her lover with a stone wall between, making 'anything like intimacy difficult' (52). Phyllis's name, conventional for shepherdesses, is ironic when compared to the artificiality of her pastoral surroundings – her garden containing box-tree borders and a yew tree unnaturally 'cut into a quaint and attenuated shape' (46).

The dwellings in *Wessex Tales* can thus represent pastoral isolation in both its positive and negative aspects. Shepherd Fennel's 'lonely cottage' (3) on the downs is an image of cosiness and domesticity, while Rhoda Brook's home 'apart' from that of the other labourers and close to 'the border of Egdon Heath' (70) suggests a contrast of settings not unlike that between Wuthering Heights and Thrushcross Grange. The rafter in her cottage showing through the thatch 'like a bone protruding through the skin' (71) symbolizes the essential deadness of Rhoda's life. The most positive house image in *Wessex Tales* is the 'Knap', which, though 'quite shut away' from King's Hintock Court (and hence from any aristocratic associations), is portrayed as a haven of permanence and stability. Its 'mullioned windows' and 'chimneys of lavish solidity' represent the house's great age and strength as a family 'homestead' and the 'large sycamore tree, whose bared roots formed a convenient staircase from the road below to the front door of the dwelling' (183) is a symbol of its still-living association with the past. Like the Norse Yggdrasil, the sycamore links earth with sky, and the world of the dead with that of the living. That it stands immediately in front of the 'Knap' validates the house's metaphorical status as a potential home for the wandering Darton – a place in which to raise succeeding generations from the ancestral roots of the past.

In a different way, the historical and cosmic imagery of 'The Three Strangers' is also related to the pastoral mode of *Wessex Tales*. Set on the downs of southern England 'little modified by the lapse of centuries' (3), the story contains biblical, classical, and medieval allusions that identify it with some of the earliest written history known to western civilization. Its comparison of the movements of the country dancers to those of the planets suggests a juxtaposition of near and remote, of small and large. This image has been considered as representing 'the small and insignificant transience of men and their actions in relation to the unresponsive, unchanging, and timeless physical world',[55] but while it is true that Nature tends to dwarf the lives of men, this view does not take into account the concept of analogy implicit in pastoralism, which always seeks generality in the particular. In 'The Three Strangers', past and present, large and small are continually juxtaposed in a way that suggests similarity as well as difference, closeness as well as distance. References to Timon, Nebuchadnezzar, and Belshazzar are made not only because these are figures from the distant past but also because their abuses of power can be compared to that of the hangman, whose every action is lawful but derived from an inhumane system of justice. Such a linkage causes the reader to extend the analogy to contemporary situations, and hence to expand the story's frame of reference even beyond Hardy's own time. The telescoping of space and time does not so much dwarf events as frame them, by suggesting parallels between the past and the present.

A pastoral vantage point is also present in the narrative technique of Wessex Tales. The stories exemplify several styles of storytelling – from the narrowly subjective point of view of 'A Tradition of Eighteen Hundred and Four' to the more distanced voice of 'The Withered Arm', and from the instructional style of 'The Three Strangers' to the more analytical method of 'Fellow-Townsmen' – but they are drawn together by a common narrative strategy: each is told in a manner that will make its specific subject matter comprehensible to the urban reader. Such a style came naturally to a writer like Hardy, whose experience included both listening to traditional tales told by old people of Dorset and socializing with the literary elite of London. In using Wessex as his fictional milieu, Hardy found a way of drawing these two worlds together – of transforming the oral culture of his native region into a literary form understandable to those who lived outside it. After a five-month stay in London, Hardy remarked in 1887 that there is a 'difference between children who grow up in solitary country places and those who grow up in towns – the former being imaginative, dreamy, and credulous of vague mysteries'. The reason, he suggested, is that 'The Unknown comes within so short a radius from themselves by comparison with the city-bred' (EL, 265). Years later, he told William Archer that

... my feeling for this county is that of the countryman born and bred. Have you ever noticed the different relation to nature of the town child and the country child? The town-bred boy will often appreciate nature more than the country boy, but he does not know it in the same sense. He will rush to pick a flower which the country boy does not seem to notice. But it is a part of the country boy's life. It grows in his soul – he does not want it in his buttonhole.[56]

By desentimentalizing and elucidating the true character of country life, the narrative technique of *Wessex Tales* ensures that a town-bred audience will not appreciate these country stories merely as one would a flower or picturesque landscape.

A rural attitude that would be foreign to the city dweller is the countryman's awareness of his own communal past as preserved in landscape and tradition. In the year that *Wessex Tales* was published, Hardy made this observation:

London appears not to *see itself*. Each individual is conscious of *himself*, but nobody conscious of themselves collectively, except perhaps some poor gaper who stares round with a half-idiotic aspect.

There is no consciousness here of where anything comes from or goes to – only that it is present. (*EL*, 271)

In Hardy's own experience, oral tradition revealed in the landscape the regional memories associated with it, and gave him a consciousness of the past that was collective rather than personal. For him a landscape was important not for its beauty but for the associations it could evoke in its beholder. As much of his poetry demonstrated, memory was for Hardy a sacred faculty and the source of his most deeply felt emotions. The regional landscape was a document of the past, full of stories for those able to read its hieroglyphics – the *locus* and catalyst of local legend: 'An object or mark raised or made by man on a scene is worth ten times any such formed by unconscious Nature. Hence clouds, mists, and mountains are unimportant beside the wear on a threshold, or the print of a hand.' (*EL*, 153) This sentiment is repeated throughout Hardy's prose and poetry. In 1878, he noted 'that the beauty of association is entirely superior to the beauty of aspect, and a beloved relative's old battered tankard to the finest Greek vase' (*EL*,

158). The same feeling governed the architectural judgments of Hardy's maturity. In his essay on church restoration he stood by the 'sentiment of association' in the 'conflict between the purely aesthetic sense and the memorial or associative'.[57] In 'The Dorsetshire Labourer' and in his famous letter to Rider Haggard, Hardy lamented the loss of 'village tradition' (*LY*, 94) and the 'instinct of association'[58] with landscape and history that had preserved the communal memories of Dorset, 'a vast mass of unwritten folk-lore, local chronicle, local topography, and nomenclature' (*LY*, 94). All of these categories of knowledge are included in *Wessex Tales*.

Hardy's respect for what he repeatedly called 'association' was not merely nostalgic or sentimental, for, as 'The Melancholy Hussar' and 'The Withered Arm' amply demonstrate, many of the memories that he linked with the Dorset landscape were sombre and even gruesome. What was essential for Hardy, rather, was the sense that these events were part of a recent past. He wrote in *The Mayor of Casterbridge*, in a passage inspired by the 1884 exhumation of Roman remains from his garden at Max Gate:

> Imaginative inhabitants, who would have felt an unpleasantness at the discovery of a comparatively modern skeleton in their gardens, were quite unmoved by these hoary shapes. They had lived so long ago, their time was so unlike the present, their hopes and motives were so widely removed from ours, that between them and the living there seemed to stretch a gulf too wide for even a spirit to pass.   (80)[59]

Clearly Hardy's interest in the past, and in the landscape that contained its remains and evoked its memories, involved the ability to see, in lives less 'widely removed' from his own, direct links with the present. What appealed to his imagination were events that occurred within or just beyond living memory, and of which he had 'heard tell' through the channel of oral tradition.

In *Wessex Tales* Hardy tried to recreate this special manner of storytelling for the reader. That he did this consciously is revealed in a conversation he once had with Margaret Newbolt:

Every historian we were saying, is now a firm believer in the value of historical documents: we go so far as to speak of them as 'authorities' and belittle those who do not strew their own margins with references. Then suddenly Hardy's mood changed, and mine with it: he turned to make a counter-attack on the whole system of records. What could they do for a writer beyond giving him order and accuracy – the qualities needed for articulating a skeleton? To make a live historical study, breath and blood should be moving, a proportion of the material should be overheard as it were coming down by oral tradition, or picked out of private letters of the time. Better still, if it could be dug for by cross-examination of ancestral ghosts.[60]

This desire to present history as it has come down through oral sources is surely the basis for the 'traditional' tone which several critics have discerned in Hardy's Wessex novels and stories.[61] Irving Howe has defined the shorter fiction by identifying it with the tradition of the tale rather than of the short story,[62] but this distinction should not imply that these narratives embody the 'naive' forms of storytelling that the word 'tale' might suggest. They belong, as the term pastoral presupposes, to a sophisticated and specifically literary genre. Written stories mimetic of the orally transmitted tale, they represent for the urban reader the subject matter and the tone of oral tradition.

There are several technical devices that Hardy uses repeatedly to create the sense that a narrative is an actual product of rural culture, while also making it understandable to the urban reader. One technique, employed more in the Wessex novels than in the stories, is to put an actual spectator on the scene, through whose particular perceptions the reader can interpret events.[63] But in *Wessex Tales*, the only actual spectator is Solomon Selby – an unreliable narrator whose perspective the reader distrusts. Instead, another technique is frequently explored, which places the narrative voice and the reader in a relationship comparable to that of teacher and student. While telling the story, the voice interprets details where necessary, but leaves the reader finally to draw his own conclusions. Neither the reader nor the narrator is an actual spectator, but the story is presented chiefly in visual and aural terms which must be understood in the same way that a knowledgeable witness would construe them. The reader, placed in the role of spectator, is initiated by the narrative voice into the countryman's mode of seeing.

Hardy once outlined a short story that would be told from the point of view of a sparrow watching the progress of a courtship; the entire plot is deduced by the bird, judging from the evidence of what it sees and hears.[64] In *Wessex Tales*, the use of sensory data as an aspect of plot development takes on an important meaning and produces a special *frisson*. William Barnes notes that in 'the olden time when there were no other books than handwritten ones, and they as such were of too high a cost for the shelves of the poor, the devising and knowledge of sight-tokens or symbols was a great branch of folklore'.[65] In *Wessex Tales*, the reader, assuming the role of an implied rural spectator, himself learns how to interpret the 'sight-tokens' of the story. The family mug in 'The Three Strangers', the unmarked graves in 'The Melancholy Hussar', the ageing Château Ringdale in 'Fellow-Townsmen', the great roots of the sycamore tree in front of the 'Knap' – all of these come to have a special significance when interpreted in terms of the pastoral perspective. Even minuscule details acquire symbolic importance in the pastoral context: the various trades of the guests in the cottage at Higher Crowstairs, the physical description of the dairy in 'The Withered Arm', and the Tudor architecture of the 'Knap'. These particulars enrich the stories, and require special explanation from the narrative voice before the reader will understand their context and importance – will recognize them, in short, as 'sight-tokens'.

The sub-title of *Wessex Tales* in its first edition added the words 'Strange, Lively, and Commonplace', a possible description for the kinds of information passed down from generation to generation in rural communities. Oral tradition, by its very nature, carries with it some details which are ordinary and others which belong more rightly to legend: it combines the 'Commonplace' with the 'Strange'. In *Wessex Tales*, these elements are blended in such a way that they repeat the form of oral tradition, while also teaching the urban reader how to understand them. Much of the 'Commonplace' material can thus also be categorized as instructive. Reacting against this sort of content, A. F. Cassis complained of Hardy's 'reliance' in the short stories 'on causality as a justification for improbabilities', and of 'the surplusage, the description, the lengthy explanation at the beginning of his stories which is often deadly to the swift launching of the plot'.[66] Such a point of view judges Hardy's tales from a twentieth-century perspective, and as a result confuses 'causality' and 'justification' with context. In Hardy's mimetic representation of the oral tale, the added consideration of a non-regional audience makes its lengthy explanations an important part of the story's structure. Practically speaking, this means that the distinction between exposition and development is less precise than in other fiction. It is interesting that Ellery Queen's own collection of detective stories should have included *Wessex Tales*,[67] for the interpretation of information is as central to a proper reading of these tales as it is to that of the mystery story. The urban reader must, in effect, assume the role of a detective who – with the aid of the guiding narrator – learns to discern a pattern of truth in a profusion of seemingly 'Commonplace' details.

The 'Strange' elements in *Wessex Tales* can also be related to its pastoral perspective by preserving for the reader the mood and the substance of a rural community's belief in the improbable. This function is itself enough to justify the outrageous implausibility of 'A Tradition of Eighteen Hundred and Four' and, at a more profound level, to illuminate the overwhelming power of 'The Withered Arm', which presents the 'Strange' and the 'Commonplace' as alternate sides of a single coin. Hardy's concern in these tales is not only with an event as it occurred, but also with the forms in which that incident has remained, however distortedly, in the memories of those who experienced it directly, and of those who learned of it indirectly, by oral tradition. In his essay on 'The Uncanny', Freud notes the relationship between the 'Strange' and the 'Commonplace' in certain kinds of primitive storytelling, and points out that the word 'uncanny' (*unheimlich*) refers to 'that class of the frightening which leads back to what is known of old and long familiar'.[68] He links this attitude to the primitive imagination's animistic conception of the universe, which sees special significance in repetition, 'an unintended recurrence of the same situation',[69] and in 'the omnipotence of thoughts':[70]

an uncanny effect is often and easily produced when the distinction between imagination and reality is effaced, as when something that we have hitherto regarded as imaginary appears before us in reality, or when a symbol takes over the full functions of the thing it symbolizes, and so on. It is this factor which contributes not a little to the uncanny effect attaching to magical practices.[71]

As Freud's remarks suggest, the world represented in *Wessex Tales* is one in which the 'Strange' and the 'Commonplace' are not in conflict, but constitute different aspects of the same thing: the compulsion of the imagination to look for the 'uncanny' in daily human experience, and to blur the lines between 'imagination' and 'reality'. In 'The Withered Arm' in particular, Hardy's narrator preserves and portrays this animistic mode of thinking in such a way the reader can both understand, and, to a degree, assume it.

Raymond Williams finds in Hardy's style an effect of 'strain' that has its source in the fact that his literary interest in his native place is 'a function of education', that he 'sees as a participant who is also an observer'.[72] Looked at more positively, however, this tension can be seen as the source and function of the pastoral mode of *Wessex Tales*, for it is precisely this dual perspective in Hardy's own mind that produced the narrative persona he created to initiate the reader into the folklore of Wessex. I use the word 'folklore' as broadly defined by William Barnes: 'a body of home-taught lore, received by the younger folk from elder ones in common life, and in the forms of knowledge or faith, or mindskills and handskills.'[73] The mixture of the 'Commonplace' and the 'Strange' in *Wessex Tales* is part of the reader's necessary instruction in the 'forms of knowledge' taken for granted by the country-dweller. Only when he has acquired these 'mindskills' can the reader rightly comprehend the meaning of these stories, and the imaginative potency that they have in the consciousness of the rural community.

This educational process extends even beyond the rich history and folklore of Dorset, for Hardy's Wessex, as he emphasizes repeatedly, is actually a dream state, which distills from the limited and actual history of Dorset what is perennially and essentially true. The Wessex tales themselves are 'but dreams, and not records' (x), while Casterbridge is 'not Dorchester – not even the Dorchester as it existed sixty years ago, but a dream-place that never was outside an irresponsible book . . . "a place more Dorchester than Dorchester itself" ' (*LY*, 144). These remarks point clearly to the intrinsically imaginative nature of Wessex, and thus to its universal quality as a symbolic representation of the human experience. This linking of the particular with the general constitutes the pastoralism of *Wessex Tales*.

2 *A Group of Noble Dames*: Ambivalent Exempla

Like *Wessex Tales, A Group of Noble Dames* is a collection of stories from the Wessex past. But, as Hardy told Harper's in 1890, the later volume is 'of a somewhat different kind' from his previous work, 'excepting The First Countess of Wessex, which comes near it in character'.[1] Since the exception Hardy cited is the volume's most documented story, it is likely that what he thought distinctive in *A Group of Noble Dames* is its whimsical use of history, different in method and tone from his other fiction about the past. Most of these stories are set in the seventeenth and eighteenth centuries – a period that Hardy could not in the majority of cases have learned of from people who were alive at the time – and their reconstruction of events is fantastical rather than retrospective, imaginary rather than imaginative. Although Hardy claimed that the women in the volume were 'mostly drawn from life'[2] and wrote to Lord Lytton that he got the stories 'from the lips of aged people in a remote part of the country',[3] his chief known source is Hutchins's *History* of Dorset. Indeed, the collection seems to have fewer direct links with oral tradition than Hardy's other stories set in the past. Whereas the preface to *Wessex Tales* cites spoken reminiscences as its main origin, the introductory remarks to *A Group of Noble Dames* stress that its roots are in the written 'pages of county histories' (vii).*

This reliance on written records is no indication that the stories are historically accurate. In the 1912 Wessex edition, *A Group of Noble Dames* is not categorized under the heading 'Novels of Character and Environment', where *Wessex Tales* is included, but under 'Romances and Fantasies'. This fact

---

*In this chapter only, page references to *A Group of Noble Dames* appear without identifying initials.

suggests that the volume is partially based on fanciful extrapol-
ation. As Hardy himself describes it, his method in *A Group of
Noble Dames* is that of 'raising images' from genealogies by
'unconsciously filling into the framework the motives, passions, and personal qualities which would appear to be the
single explanation possible of some extraordinary conjunction in times, events, and personages' (vii) – a process significantly different from that described in the preface to
Wessex Tales, of preserving 'the fresh originality of living fact'
(viii).

    In its subject matter, however, *A Group of Noble Dames* has
interesting links with Hardy's earlier work. The book is one of
his many attempts, beginning with *The Poor Man and the Lady*,
to portray the fascination and the difficulty of sexual alliances
that cross class boundaries. It also has common themes with
Tess of the d'Urbervilles, the novel immediately preceding it. As
Hardy himself suggested in 1892, the dames have a kinship
with Tess, despite their different circumstances: 'One often
notices in the woman of position the same transparency of
passions, the same impulses, the same gentle, candid feminin-
ity that you meet with in dairymaids. The higher or the lower
you go, the more natural are the people – especially the
women.'[4] Like Tess, the dames are different from other
women in their purity and intensity of feeling, and their lives
represent the natural reactions of human beings placed in
extreme circumstances. Both *A Group of Noble Dames* and *Tess*
are also critical of those who romanticize noble lineage, while
revealing equivocal feelings toward old titled families, feelings
Hardy may himself have shared. As Angel Clare says,
'Politically I am sceptical as to the virtue of their being old.
Some of the wise even among themselves "exclaim against
their own succession," as Hamlet puts it; but lyrically, dramatically, and even historically, I am tenderly attached to them.'
(*T*, 213) Hardy's own curiosity about upper-class women may
have originated in his childish fascination with Julia Augusta
Martin of Kingston Maurward House, and in his 'romantic
interest' (*EL*, 12) in the story of Lady Susan O'Brien. But it is
not necessary to invoke such biographical details to explain his
interest in the past of Dorset's titled families. As Lord David
Cecil has noted, Hardy's architectural experience gave him a
familiarity with, and an imaginative interest in, the great

houses of the local countryside,[5] and his knowledge of the area's history added to his fascination with the people who inhabited such mansions in the centuries before his birth.

Hardy shares his historical preoccupations with the members of the Antiquarian Club who tell the stories. But he adds a further concern extending beyond their range of perception: a desire to present the less happy underside of upper-class life. His focus is on the women, and the injurious effect upon them of the clash between convention and sexual passion. They are the victims of social rules, of men, and sometimes even of their own prejudices. Each noble dame tries to make a marriage that will allow for the fulfilment of her desires and affections within the framework of a society which requires in a spouse education, social accomplishment, inherited wealth, and title. Differences in class both attract and repel lovers, and youth and physical beauty are placed in opposition to age and established rank. By extension, the book also presents children as victims of the insidious claims of class. Legitimate children stand above illegitimate, male above female, and all are seen by their parents in terms of the laws of inheritance. It is not accidental that *A Group of Noble Dames* portrays more children than the rest of Hardy's work. Many of the dames themselves, indeed, remain children throughout their lives because they are denied the affection and guidance that nurture maturity. Hardy may have meant his epigraph from 'L'Allegro' – 'Store of Ladies, whose bright eyes/Rain influence' – to be applied ironically to his noble dames. These women are more sinned against than sinning, more likely to be controlled by the restrictions of their birth than to 'Rain influence' over others.

The first and last stories in *A Group of Noble Dames* are the only ones with truly 'happy' endings. Each of the others is a fairy tale gone wrong, a perversion of the convention in which princess and prince finally discover each other and live happily ever after. The first two and the last two stories all portray desperate elopements, while the middle six depict the various ways in which the family as a group can be damaged by class pressures. With few exceptions, each story can be seen as a repatterning or ironic refutation of the ostensible moral of the one preceding it. This method of organization impresses upon the reader both the extent and the diversity of unhappiness possible in a society that cherishes birth above human qualities. The contrapuntal structure also gives to the volume a rich ambivalence. Like a collection of exempla, the stories present different moral situations, each illustrating an ethical precept, but no single one of them can be seen as embodying an all-encompassing truth. Like Hardy's poems these stories are a series of 'impressions . . . humbly recording diverse readings' of life's 'phenomena' (*PPP*, vi) – each revolving about one theme, and all together expressing a general moral view only in their complex manner of contradicting, reflecting upon, and modifying one another.

Another aspect of the volume's ambivalence lies in the relationship between the content of the stories and the manner in which they are told. Because accuracy and thoroughness of detail are natural attributes of the pastoral point of view, most of the traditional stories in *Wessex Tales* lead the reader to adopt the judgments made by the narrative voice. But the constant presence in *A Group of Noble Dames* of the Wessex Field and Antiquarian Club forces the reader to separate himself from both storyteller and audience and to see events from a different perspective altogether – to transcend the complacency of the Club members, whose judgments simply do not accord with the presented facts. In no sense 'pastoral', these histories contain an ambivalence built into their very form: they are 'exempla' in two senses, each a contradiction of the other. In the eyes of the narrators they possess a convention-bound moral, while to the enlightened reader they embody a human problem which must be judged according to separate standards, unfettered by the prejudices of class. This ambivalence, or double perspective, makes *A Group of Noble Dames* essentially different in tone and narrative technique from all of Hardy's other fiction.

'The First Countess of Wessex' contains many of the standard character types and situations in *A Group of Noble Dames*: a young and innocent maiden, her manipulative parents, and two suitors – one youthful and attractive, the other, a titled man, older and more calculating. As in a fairy tale, Betty Dornell must choose the suitor who is truly loving over the one who merely appears to be so – a task that can only be performed after she has achieved maturity. Betty's entrance to adulthood is obstructed, however, by the aims of her parents, who place their own desires for her future above her welfare. Her situation illustrates a central theme in *A Group of Noble Dames*, that the requirement for a woman to make a good match may prevent her ever making an independent decision: by pushing Betty prematurely into the position of a woman, the Dornells are inviting the possibility that she will always remain a child. 'The First Countess of Wessex' charts the progress of Betty's attempts to transcend the wills of her parents, and to govern her own life as she moves – despite their efforts to prevent it – 'from girl to woman' (46).

More space is devoted in 'The First Countess of Wessex' than in any of the later stories to the relationship between the heroine's parents, and so the crisis of Betty's marriage choice is seen to be a repetition of that faced by her mother and father and by generations before them. The Dornells' disagreement about Betty's fate reveals their own incompatibility, which stems from their differences in temperament and in background. The Squire is too crude for the more refined social world of 'the greatest heiress in Wessex' (5), and he has lost much of his authority and autonomy by moving to her estate. Dornell's own ancestral house expresses his pathetic attempts to preserve his identity and virility in the face of a domineering wife and the pre-emptive claims of her class. Like Ravenswood's castle in *The Bride of Lammermoor*, Falls-Park is a 'lonely place, where a few rooms only' are 'kept habitable' (6) by faithful servants (Tupcombe is not unlike Caleb Balderstone in his unflinching fidelity to his master), and Dornell's only social contacts here are with fellow 'members of the hunt' – 'all smaller men than himself' (9).

Dornell seems at first to be more concerned than his wife Susan for their daughter's welfare, but, like Henchard in *The Mayor of Casterbridge*, he is a violent man whose instincts sometimes lead him to actions destructive of his own happiness and the happiness of those he loves. His 'uncalculating passionateness' (5) toward Betty is as harmful as her mother's ambition. The premature marriage is arranged when he has temporarily abandoned her for his masculine retreat, and his tardy efforts to rescue Betty from her mother's tyranny are only 'vague and quixotic' (7). He often mistakes his daughter's interest for his own, a tendency which takes a menacing form when he urges Betty to feign interest in Phelipson merely to sting her mother's conscience. Dornell's dying words reveal most profoundly that his love for his child is inseparable from a desire to defeat his wife: 'What – Betty – a trump after all? Hurrah! She's her father's own maid! She's game! She knew he was her father's own choice! She vowed that my man should win! Well done, Bet! – haw! haw! Hurrah!' (39) Mrs Dornell's more calculating concern for her daughter, though like her husband's self-interested, takes a more practical form. Her concern is to find Betty not a romantic mate but a man who has prestige at Court and thus the potential for a title. She is seeking, in short, the qualities which her husband lacks – perhaps in order to enjoy vicariously her daughter's social triumph.

Betty transcends the selfish machinations of both her parents by choosing her true suitor, a decision which requires her to see through conventional appearances to the reality behind them. Until the elopement, Phelipson is perceived by both Betty and the reader as the ideal romantic hero. In contrast to the thirty-five-year-old 'pale, tall, sedate' and 'self-possessed' Reynard (28), he is young, physically attractive, and seemingly a more appropriate mate for Betty.[6] But this conventional dichotomy between the two suitors is turned upside down by the smallpox incident, and Phelipson's character, hitherto judged as appealingly 'frank and impulsive' (16), is seen to be disingenuous and cowardly. Reynard, however, appears suddenly in a new and more flattering light: the very qualities in him which had seemed villainous – his cunning, self-possession, and apparent distance from events – become the attributes of a particular kind of hero. As Morrell notes, Reynard's kiss is 'a dramatically heroic and theatrical gesture'[7] that makes his capacity for calculation appear the more attractive quality of prudent resourcefulness. The 'little ewe lamb' (9) is safer in the hands of the fox than in those of its parents, the true predators, who between them had nearly torn it apart. Reynard combines the calculating qualities of Mrs Dornell, without her self-absorbed coldness, and the loving attributes of the Squire, without his selfish impulsiveness. Embodying the virtues but not the faults of Betty's parents, he can act in her best interest and become her ideal mate.

For this reason, it is important that Betty's sexual union with Reynard is an act repudiating both her mother's and her father's wills.[8] The historical figure on whom Susan is based had contrived her daughter's secret meetings with her husband,[9] but Hardy's fictional character – in a manner anticipating Sue Bridehead's remorseful return to Phillotson (note the similarities in name) – suddenly embraces the very opinion she formerly had passionately opposed. This change in Mrs Dornell's behaviour permits Betty to act for the first time as a mature woman. Her initial opposition to her parents had been childish passivity, and her first attempt to act on her own behalf by contracting smallpox[10] was recklessly carried out in a 'wild' (24) state of mind similar to that of Lucy Ashton at the moment of her forced marriage in *The Bride of Lammermoor* (the two works have a similar social theme). This behaviour is crazed and adolescent, as is Betty's later attempt to elope with Phelipson. But her final surrender to Reynard is made with the careful deliberateness of a mature woman who knows both her mind and her rights. Betty's clever retort to her mother's reproaches about her pregnancy is irrefutable, and manifests the self-possession she has finally achieved: 'But, my dearest mamma, you made me marry him! . . . and of course I've to obey him more than you now!' (48) The impact on Betty of Stephen Reynard – ostensibly the romance villain and the cunning fox of the beast fable – propels Betty into adulthood, and makes her story, as the Local Historian summarizes it, an instance of the 'small count taken of the happiness of an innocent child in the social strategy of those days, which might have led, but providentially did not lead, to great unhappiness' (48). In subsequent stories, the same social strategy does indeed produce great unhappiness.

'Barbara of the House of Grebe' duplicates – though with an entirely different outcome – the dramatic configuration of character types in 'The First Countess of Wessex': an heiress too young to know her own mind, her ambitious parents, an attractive admirer of modest descent, and a titled suitor who seeks by a series of calculated moves to conquer her affections. In Betty's story, the conventional hero is exposed as a coward, and she finds happiness with the older suitor, whose 'mild, placid, durable' affection is the sort that 'tends most generally to the woman's comfort under the institution of marriage'

(44). In 'Barbara', Hardy uses these same two conventional types of suitor to explore the distinction between physical and moral beauty, but the values are shifted so that the handsome suitor is indeed good and beautiful – in a moral as well as a physical sense – while the man of title is as 'perverse and cruel' (90) as one at first suspects Stephen Reynard to be. To see life as a 'philosopher' (43, 58) and to act with careful calculation – abilities which are finally seen as virtues in Reynard – become translated in Lord Uplandtowers into a sinister and sadistic skill in manipulating events and persons for his own selfish ends. As a result, Barbara's fate is the converse of Betty's. Because Betty's husband is patient enough to wait for her to mature into womanhood, and woos rather than coerces her affections, she achieves happiness and produces a multitude of descendants. Barbara, however, is prevented from developing in herself more than the 'capricious fancies of girlhood' (77), first by her overambitious parents and later, more maliciously, by the cold and 'subtle' (84) Uplandtowers. Emotionally, she remains an adolescent.

Barbara's behaviour with both her husbands can be attributed to her lack of maturity. Like Betty, she elopes to escape the suitor chosen for her, and is initially attracted to superficial beauty. Barbara's feeling for Edmond Willowes is so dependent on his attractive presence that her happiness with him wanes as his social inadequacies are revealed, and is entirely undermined by his grotesque disfigurement. Her 'infantine' (63) nature then leads her to turn to Uplandtowers for condolence and assistance. He invariably appears, devil-like, at the precise moments when she is most vulnerable: while she walks alone in the garden at Yewsholt Lodge, while she awaits the arrival of her scarred husband at Lornton Inn, and finally after Willowes's departure, when she is still numbed by horror at her husband's appearance. In these circumstances, with little guidance from her parents, Barbara turns to Uplandtowers as the 'brother' she lacks, and her marriage to him is an expression of her need as a child to cling like a 'sweet-peaor with-wind' to a nature of 'stouter fibre' (78) than her own.

Barbara's capitulation to Uplandtowers is not reached, however, without a struggle to achieve maturity and autonomy. She feels guilt when her affection for Willowes begins to diminish in his absence, regrets having spoken 'earnestly and warmly' (70) to Uplandtowers, and in a spirit of 'self-chastisement' (71) stays awake for her husband's return. Her panicked reaction to his appearance demonstrates her child-ishness, but she afterwards tries heroically to overcome it. Fleeing, she crouches foetus-like on a flower-stand in the 'hot-house' (75) – attempting in this place where infant plants are nursed to early adulthood to force herself to the maturity her predicament demands. But when she returns to find him gone her only recourse is to divert her contrition in other directions – first into a misguided philanthropy and later, after her marriage to Uplandtowers, into a mystic 'beati-fication' (82) of her dead husband.

Emotionally, Uplandtowers is a jarring complement to Barbara. While she is fixed in a state of malleable adolescence by her untimely advancement into the position of an adult, he, also by reason of his privileged position in society, is propelled into manhood before ever going through the natural stages of youth:

> His matured and cynical doggedness at the age of nineteen, when impulse mostly rules calculation, was remarkable, and might have owed its existence as much to his succession to the earldom and its accompanying local honours in child-hood, as to the family character; an elevation which jerked him into maturity, so to speak, without his having known adolescence. (55)

For Uplandtowers, this premature leap is as emotionally incapacitating as Barbara's arrested development. The very susceptibility to feeling that paralyses her, were it blended with control and altruism, would be the mark of a humane and mature person. But in contrast to Stephen Reynard, who possesses the compassion of maturity, Uplandtowers rep-resents calculation without kindness, self-mastery without sympathy for others. Even Uplandtowers's desire to possess Barbara is 'an idea, rather than a passion' (55). For him, emotion is a weakness to be exploited in others.[11]

Edmond Willowes embodies all the passion and beauty that Uplandtowers lacks. His Christian name cannotes nobility and kingship, while his surname suggests the traditional associations of the willow tree with grief for unrequited love or the loss of a mate. As a descendant of 'the last of the old glass-painters in that place, where . . . the art lingered on when it had died out in every other part of England' (59–60), he belongs to the highest level of the peasant classes, the village artisans whom Hardy praised in 'The Dorsetshire Labourer'. His sexual vitality is emphasized throughout: he is 'one of the handsomest men who ever set his lips on a maid's' (63) and his statue is compared to Adonis and Phoebus Apollo. He possesses furthermore a 'superhuman' (67) moral courage. In short, he is the hero of fairy tale and romance, willing to undergo a series of tests to win the hand of his princess – in this case by the acquisition of education and social graces – and, subsequently, to risk his own life in order to guard those of others.

But Hardy's fairy tale is told in a realistic mode rather than a mode of romance, and as a result his hero loses physical beauty in proving his moral worth. Willowes also exhibits some human fallibility. He magnanimously leaves Barbara free to disclaim him, but phrases the choice in such a way that she has little room or time to adjust her emotions to the shock of his physical alteration: 'I was aware that no *human* love could survive such a catastrophe. I confess I thought yours *divine*.' (76) He too tries to propel Barbara into maturity at a single stroke and before she is ready for it. But although – and perhaps because – Willowes accepts so hastily what he most fears, he remains a hero and a figure of goodness in every sense, physical and moral. Contrary to T. S. Eliot's accusation that 'Barbara of the House of Grebe' presents a 'world of pure Evil',[12] the story portrays almost allegorically the polarized forces of Good and Evil in the persons of Barbara's two suitors, Willowes and Uplandtowers.

Willowes's status as the embodiment of beauty and goodness makes the statue representing him – a 'specimen of manhood almost perfect in every line and contour' (81) – the central symbol of the story. The statue's very existence stems from Barbara's attempt to behave as a woman, 'to act faithfully and uprightly' toward her husband. Lacking the mature emotions to nurture an abiding love for him during his absence, she seeks a visible copy of him so that 'she might look at it all day and every day, and never for a moment forget his features' (65). At least subconsciously, Barbara knows that it is Willowes's physical features she loves and that she requires his image, rather than his intelligent and 'affectionate' (65) letters, to sustain her feelings. The arrival of the statue is especially charged with significance because it occurs after Barbara's marriage to Uplandtowers and the announcement of Willowes's death.[13] Her affection and reverence for the statue are a measure both of her unhappiness with Uplandtowers and of her sense of guilt and grief at having rejected Willowes. In a sense, her only choice is between two statues: Willowes's dead image of beautiful warmth and Uplandtowers's living embodiment of cold 'sculptural repose' (56). Without an animate love-object, Barbara turns to a marble image, and adores it with a religious passion, attempting to make of it a reality. Like Pygmalion, she kisses an inanimate statue and addresses it with fond words of love; but while Venus brought Pygmalion's statue to life and thus into the world of time and change, Barbara brings about the opposite effect, becoming herself another statue, cold and lifeless: 'her long white robe and pale face lent her the blanched appearance of a second statue embracing the first.' Barbara addresses the statue in 'a low murmur of infantine tenderness' (83) like a child expressing contrition and promising never again to transgress.

It is this 'infantine' quality in Barbara's personality that allows Uplandtowers to coerce her affections. Because she cannot distinguish between the ideal and the actual, he has only to tamper with the 'copy' in order to alter her feelings about the 'original' (85). In keeping with her childish emotional state, he manipulates her with baby-talk: 'Frightened, dear one, hey? What a baby 'tis! Only a joke, sure, Barbara – a splendid joke! But a baby should not go to closets at midnight to look for the ghost of the dear departed! If it do it must expect to be terrified at his aspect – ho-ho-ho!' (86) By means of a grotesque and sinister stratagem, Uplandtowers seals Barbara in a state of childhood, eliciting from her an unrealistic promise that she will control her thoughts as well as her actions – and so preventing her ever making a more mature and authentic declaration of love. It was for the first edition of *A Group of Noble Dames* that Hardy made Barbara 'adjectly' kiss Uplandtowers 'with gasps of fear',[14] a change which emphasizes that Barbara's pathologically 'servile mood of attachment' (89) to Uplandtowers is created by irrational terror. The unnatural quality of this allegiance is judged by Nature itself in Barbara's stillborn children, symbolic representatives of a perverse sexual union. Barbara and Uplandtowers reflect in their different ways the danger of a premature immersion in adulthood. She is an infantile woman who lacks all control over her feelings, he an emotionally decrepit man devoid of any feeling at all.

'Barbara of the House of Grebe' has been the subject of fierce critical debate ever since *A Group of Noble Dames* was published. The *Spectator* reviewer who called it 'as unnatural as it is disgusting' is typical of contemporary response,[15] and the story drew more criticism in later decades from George Moore, who wrote a satirical summation of it, viciously parodying its style,[16] and from T. S. Eliot, who asserted that the story 'would seem to have been written solely to provide a satisfaction for some morbid emotion'.[17] More recently, one critic has tried to explain and justify the story's grotesqueness by seeing it as written 'in a consciously Gothic mode',[18] and it has been interpreted as a 'fable' having affinities with myth and fairy tale.[19] Barbara's predicament recalls 'Beauty and the Beast', a tale about appearance and reality and the maturing of a young woman as she comes to accept the bestial aspects of sexuality. Barbara, however, fails to learn what Beauty learns, that in sexual love ugliness can become beauty. But while these interpretations vindicate the morbidity of 'Barbara', it is important that the reader see it as a naturalistic story as well as a fairy tale – or rather, as a fairy tale enclosed and determined by a naturalistic environment. Barbara's moral weakness is not intrinsic to her nature, as it would be in a pure fairy tale, but a natural outgrowth of her position in society. A failed heroine of romance, she is also a victim of circumstance. This is the double role that in varying degrees defines the predicament of each of the noble dames.

'The Marchioness of Stonehenge' presents yet another instance of how class-consciousness can stifle or corrupt normal human emotions. Lady Caroline is not forced into a premature marriage, but she is like her two predecessors in *A Group of Noble Dames* in that her social position undermines her stability and maturity. Here there are no manipulations by parents or suitors impeding Caroline's development to womanhood, but a more subtle set of forces is at work. The very plenitude of her upbringing prevents her discovering the range and limits of her emotional needs: 'satiated with the constant iteration' of the best in life, she develops an appetite for what is conventionally beyond her reach, merely because it is foreign to her. So Caroline's romantic feeling for a 'plain-looking young man of humble birth and no position' (95) is 'a little stimulated' by his 'casual' (96) attentions to another woman. Her emotions are those of a spoiled child wanting what another possesses. As it is for Eustacia Vye in *The Return of the Native*, so jealousy is for Caroline an essential element in sexual attraction. This fact is complicated by Caroline's social pride, which prevents her openly declaring her love for a man of lower station. Her secret elopement is an unrealistic sidestepping of her inability either to marry or to renounce the youth to whom she is attracted, and she soon discovers that in satisfying a sexual need, she has denied herself the gratification of her social expectations. In her reckless indulgence of a new sensation, she discovers her reliance on the old conventions she had taken for granted.

The scene in which Caroline's husband dies of a heart attack both dramatizes her dilemma and resolves it, at least temporarily. The incident has been called one of Hardy's more 'improbable plot devices',[20] and this accusation may be true enough, but it fails to take into account the story's persistent dependence on melodrama to portray the radical shifts between jealousy and pride in Caroline's emotions. When she realizes that her husband is dead, her feelings change with almost unnatural speed from 'passionate grief' to 'concern at her own position as the daughter of an earl' (98). In the manuscript Hardy had Caroline address the dead youth first as a 'darling husband' and then as a 'dearest Husband' before he finally decided on the adjective 'unfortunate'[21] – a choice emphasizing the state of dispassionate self-interest at which Caroline arrives almost immediately after she has comprehended the fact of her husband's death. Caroline overlooks nothing when she drags the youth's body back to his father's cottage. She leaves the sash of the window open in order to return undetected, lifts the body across the gravel 'to avoid leaving traces in the road', and even remembers to find the key to the cottage and place it in the dead man's hand. Only then does she kiss his face 'for the last time, and with silent little sobs [bid] him farewell' – a gesture which does not interfere with her composedly returning to her room, where she sets everything in order, and returns to bed (100).

Caroline's self-possessed and level-headed manner is a cold reversal of Barbara's intense and tempestuous embrace of Willowes's statue. Caroline can without flinching lay the arms of her dead husband 'round her shoulders' in order to gain 'immunity from the social consequences of her rash act' (99), while Barbara loses all control in seeing even the image of her former husband. In the light of this precipitous change in Caroline's affection, the story's earlier comparison of her to Alcestis, the model wife in Chaucer's *Legend of Good Women*, becomes especially ironic: Hardy purposely overlooks the fact that Alcestis taught not only 'all the craft of fine loving', but also, in the lines immediately following, 'of wyfhood the livinge,/ And alle the boundes that she oughte kepe' (11. 545–6)– skills of altruism and self-control which Caroline has obviously never cultivated.

If there is an ideal wife in the story, it is not Caroline but Milly, whose love for the youth remains constant though unrequited. Just as Barbara's reverence for an image becomes a palpable physical experience, so Milly's imagined marriage becomes for her a living truth. The first graveyard scene, contrived by Caroline at a 'solemn place and hour' (102) in order to manipulate the 'impressionable and complaisant Milly' (104), results in a submission by the 'rustic maiden' to the woman of 'birth and beauty' (102), chiefly on account of the latter's use of her wealth and position. But the remainder of the story shows Milly's turning the tables on the lady who has stolen her lover. This dramatic reversal results from the change that takes place in Milly as soon as she has claimed the youth as her dead husband. The perverse ceremony at the graveside assumes a strange kind of truth in her mind, and her 'spirit of ecstasy' (103) at being the youth's widow gives her a power that allows her to oppose Caroline in their second confrontation. Here Caroline's social pride is matched by Milly's: 'My character is worth as much to me as yours is to you! . . . No such dishonour for me! I will outswear you, my lady; and I shall be believed. My story is so much the more likely that yours will be thought false.' (106) For the first time Lady Caroline's will is subverted, not by the perversity of her own contradictory nature, but by the equally vehement feelings of another, and her rank fails to gain her the triumph she desires.

The final confrontation between the two women reiterates the pattern of the second, though a different emotion is now involved: not honour but the gratification of 'maternal instincts' (108). Upon learning of the growing success of her unacknowledged son, Caroline suddenly craves to possess him, just as she had impulsively desired the affections of his father. A still greater irony lies in her continued inability to recognize the failure of social position to win human affection. The incident in which the son chooses Milly over Lady Caroline has the schematic structure and the dramatic force of a biblical parable and brings to mind the Old Testament story in which Solomon discovers the true mother of an infant by threatening to have it cut in half. In Hardy's story the child is old enough himself to choose the better mother, and does so in terms of a morality and a logic which has never occurred to the woman of title, for whom the parental role is by convention more closely allied to inheritance than to affection. The contrast between the young man's kisses for his two mothers, one given 'with the tenderest affection' and the other 'with a difference – quite coldly' makes of this 'painful scene' (110) a miniature moral exemplum. Still, however, Lady Caroline comprehends only the pain and not the truth lying behind it. Even her death of a 'broken heart' is caused not by a tragic awareness of her past mistakes but merely by an intensification of the jealousy that had put her in such a difficult situation in the first place: 'It was in the perverseness of her human heart that his denial of her should add fuel to the fire of her craving for his love.' This makes the reference to King Lear's 'anguish that is sharper than a serpent's tooth' (111) – added to the manuscript as an afterthought[22] – especially ironic: blinder even than Lear, Caroline never sees that parenthood is as much the raising of children as the begetting of them. The ostensible 'perversity' of Milly's fictional marriage generates a stronger and truer emotion than Caroline's sexual jealousy and social pride. Caroline's love is self-absorbed, while Milly's takes on increasing reality as she directs it to a living object, the son she never bore.

The link between 'The Marchioness of Stonehenge' and 'Lady Mottisfont' is the presence of an unwanted child, and in both stories there is a struggle between two women – one noble and wealthy, the other of simple origins – as to whether the claims of flesh and blood should take precedence over those of affection. The female characters seem at first to fall into stereotyped moulds and to correspond in type to Milly and Lady Caroline. Philippa, 'the gentle daughter of plain Squire Okehall', is an 'amiable girl' (116), willing in her simplicity to love another woman's child 'as if she had been her own by nature' (118). The Italian Countess is a woman of great beauty and accomplishment who has given up her child for the sake of convention, but who still longs for the offspring of her passion. It appears at first sight that, as in 'The Marchioness of Stonehenge', the adoptive mother has a more durable affection than the natural mother, but the two stories finally refute each other. The very moral which the preceding story had so dramatically pointed is contradicted by 'Lady Mottisfont', in which parental affection is seen as a selfish need easily gratified by replacement. This is demonstrated by all three of the adult characters, and especially by the surprising about-face in the demeanour of the 'tender and impulsive' Philippa (117).

Until the middle of the story, Philippa behaves toward Dorothy, her husband's illegitimate daughter, in a manner reminiscent of Milly's maternal devotion to Lady Caroline's son. Motherly feeling, it seems, is more emotional than biological. Subsequent events tend to argue, however, for the power of the physiological tie. When Philippa discovers that the Countess is Dorothy's mother, her distress is chiefly 'at the spectacle of herself as an intruder' (123) between them; Dorothy is attracted to the Countess 'with a strange and instinctive readiness that [intimates] the wonderful subtlety of the threads which bind flesh and flesh together' (125); and after the Countess has saved Dorothy's life, Mottisfont is 'in a dream of exaltation which [recognizes] nothing necessary to his well-being' outside the 'welded circle' (126) of himself, the Countess and Dorothy. Just before this incident, Philippa had declared to her husband with conviction, 'But she's *mine* –

she's mine!' (126) Afterwards, however, she seems less certain about the question of Dorothy's parentage, especially when the child herself expresses a preference for the Countess: 'I can do no less than grant to the Countess her wish, after her kindness to my – your – her – child' (127). Finally Philippa changes her position completely when she becomes pregnant. Now she can respond to the Countess as an equal, with whom she need not compete: '"I am not a beggar any longer," said Lady Mottisfont, with proud mystery' (129). Whereas Milly defies Lady Caroline's power by clinging to her adopted child, Philippa responds to the Countess by forsaking the young Dorothy. A change Hardy made in the manuscript emphasizes the literal replacement of one child by the other. Originally, the Countess's last interview with Sir Ashley occurred 'three days before his wife had presented him with a son and heir', but Hardy changed the word 'before' to 'after',[23] making Philippa's rejection of Dorothy a direct response to the birth of a male heir who usurps Dorothy's place by both his legitimacy and his sex. Philippa's sudden refusal to employ the words 'my' and 'our' in referring to Dorothy is an expression of this change:

> 'But, my dear Philippa, how can you argue thus about a child, and that child our Dorothy?'
> 'Not *ours*,' said his wife, pointing to the cot. 'Ours is here.'
> 'What, then, Philippa,' he said, surprised, 'you won't have her back, after nearly dying of grief at the loss of her?'
> 'I cannot argue, dear Ashley. I should prefer not to have the responsibility of Dorothy again. Her place is filled now.'
> (130–1)

As surprising as Philippa's change of heart is the assertiveness of her tone. Once over-submissive to Ashley's every suggestion, in her role as mother she assumes a position of authority. She refuses to acknowledge Ashley's right to share in a decision concerning his own child, and he responds to her dictum with the acquiescence that formerly had characterized her.

In his *Academy* review of *A Group of Noble Dames*, William Wallace questioned the plausibility of 'Lady Mottisfont' on the grounds that Philippa's 'double passion for and rejection of

Dorothy . . . involve too large a draft on one's credibility'.[24]
Such a comment can best be answered by a consideration of
the story's narrative tone. The tongue-in-cheek irony obvious
in the description of the cathedral at Wintoncester as a place
of meditation and romance also appears in the language of
Ashley's proposal to Philippa, in the formal aspects of their
wedding ceremony, in the details of their life together 'with as
near an approach to bliss as the climate of this country allows'
(117), and finally in their familial harmony after Dorothy has
been taken in:

> and when he came home he looked pleased to see how the
> two had won each other's hearts. Sir Ashley would kiss his
> wife, and his wife would kiss little Dorothy, and little
> Dorothy would kiss Sir Ashley, and after this triangular
> burst of affection Lady Mottisfont would say, 'Dear me – I
> forget she is not mine!'   (118)

The farcical quality in these scenes of idyllic happiness causes
the reader, especially in the light of the story's subsequent
incidents, to question the initial appraisal of Philippa as an
entirely 'innocent' and 'amiable' woman (116). Her early
conclusions about Dorothy's parentage disprove any claim
that she is completely naive, and even in the moment of
sublime domestic bliss quoted above, Philippa does remember
to forget that Dorothy is not her own child. Philippa's
about-face is more believable if the early remarks about her
character are regarded as a conscious glossing over of those
aspects of her personality that later cause her to reject
Dorothy so heartlessly. An 'ecstatic' (116) and 'impulsive' (117)
temperament, after all, is quite capable of a complete trans-
ferral of affection.

   It is also illuminating to look at Philippa in terms of the
aristocratic world into which she has married. In *A Group of
Noble Dames* the nobility regard children as first and foremost
the inheritors of their parents' titles and wealth. There is little
room for illegitimate children in the scheme of things, and
daughters are important chiefly for the social and financial
value of the marriages they contract. Philippa enters this
world unable to understand 'how she had deserved to have
sent to her such an illustrious lover, such a travelled person-

age, such a handsome man' (116) as Lord Mottisfont. Later, she is overwhelmed by the Countess's beauty, and even more forcefully by her acquired social graces and knowledge of the world. Philippa's very lack of familiarity with the glamour of the aristocracy subsequently causes her to assume too readily its most unattractive aspect: a disregard for the happiness of those of inferior rank. The Sentimental Member tells a most unsentimental story with an ending that, far from romanticizing aristocratic values, exposes their failure to nurture normal human affections. Wintoncester Cathedral, whose rarefied atmosphere is distinguished from 'spots where all is life, and growth, and fecundity' (115), is thus an appropriate setting for the cold courtship of the Mottisfonts. And Dorothy's final fate as the wife of a 'respectable road-contractor . . . who repaired and improved the old highway running from Wintoncester south-westerly through the New Forest' (132) is a turning to the security and love denied to her by both her natural and her adoptive parents – as well as to the centres of 'life, and growth, and fecundity' that her husband's highway symbolically and actually connects.

'The Lady Icenway' continues to explore the various aberrations that can exist in marital and parental affection when they are subject to the conventions of upper-class life, and the complications that accompany the inheritance of wealth and title. When the central concern is disposing of one's property by producing a 'lineal successor' (79, 147), the sexual act becomes a practical means to a necessary end rather than an expression of love or passion. This attitude toward sex can produce such cold men as Uplandtowers and Icenway, who marry merely to produce an heir. The women who emerge from the same context display different types of dislocation, ranging from Barbara's deranged servility to the selfishly possessive yet inconsistent passions of the Marchioness of Stonehenge and Lady Mottisfont. The Lady Icenway is still another variation of the type, and moves a step closer to a complete subsuming of natural affection by pride and position. In her story, maternal affection is barely mentioned, and her coldness to her child is measured by her lack of sympathy for his father's paternal feelings – feelings we are not meant to undervalue despite the excessively romantic manner in which he expresses them. Maria's disregard for Anderling, except in so far as he can provide her with the child she desires, is a denial of both his humanity and her own sexual nature.

Maria Icenway's inhumanity is heightened by repeated references to conventions of romance. She is the haughty lady of the courtly love tradition, while Anderling is her humble suitor. He first appears to Maria just 'at the moment' (137) when she needs to be rescued, promises to 'devote himself to her service for the rest of his days' (142), and calls her 'cruel mistress' (144). His 'chivalrous respect' for his lady takes the conventional form of 'submission' (145) to her will, and his attachment to her increases 'in proportion to her punitive treatment of him' (146): 'He sunned himself in her scornfulness as if it were love, and his ears drank in her curt monosyllables as though they were rhapsodies of endearment.' (147) Anderling is, moreover, a courtly lover with the self-destructiveness of a Byronic hero, whose hopeless love for his mistress is expressed in an unending physical and emotional struggle with the forces of life. His bigamous marriage to Maria – like Manfred and Childe Harold he has broken a sexual taboo – is described as a 'crime' to which he has 'been tempted . . . by her exceeding beauty, against which he had struggled day and night, till he had no further resistance left in him'. In a state of remorse as passionate as his lust, Anderling then becomes in the fashion of Childe Harold 'a wanderer on the face of the earth' (140), assumes 'strict religious habits' (142), and recklessly gambles away his fortune 'in the Continental hells' to which Maria has 'banished' him (144).

'The Lady Icenway' is not a romance in the strict sense of the word, however. The story mocks sentimentality, qualifying a reference to 'tender feeling' by parenthetically adding that such are the terms used by 'the romantic' (138). But here the commonplaces of the romantic tradition are used for a particular purpose, linking the stereotyped behaviour of the humble suitor and the haughty lady to a different structure of action and a new range of meanings in which the traditional postures are seen as expressions of the characters' historical circumstances and symptoms of their particular psychological types. Maria's position as a wealthy orphan makes her isolated and vulnerable, and the haughtiness she adopts to cope with this eventually becomes a true and dominating aspect of her personality. Subject to the conventions of the insulated life of the landed aristocracy, she must guard her pride and 'honour' (143), even to the point of lying, in order to survive. She is attracted to Anderling because of the intensity of his passion for her and the 'pleasure of power' (138) she derives from his devotion. The more he degrades himself for her sake, the more she is satisfied. Pride has transmuted her sexual affections into complete self-absorption, a need for an adulation which can never be reciprocal.

Anderling – the first part of his name is the German word for 'other' – is in comparison to Maria rootless: while her wealth is inherited, his is acquired from his own investments. His readiness to turn landed wealth into portable assets represents an attitude toward money, and toward life, which is utterly foreign in Maria's world. For him, wealth is not a legacy from the past, to be guarded and carefully distributed among one's descendants, but a liquid asset, to be diminished or expanded according to one's whims. For similar reasons, he is prone, in contrast to Maria, to place his passion before his pride. He takes pleasure in degrading himself by extravagantly revering the object of his passions – making of himself the 'underling' which his name brings to mind. The relationship between Maria and Anderling is perversely symbiotic: his humility and her haughtiness feed on each other.

Linked to these romantic poses is the contrast between the two lovers in their attitudes toward legal contracts. Maria is aghast at Anderling's bigamy and leaves him, fearing that she will be discovered as 'having been fooled, or deluded, or nonplussed in her worldly aims' (141). All her former sexual passion for Anderling – admittedly never as strong as his for her – is subsumed in vanity. Neither is Maria's marriage to Icenway a passionate act, but rather 'a method of fortifying her position against mortifying discoveries' (141). For her, the marriage contract is a formal document, preserving position and reputation: Anderling's bigamy, not his adultery, distresses her. Anderling looks at the situation from a different perspective, placing passion before pride. He regrets his mistake in marrying a woman of 'bad and scandalous' reputation, but is little concerned by the legal ramifications of his second marriage, hoping 'that such a condition of things would make no difference in her feelings for him, as it need make no difference in the course of their lives' (139). Anderling's greatest shock is at Maria's failure to give due regard to her feeling for him before signing another marriage contract: 'it had never occurred to him that a woman who rated her honour so highly as Maria had done, and who was the mother of a child of his, would have adopted such means as this for the restoration of that honour, and at so surprisingly early a date' (143). The key word here is 'honour', for Maria and Anderling have mutually exclusive ideas of what it means. Anderling believes only in an inner integrity, with no regard for formalities; Maria thinks of 'honour' in terms only of outward show. For him the contract of marriage is the means of acquiring licence to follow one's passions; for Maria, it is not a means but an end.

This moral stalemate is presented chiefly in comic terms – neither character commands all the reader's sympathy – but with the appearance of the child an issue is introduced which lies outside the bounds of humour. The romantic counterpoises of humility and haughtiness may be useful during courtship but are absurdly inappropriate in marital and parental love. In the story's concluding incidents, therefore, the reader's sympathy is swayed toward Anderling, whose love for his son is described in terms more genuine – uncluttered by the language of any convention – than is his adulation for Maria. His forsaking of Roman Catholicism in order to see the boy in church is a much more touching gesture than all his remorseful self-denial. This most stylized of lovers is, as a father, pathetically true to life. The Churchwarden correctly sees Anderling's sexual behaviour as evidence of a 'culpable' (133) nature, while commending warmly his paternal affection for his child.

This admirable side of Anderling's character creates in the final encounter between him and Maria an ironic mixture of comedy and pathos. The dialogue recalls the language of deathbed protestations in stage melodrama:

'You must get well – you must! *There's a reason*. I have been hard with you hitherto – I know it. I will not be so again.'
    The sick and dying man – for he was dying indeed – took her hand and pressed it to his lips. 'Too late, my darling, too late!' he murmured.

'But you *must not* die! O, you must not!' she said. And on an impulse she bent down and whispered some words to him, blushing as she had blushed in her maiden days.

He replied by a faint wan smile. 'Ah – why did you not say so sooner? Time was . . . but that's past!' he said. 'I must die!' (147–8)

Deliberately cliché-ridden, the scene is both heartrending and ridiculous in its mixture of conflicting and misunderstood aims. The melodramatic 'Too late, my darling, too late!' (a variation of an early title for *Tess*)[25] has an utterly different meaning for Anderling than for Maria. Typically, he speaks of the fulfilment of his longstanding passion, while she entertains a desire that is merely ambitious. He is deceived by her cajoling submission, actually a pretence to acquire the object she desires, and never sees the opportunism so apparent to the reader from her previous discussion with Lord Icenway and from her emphatic words (added for the first edition), '*There's a reason*.' In what seems to be her moment of greatest compliance, Maria is actually in perfect control. Her 'softening heart' (147) is shocked at Anderling's condition, not out of compassion, but because she regrets his inability to carry out the role for which she has selected him.

To see Maria's dismay at Anderling's death as mere frustration at having her ambitions thwarted might make her stained-glass 'tribute to his memory' (148) a conflicting detail. But Maria's grief is only a recognition that though she did not love Anderling, she was psychologically dependent on the devotion she had always taken for granted. A haughty lady needs a humble servant in order to maintain her superior posture, and Icenway can hardly perform such a role. The secretive manner in which Maria plans the tribute is, moreover, perfectly in character: she indulges herself while preserving position and appearance. The final words of her dialogue with Icenway reveal all the absurd implications of her supposed grief. Her remorse stems not from her guilt at having scorned Anderling, or at having tried subsequently to use him, but rather from the fact that his utility was not obvious soon enough for her to take advantage of it. The memorial erected for Anderling '*by his grieving widow*' (148) expresses regret not for the death of a mate but for the loss of an opportunity. Barbara Grebe is by Uplandtowers's manipulations a pathetic victim. But Lady Icenway, like Uplandtowers himself, is an example of how the demands of a social role can alienate a person from his own sexuality.

'Squire Petrick's Lady' depicts a process of moral impairment more insidious still: an acceptance by those outside the nobility of precisely that elitist code of values that excludes them from the upper classes, and a resulting lack of self-regard that debases their affections as surely as pride taints the affections of the nobility. Like the most pretentious members of the aristocracy (or for that matter like John Durbeyfield), Squire Petrick thinks of the highly descended as superior not only in their wealth and prestige but also in their physical and mental attributes – an attitude that seems especially preposterous because he possesses as much wealth as many aristocrats, and lacks merely the 'backward historical perspective' (159) of a title. Like Paula Power of *A Laodicean*, he finds his financial holdings insufficient to satisfy his romantic ideas. His story is a psychological study of the process by which adulation of the aristocracy can cause a man to disregard his natural instincts and spurn his own son. As elsewhere in *A Group of Noble Dames*, parental affection deteriorates into a selfish attempt to compensate for disappointment by projecting unfulfilled desires onto one's child.

It is especially ironic that a man such as Petrick should so adulate the aristocracy, since he is descended from a family whose fortune is founded on its unscrupulous transactions with the upper classes. But this propensity in the Petricks to 'torture and to love simultaneously' (159) the very people they are exploiting is actually a jealousy of their opportunities. The aspects of the Southwesterland family which Petrick most desires to see in his son are precisely those gifts that accompany wealth transmitted through several generations – not on account of the inherent superiority of a particular family, but because of the mixture of education and leisure that constitutes their way of life. While Petrick's ancestors were discovering the 'revelation' and 'legal lore' (153) of financial opportunism, the 'illustrious house ennobled as the Dukes of Southwesterland' (159) had been accomplishing 'political and military achievements' and 'performances in art and letters' (160) – attainments of which Petrick's family could never boast. Petrick's desire is that his son Rupert will become a man of a type his own family has never been able to produce.

Petrick's fluctuating feelings for his child sharply reflect his confused and contradictory attitudes toward his background. After believing Rupert to be the offspring of his wife's affair with another man, he embraces the idea that his son has an aristocratic father in order to justify what he finds to be a 'weakness' (158) in himself – his natural inclination to love a child not his own. By this perverse convolution of logic, Petrick's love for Rupert is translated into an adulation for the boy's presumed roots. Petrick transforms illegitimacy into nobility, and shame into honour – thus turning the very reason for his original alienation from the child into a bond of intimacy and a basis for adoration. In this way, Petrick manages to attach his common blood to that of the aristocracy and to disown the heritage he despises: 'He is of blue stock on one side at least, whilst in the ordinary run of affairs he would have been a commoner to the bone.' (158) The implicit self-hate in such a statement is vividly dramatized in the dialogue, added for the first edition, in which Petrick learns that Rupert is his own son:

'You look down in the mouth?' said the doctor, pausing.
'A bit unmanned. 'Tis unexpected-like,' sighed Timothy.
(161)

Preposterously, Timothy is 'unmanned' by the fact that he has not been cuckolded. The question he puts to his baffled child is a rhetorical expression of his absurd position, torn as he is between his natural affections and his belief in the superiority of noble blood: 'Why cannot a son be one's own and somebody else's likewise!' (163)

'Squire Petrick's Lady' is not directly concerned with an aristocratic or upper-class family, as are the other stories in *A Group of Noble Dames*, and it is feebly defended by the Crimson Maltster on the ground that he has never had the 'good fortune to know many of the nobility' (149). But the Maltster's apology is not Hardy's, for the story is important precisely because its characters are not noble. Appropriately located at the centre of *A Group of Noble Dames*, it portrays the extent to which the common man can be corrupted by the romantic

illusion he has learned to share with his social betters: the
belief that there is a 'glory' and a 'halo' (162) surrounding the
aristocracy. For both the nobleman and the commoner, the
effects of such a misconception are especially destructive
because their victims are children, born into a society which
confuses their lineage with their humanity.

'Anna, Lady Baxby' marks a departure from that theme of
childhood which in various ways links all of the preceding
stories. Anna's younger days are not presented (as Betty
Dornell's and Barbara Grebe's are) and no mention is made of
any offspring of the Baxby marriage. Yet the story does
explore the subject of flesh-and-blood ties. Here sexual
constancy and familial devotion are seen as conflicting instincts, and the English Civil War, in which political allegiances divided families and brother fought brother, is a
convenient background for the story's theme: the emotional
wellsprings, personal and political, of loyalty to family,
spouse, and country. For the story's *Graphic* publication,
Hardy was forced to remove the threatened adultery of the
manuscript and to reduce it to a story about politics. In this
version, Anna begins to flee, but upon overhearing the plan of
the parliamentary forces to lure her away and to kill her
husband, returns to the castle to save his life; none of Baxby's
faults is mentioned, and Anna's 'domestic rebellion' is seen as
a temporary threat to 'the inviolability of the castle and its
garrison'.[26] But the manuscript version that was restored in
virtually all its particulars in the first edition treats the
concepts of domestic rebellion and loyalty in a much more
complex manner. In a consideration of the dissimilar personalities of Bedford and Baxby, and the different emotional
relationships they bear to Anna, the worthiness of each must
be weighed against the power of the sexual tie. While Anna's
husband is a formidable force in her life, her brother's moral
qualities also have a claim on her fidelity.

Anna's secret departure from Sherton Castle is a parodic
version of the love-inspired elopement in romance. Whereas
conventionally the maiden leaves secure home and family for
the adventurous lover, Anna flees the 'long and reposeful
breathings' of her husband 'in his comfortable bed' (171) for
her imperilled and unsheltered kinsman. Her nostalgic affection for William and sympathy for his suffering are linked to

her innate attraction to excitement and danger – as well, of course, as to a sentimental attachment to her past and the presexual love of her childhood. These feelings are thrown over, however, by Anna's accidental discovery of her husband's appointment with the young girl. Suddenly, all of her outbursts about loyalty, previously abstract and contradictory, are concrete and impassioned: 'Here was a pretty underhand business! Here were sly manoeuvrings! Here was faithlessness! Here was a precious assignation surprised in the midst! Her wicked husband, whom till this very moment she had ever deemed the soul of good faith – how could he!' (173)

The reason for Anna's return to the castle (and her reversion from parliamentary to royalist principles) is consistent with Hardy's conviction, obvious in much of his writing, that jealousy is an important, if not necessary, component of sexual attraction. The turning point is not Anna's discovery that her husband has been disloyal to her, but rather her realization that another woman is drawn to him: ' "How the wench loves him!" she said to herself, reasoning from the tones of the voice, which were plaintive and sweet and tender as a bird's. She changed from the home-hating truant to the strategic wife in one moment.' (172) Until the first edition, this passage had read 'timorous' for 'home-hating'.[27] The change emphasizes Hardy's intention to make Anna's decision to join her brother a rejection of her husband, and not a fearful flight from physical danger. The knowledge that Baxby is desirable to someone else revives in Anna the sexual feeling that had led her in the first place to leave family for husband. Her return to the castle is a symbolic gesture, representing her determination to protect the fortress of her marriage. Her manoeuvres to keep Baxby literally in his marital bed – locking the castle door, keeping the key under her pillow, and tying his hair to the bedpost – are in a comic sense as direct and forceful as those of Charles himself in trying to keep his power in the face of the Parliamentary Rebellion. But kingdoms and marriages are different realms, as the story itself amply demonstrates, and Anna's repressive measures lead simply to a happy resumption of power. In conventional terms, at least, 'Anna, Lady Baxby' has a happy ending, which attaches little importance to Baxby's forgotton tryst.

But there are unmistakable notes of discord and irony in the closing allusions to Baxby's later 'vicissitudes' and 'eccentric' conduct (174) which imply that perhaps Anna's exaction of loyalty from her husband is less complete than the evidence suggests. It is possible that Hardy intended the reader to treat Baxby's 'culpability as regards the intrigue' (173) more seriously than does the narrator, especially when one considers the fact that Edred Fitzpiers of *The Woodlanders* is 'on the mother's side . . . connected with the long line of the Lords Baxby of Sherton' (*TW*, 192). If one thinks of Baxby in terms of the more serious consequences of his descendant's infidelity, then the ending of 'Anna, Lady Baxby', with the heroine's forsaking of the faithful brother for the feckless husband, is a disturbing statement about the conflicting claims of familial and sexual love. It is also a comment on the nature of history, in which great events are shaped by trivial accidents. But more than any of the preceding stories in the volume, this narrative – perhaps because it has no single victim like Barbara or the abandoned children in 'Lady Mottisfont' and 'Squire Petrick's Lady' – is finally farcical rather than serious. Lacking the explicit didactic content of the moral exemplum, it represents the same form in its comic mode: a parable embodying not a moral but an absurdity that seems a natural part of life's experience. As in Hardy's later 'Satires of Circumstance' poems, the focus of 'Anna, Lady Baxby' is more on the comic situation than on the suffering that results from it.

'The Lady Penelope' returns to the more sombre emphasis of some of the earlier narratives. Its heroine is an innately likeable woman who becomes a victim of the renown that accompanies her beauty and title. As with Betty and Barbara, her fault is merely the 'unseemly wantonness' (188) and 'precipitancy' (180) that characterize youth, but because of her highly visible position in the community, she can never transcend the natural mistakes of her flirtatious adolescence. If 'Squire Petrick's Lady' depicts how a commoner can be corrupted by romantic notions about nobility, then 'The Lady Penelope' portrays the reverse process: the destruction of a beautiful and gifted woman of title by the hurtful interest of the community in her private life. Penelope is depicted at the start as a fairy-tale princess courted by three knights of varying age and character, and her attractiveness to men is as compelling as that of her classical namesake: 'Her beauty was so perfect, and her manner so entrancing, that suitors seemed to spring out of the ground wherever she went' (177–8). She is also like Homer's Penelope, however, in unwittingly inspiring among the men who court her a potentially violent conflict. Only in response to this grave possibility, and not out of coquettish impulse, does Penelope utter her famous 'roguish' quip: 'Have patience, have patience, you foolish men! Only bide your time quietly, and, in faith, I will marry you all in turn!' This comic 'sally' – a seemingly harmless verbal thrust meant to deflect more injurious blows – prevents the physical resort to sword and pistol. And although Penelope's stratagem is successful, she is conscious immediately of the impropriety of her 'arch jest' (179). It is not she, but her supposed friends, who turn Penelope's momentary indiscretion into a commonplace of gossip, and only with the communal elaboration of her playful remark does it begin to shape her life and to fulfil itself as a prophecy.

A second contributing factor in Penelope's unhappy fate is the reticence of Sir William Hervey, her preferred lover, in making his 'unaltered devotion' (180) known to her after the death of her first husband. Like Charles Barnet of 'Fellow-Townsmen', he reproaches the woman he loves for not sending him 'a more overt letter' (182), although he fails himself to make any overture. The irony of the misunderstanding is intensified by the fact that Penelope's marriage to her second husband is a frustrated response to William's hesitancy in approaching her – an expression of her pique 'at the backwardness of him she secretly desired to be forward' (180). After his marriage to Penelope, William is again at fault when he believes the rumours involving the death of her last husband without even asking her about them. Had he confronted Penelope with the accusations, the matter might have been easily cleared up. As it stands, it is a combination of Penelope's precipitancy, the community's gossip, and William's inaction that reduces her from a 'brave and buxom damsel' (178) to a woman 'dwindled thin in the face' whose rings fall 'off her fingers' and whose arms hang 'like the flails of the threshers' (186).

In its incrementally repeated incidents leading to the tragic fulfilment of a prophecy, and its image of rumours that 'rustled in the air like night-birds of evil omen' (186), 'The Lady Penelope' sets up a quasi-balladic pattern of recurrent events. But in the final analysis, it is the community's desire to see the prophecy borne out, and not the power of the prophecy itself, that seals Penelope's doom. Her marriage to Gale is in part a response to the manipulative appeals of her jesting friends that she live out her 'careless speech' (180), and when the story moves outside her circle of acquaintance it becomes dangerously distorted. The dialogue among the basket-weavers, the actual words of which were added for the first edition, demonstrates the way in which unfounded rumours can take on minute detail. The more detached from fact, the more precise untruths can become:

> 'A cupboard close to his bed, and the key in her pocket. Ah!' said one.
> 'And a blue phial therein – h'm!' said another.
> 'And spurge-laurel leaves among the hearth-ashes. Oh-oh!' said a third.   (185)

There is an incantatory quality to these words, as though the basket-weavers were a Greek chorus both telling and orchestrating the events, or witches working a spell. But the dialogue is given a power over Penelope's life by entirely explicable causes: the readiness of Sir William to believe what he overhears, and the failure of the community to express these insidious rumours 'openly' on account of Penelope's 'noble birth' (185). This story bears some resemblance to 'Anna, Lady Baxby': in both narratives, overheard conversations are a crucial element in the plot, and their consequences are especially profound because of the elevated positions of their heroines.

'The Duchess of Hamptonshire' raises some of the same questions as do the first two stories in *A Group of Noble Dames*, and returns to the issues that had opened the volume. Emmeline Oldbourne, like Betty Dornell and Barbara Grebe, is forced into marriage by a parent who places wealth and social prestige over affection and sexual passion. Again the main characters form a triangular pattern, with an impressionable and impulsive girl poised between an attractive youth and a wealthy titled man. Emmeline's tragedy, however, unlike Betty's or Barbara's, is that neither of her suitors can fulfil her sexual and emotional requirements. The Duke of Hamptonshire is cruel and selfish throughout, but the Reverend Alwyn Hill, in his principled refusal to rescue Emmeline from her suffering at her husband's hands, comes to represent a subtler form of egoism. Her death is caused as much by a state of grief and frustration at being left defenceless with the Duke as by the rigours of her journey; her plea to Alwyn – 'O, if you only knew how much to me this request to you is – how my life is wrapped up in it, you could not deny me!' (197) – is as much an anticipation of her fate as it is an expression of her desperation.

Emmeline is presented as a woman who, while naive and ignorant, embodies utter simplicity and unmixed goodness. Like Shakespeare's Miranda, she has 'been bred in comparative solitude' and is 'troubled and confused' (193) by encounters with men. Her predicament is like that of an imprisoned princess in a fairy tale, or a heroine in a Gothic romance. The castle in which the Duke confines her is reminiscent of Mrs Radcliffe's Udolpho:

> On still mornings, at the fire-lighting hour, when ghostly housemaids stalk the corridors, and thin streaks of light through the shutter-chinks lend startling winks and smiles to ancestors on canvas, twelve or fifteen thin stems of blue smoke sprouted upwards from these chimney-tops, and spread into a flat canopy on high.   (192)

Insufficiently aware of the legal and moral complexities involved in leaving her husband, Emmeline turns to Alwyn Hill to rescue her from his tyranny. The imagery used to introduce Hill suggests an untainted youthfulness that makes him a perfect physical match for the innocent Emmeline: 'He was a handsome young deacon with curly hair, dreamy eyes – so dreamy that to look long into them was like ascending and floating among summer clouds – a complexion as fresh as a flower, and a chin absolutely beardless.' (192–3) Hill's reaction to Emmeline's plan, however, indicates that his moral perceptions are far more subtle and more socially conscious than hers: she is an unfallen woman entreating a man who inhabits a fallen world.

Neither of the lovers is entirely right, however, and each is incapable of comprehending the other's logic. Emmeline can only appeal to natural law: 'Is it wrong to run away from the fire that scorches you?' Hill places social and moral law – or rather, the appearance of conforming to them publicly – above Emmeline's unhappiness: 'But it is wrong, Emmeline, all the same. . . . It would look wrong, at any rate, in this case.' (197) Hill knows that the Duke is ill-using Emmeline, but his impulse to protect her is stayed by his rigid sense of the proprieties of the married state. It is ironic that Hill should himself unwittingly bury Emmeline during his journey on the *Western Glory*: he is responsible to some degree for her death.

Hill may have a literary antecedent in Hawthorne's Arthur Dimmesdale, whose refusal to succumb to temptation is an expression less of moral strength than of rigorous, life-denying concern for reputation.[28] Together with Joshua Halborough and Randolph Twycott of *Life's Little Ironies*, these ministers can be placed in a line of literature's hypocritical clerics, represented later in the century by Ibsen's Parson Manders.[29] Hill seems to derive some characteristics from Clym Yeobright (*The Return of the Native* was still being serialized when the story first appeared). Though different in calling and outward appearance, both men possess a self-absorbing idealism equivalent at times to moral blindness, and turn to rhetoric and preaching as a professional expression of their personal preoccupations. Hill also immediately foreshadows the more comically hypocritical Stockdale of 'The Distracted Preacher' (published a year after 'The Duchess of Hamptonshire' first appeared) in his moral naivety, youthful beauty, and general fastidiousness – attributes that will later assume a more sinister form in Angel Clare.

But Hill is not an interesting portrayal of this type, partly because Emmeline, the victim of his moralistic attitudes as Tess is of Angel's, lacks the tragic grandeur necessary to dramatize her lover's self-absorption and priggishness. The story lacks effectiveness, too, because of the distracting contrivance of its plot – too much space is devoted to unravelling the mystery of Emmeline's disappearance – and the unsatisfying ambiguities of its moral situation. Angel's censure of Tess is an entirely selfish and unmoral act, while

Alwyn's refusal to elope with Emmeline, though heartless and cowardly, is based on his recognition of her legally and morally binding marriage – a tie made all the more restricting because she is a duchess. The reader is left condemning Alwyn for his lack of sympathy but unable to imagine an alternative plan of action. These problems may be attributed to the story's early composition. 'The Duchess of Hamptonshire' contains the mixture of absurdity and pathos that characterizes the *Noble Dames* stories written in the early 1890s, but lacks the moral coherence and sociological acuity of the later narratives.

To a much greater degree, the same fault mars 'The Honourable Laura', first published in 1881. Superficially, the story has situations paralleling those faced by other noble dames – for example, a conflict between two men over the affections of a wealthy young woman, and an elopement – but it fails to present the heroine's weaknesses and mistakes in terms either of a fully realized characterization or, as in other *Noble Dames* stories, of the environment that produced her. In the story's original version, Laura (first called Lucetta)[30] was not of noble birth,[31] and few changes were later made to signal that she was a member of the aristocracy, or to link her circumstances with this background. Instead, 'The Honourable Laura' exploits sensational melodramatic elements – the sham opera singer complete with moustache, the dramatic confrontation between husband and lover leading to a challenge for a duel, and the supposed murder at the cliff – in place of genuine dramatic content. But Hardy may still have considered 'The Honourable Laura' as a suitable last story for *A Group of Noble Dames* because of its happy marriage, achieved after years of penitential suffering. This optimistic conclusion parallels the ending of 'The First Countess of Wessex', while also representing, with its references to tricycles and railway stations, a story 'more modern in [its] date of action' (206) than the previous narratives. This late nineteenth-century setting points to the similarities rather than the differences between past and present: as in earlier centuries, the heroine's fate is decided by the men who lay claim to her (she does not even know of the duel). Her predicament is a version of that of the other noble dames – here expressed in the contemporary mode of stage melodrama. But because no explanation is given either for Laura's transgression or for her sudden turn from pouting tantrums to mature contrition, the story remains an unsatisfactory conclusion to the collection as a whole.

The serious weaknesses of the last two stories in *A Group of Noble Dames*, and the varied quality of all the narratives, point to the essentially miscellaneous nature of the volume's contents. Hardy did attempt to establish some superficial links among the stories by a series of internal cross-references. It is first mentioned at Dornell's dinner at Falls-Park that 'Baxby of Sherton Castle' (9) is a lady's man; Uplandtowers's 'intimate friend' is 'one of the Drenkhards' (56); and among those whom the Mottisfonts see in Bath are 'the Earl and Countess of Wessex, Sir John Grebe, the Drenkhards', and 'the old Duke of Hamptonshire' (125).[32] Hardy also improved the structure of the volume as a whole by changing the sequence of the stories. In the *Graphic* version, 'Anna, Lady Baxby' comes after 'Barbara of the House of Grebe' and 'The Marchioness of Stonehenge', and is followed by 'The Lady Icenway', 'Squire Petrick's Lady', and 'Lady Mottisfont'. But Hardy's rearrangement of the tales for the first edition is more coherent. 'The First Countess' and 'Barbara' are contrasting versions of a similar pattern, as are 'The Marchioness of Stonehenge' and 'Lady Mottisfont'. 'The Lady Icenway' and 'Squire Petrick's Lady' continue the theme of the child as victim begun in the previous two stories, and 'Anna, Lady Baxby' treats the related subject of fraternal affection. The final three stories, though they have thematic affinities with the earlier material, fit less neatly into the pattern – probably because they were conceived separately from the rest of the volume. It is possible that Hardy only added these concluding stories in order to pad the book out – giving it a numerical roundness like that of the *Decameron*.

   That Hardy himself perceived some of the weaknesses of *A Group of Noble Dames* is evident from the letter he sent to Lord Lytton, in which he described the book as 'rather a frivolous piece of work, which I took in hand in a sort of desperation during a fit of low spirits'[33] – perhaps a symptom of his mental and physical exhaustion upon completing *Tess*. But although Hardy said that he wrote *A Group of Noble Dames* merely 'by

way of relaxation',[34] he did pursue his material quite energeti-
cally, and his selective use of the historical sources reveals that
he had a clear sense of his own fictional intentions when
adapting the facts for his stories. Five of the ten narratives are
based on Hutchins – two in skeletal details only, three more
specifically. One, 'The Duchess of Hamptonshire', incorporates an incident recorded in *Early Life*.[35] 'The Lady Icenway'
has no discoverable basis in fact, but bears some resemblance
to a proposed 'story or play' set down in a notebook in 1873.[36]
The remainder of the stories – 'The Marchioness of
Stonehenge', 'Lady Mottisfont', and 'The Honourable
Laura' – have no known sources.

The cases where Hardy was working with familiar historical
material indicate that his aim was not accuracy, but a particular symbolic configuration of events. 'The First Countess of
Wessex', the story with the best documented historical basis,
illustrates this point. Squire and Mrs Dornell are based on the
grandparents of Lady Susan O'Brien, Thomas and Susannah
Strangways-Horner. Their daughter Elizabeth, Lady Susan's
mother, married Stephen Fox (Reynard) in 1735 when she
was thirteen years old, but because of Thomas Horner's
opposition to the union they did not live as husband and wife
until 1739.[37] As in the fictional story, Horner had an estate
considerably smaller than his wife's and, as a simple country
squire, shared few of her passionate ambitions.[38] He died in
1741, after which Susannah 'spent the latter part of her life in
acts of piety, charity, and generosity'.[39] There are other details
in the story, however, which do not correspond with the
historical facts. During their years of separation, Stephen and
Elizabeth met occasionally, but not against the will of Susannah. On the contrary, she plotted their trysts, and even
planned a second marriage ceremony in order to confirm
their elopement.[40] There is no evidence that Elizabeth fell in
love with anyone else while separated from Stephen, nor that
her mother opposed the union after Horner's death. Historically, indeed, Elizabeth began to live with her husband two
years before the death of her father in 1741.[41] Hardy also
ignores – or perhaps never realized – the political basis for
Horner's objection to Fox. An old Tory, he opposed his
daughter's marriage not only because of her tender years, but
also because Fox (later the uncle of Charles James Fox) had

affiliations with some of Walpole's Whig cohorts.[42]

Hardy's changes and omissions serve chiefly to enhance the subtleties in characterization and motive that he works into the historical story. He places the Squire's death before Betty's marriage in order first to remove the father's active opposition, and then to set into motion Mrs Dornell's 'remorseful *volte-face*' (44) – perhaps Hardy's fictional explanation for the historical Susannah's sudden burst of philanthropy after her husband's death. Hardy orchestrates the details – and hence distorts them – in order to dramatize the domestic conflict between the Horners over their daughter's future.

A similar mixture of fact and fictional transformation characterizes Hardy's use of sources in 'Anna, Lady Baxby'. Anna is based on Lady Anne Russell, who was married to George, Lord Digby (Baxby),[43] and whose brother, William Russell, Earl of Bedford, led the parliamentary forces which camped outside the loyalist stronghold of Sherborne Castle (Sherton) in 1642. It was the lodge at Sherborne (not, as Hardy has it, the castle itself) from which Lady Anne emerged to confront her brother, but other details of the encounter seem to come directly from Hutchins:

> While the Earl of Bedford besieged the castle, tradition reports that the wife of George, Lord Digby, son of the Earl of Bristol, his sister, was then at the lodge. He sent a message to desire her to quit it, as he had orders from the Parliament to demolish it. She immediately went on horseback to his tent, at the camp now called Bedford's Castle, and told him, 'if he persisted in his intention, he should find his sister's bones buried in the ruins,' and instantly left him; which spirited behaviour in all probability preserved it.[44]

In the historical circumstances, Lady Anne was using her relationship to her brother as a defensive weapon for the then outnumbered loyalists – a strategy pursued again later by the Marquis of Hertford who ended his terms of partial surrender to Bedford by threatening that if these were not accepted, he would 'place the Earl of Bedford's sister on the battlements, who should serve as a flag of defiance to him and all his followers'.[45] This use of Anne as a political pawn to control the military moves of her brother is not depicted in Hardy's version of the story. Instead, he intensifies and fills out the emotional meeting between brother and sister – William's tearfulness, their impassioned argument, and the embrace within the tent are all plausible extrapolations from the original situation – and history becomes pure imaginative speculation at the point when Anne experiences a change of heart (and political allegiance) in favour of her brother. Here it becomes clear that the real substance of Hardy's story lies in Anna's choosing between the antithetical personalities of the two brothers-in-law, and not between their political beliefs.

This emphasis on the differences between Baxby and William has historical authenticity. The original George Digby was condemned by the parliamentary party for suddenly turning on them in the case against the Earl of Strafford and was notorious for his impulsive ambitiousness,[46] while the Earl of Bedford was well known for his courage and constancy.[47] In the fictional story, Hardy never attempts any justification for the political commitments of either of the two men, but rather translates their public characteristics into terms of private conduct concerning familial and sexual love. This shift from a political to a personal and emotional emphasis directs the reader to Hardy's actual focus in this story – separate from, if not superfluous to, the historical circumstances: the fluctuation of a woman's feelings between her ties to family and to a sexual partner, between her loyalty to the past and a practical commitment to the present.

'The Lady Penelope' also veers from the actual at precisely the points that define Hardy's artistic concerns in writing it. The plot is based on the description in Hutchins of Lady Penelope Darcy, daughter and heiress of Mary, Countess of Rivers, who married Sir George Trenchard at Wolveton House in the early years of the seventeenth century:

Sir George dying soon after his marriage, she remarried Sir John Gage, of Firle, co. Sussex, bart. by whom only she had issue; and being again left a widow, she then married William Hervey, of Ickworth, bart. She was courted by her three husbands at one time; but quarrels arising between them, she artfully put an end to them, by threatening the first aggressor with her perpetual displeasure; and humorously told them, that if they would be quiet and have

patience she would have them all in their turns, which at last
actually happened.[48]

Because this story is set at an earlier date than any of the others
in *A Group of Noble Dames*, Hardy had hardly to disguise even
the names of its historical figures, but the elements he adds to
the skeletal plot found in Hutchins are significant. The
characters of the four chief persons in the story are filled out
in such a way that Penelope's innocent roguishness is set
dramatically against the potential violence of her three
suitors. Both her preference for Sir William and his reticent
character are established soon after her first marriage. The
historical offspring of the second marriage is replaced by a
stillborn child of the third – emblematic here as in 'Barbara' of
a serious defect in the sexual union which created it. Most
importantly, the story emphasizes, what the chronicle never
even suggests, that the gossip of Penelope's contemporaries
was to some degree responsible for the tragic fulfilment of her
flippant prophecy.

Two other stories reveal an even freer elaboration of the
facts. Barbara Grebe is based on Barbara Webb, sole heiress to
her parents' fortune, who married the fifth Earl of Shaftesbury in 1786 and died at Florence in 1819. It is clear that
Hardy got his information initially from Hutchins because
Mabella, a name which he considered for Barbara at the
manuscript stage, was also a Webb family name.[49] But there is
nothing in Hutchins to suggest either Barbara's first marriage
or her grisly history. Indeed, the historical fifth Earl of
Shaftesbury, unlike Lord Uplandtowers, died more than
eight years before his wife.[50] Similarly, the plot of 'Squire
Petrick's Lady' is based only selectively on the facts reported in
Hutchins. The Petrick family is drawn from the descendants
of the historical Peter Walters who bought numerous estates
from the aristocracy during the first half of the eighteenth
century and was known as the most enterprising and oppor-
tunistic businessman of his time. Like Hardy's fictional
character, Walters 'would not lend money or buy without
seeing every acre', outlived his son, and entailed his entire
estate to his eldest grandson and his male heirs. Beyond these
details, however, Hardy's story turns into fiction. Peter
Walters had three grandsons instead of two, and the eldest left

only a fifteen-year-old daughter at his death.[51] The presumed adultery with the Marquis of Christminster and the image of the rejected son were both added to the historical circumstances. Hardy's alterations and embellishments make the stories essentially different from their written sources. One must not accept too literally his claim that while names in the volume are 'disguised', its incidents are 'approximating to fact'.[52]

The nominal basis in local fact which some of the stories did have, however, made publication risky because there were living descendants of these historical figures still living in Dorset. Perhaps for this reason, Hardy disguised the names and disclaimed his responsibility as author by establishing a narrative setting involving the Wessex Field and Antiquarian Club. This strategy allowed him to insist upon the status of the stories as fiction rather than as historical fact. These stories lack even the authoritative narrative voice found in such Wessex tales as 'The Three Strangers' and 'The Withered Arm'. The Club members represent not an oral tradition of a general and impersonal nature but rather the limited viewpoints of individuals whose judgments are prejudiced by their sex, their social station, and their conventional morals. As Lascelles Abercrombie puts it, the narrative framework of *A Group of Noble Dames* contains 'the quiet irony of the whole – these comfortable representatives of a world satisfied with unexamined formulae, telling each other tragical tales which reveal, though they never suspect it, the reality of life's processes as something by no means to be contained in easy-going formulae'.[53]

Hardy emphasizes both at the beginning and at the end of *A Group of Noble Dames* the unusually 'inclusive and intersocial character' (49) of the Antiquarian Club, with a range of types including a maltster and a churchwarden, an ageing spark and a gentleman. They share in common, however, their sex and their engrossing interest in the lives of their social betters (none of them has a noble title), causing them to make of the women their own private romances: 'curious tales of fair dames, of their loves and hates, their joys and their misfortunes, their beauty and their fate' (50). These narrators are similar to the people described in *A Laodicean* who come to see the local ladies act in a performance of *Love's Labour's Lost* because they were eager to see well-known notabilities in unwonted situations. When ladies, hitherto only beheld in frigid, impenetrable positions behind their coachmen in the High Streets of the county, were about to reveal their hidden traits, home attitudes, intimate smiles, nods, and perhaps kisses, to the public eye, it was a throwing open of fascinating social secrets not to be missed for money. (261–2)

It may not be accidental that the word 'benighted' (meaning unenlightened as well as confined by weather), which appears in the original title of 'The Honourable Laura', is also used to characterize the members of the Antiquarian Club as they leave the museum to go their separate ways. The storytellers are themselves unenlightened – seeing these women only as sexual objects, and judging them merely as vessels of honour or dishonour.

In this context, even the title of the volume becomes ironic. The phrase *A Group of Noble Dames* was probably broadly modelled on Chaucer's *Legend of Good Women* and Boccaccio's *De Claris Mulieribus*, but the particular words Hardy chose for his title are curiously and richly ambivalent in their meaning. The word 'Noble' is used as a pun. In its technical sense of 'titled', it is appropriate only for some of the women, and its other definition – having high moral qualities or ideals – draws attention, by its varied aptness of application, to the narrators' convention-bound understanding of the word. Lady Icenway is noble in title but not in character, while the Lady Penelope possesses a degree of moral nobility for which the narrators fail to give her credit. The word 'Dames' also has a range of contradictory and suggestive interpretations. As a title, it is confined to the wife of a knight or baronet or below (contradicting the first meaning of 'noble') and applies to few of the women in the volume; its more archaic meaning, the head of a household, can only be used accurately to describe Betty Dornell or 'The Honourable Laura'. In any case, Hardy may have invoked the term 'Noble Dames' – used also in Scott's *Marmion* (VI.v) – simply to give the title of his book an historical flavour.

The titles of the stories similarly suggest additional levels of meaning. Each can be seen as representing the position –

emotional rather than titular – which its heroine has achieved. It is symbolic that Barbara Grebe's story should bear her childhood name instead of that of either of her husbands (emotionally she never reaches the status of an adult); that Annetta Petrick should be called both Petrick's wife, as she truly is ('lady' can mean 'wife' when linked to a possessive noun), and the 'Lady' of title she imagines herself to be; that 'The Lady Penelope' should bear none of her three married names but the Christian name symbolizing her attractiveness to men; and that 'Anna, Lady Baxby' should appear under both the Christian name by which her brother addresses her, and her married title. It is appropriate too that those women who place rank above natural instinct – 'The Marchioness of Stonehenge', 'Lady Mottisfont', and 'The Lady Icenway' – should bear the titles for which they sacrifice their sexual and maternal passions. Only the first and last stories seem to have names utterly lacking in irony. 'The First Countess of Wessex' suggests that Betty is the first aristocrat of Hardy's Wessex and indicates that she mothered a whole line of descendants to succeed her in title, while 'The Honourable Laura' is distinguished not only by a formal designation of her social status but also by the virtue she finally acquired.

These levels of meaning lie far beyond the comprehension of the narrators, who see the women only as objects of fanciful daydreaming and complacent moral assessment. This tendency in the Club members to judge rather than to sympathize forms the basis for the distinctive narrative tone of the stories in *A Group of Noble Dames*. Apart from 'A Few Crusted Characters', it is the only work by Hardy which consistently uses first-person point of view, and yet, paradoxically, never do Hardy's narrators seem more smugly removed from the sufferings of the characters they describe than in this volume. In most of the stories, the woman's rashness is deemed worthy of censure, while no account is taken of the wrongs performed by father, lover, or husband – nor of the social conventions that have served to stunt her emotional growth. So the Local Historian concludes 'The First Countess of Wessex' with the condescending declaration, 'Such is woman; or rather (not to give offence by so sweeping an assertion), such was Betty Dornell' (48). The Old Surgeon ends 'Barbara of the House of Grebe' by commending the Dean of Melchester's 'excellent sermon' about 'the folly of indulgence in sensuous love for a handsome form merely' (91). The Colonel ignores Lord Baxby's infidelity and sees Anna as an instance of how 'the more dreamy and impulsive nature of woman engendered within her erratic fancies' (164). The judgment of some of the Club members that the fate of Lady Penelope 'ought to be quite clearly recognized as a chastisement' (188) is an indication that the story's full complexity has not reached them, and the Quiet Gentleman's similar evaluation of Emmeline Old-bourne repeats this insensitivity.

Anderling of 'The Lady Icenway' – surely not the most evil man in the volume – is the only male character to receive any disapproval, and 'The Marchioness of Stonehenge' is unique in eliciting criticism that is analytical as well as judgmental: 'The sentimental member said that Lady Caroline's history afforded a sad instance of how an honest human affection will become shamefaced and mean under the frost of class-division and social prejudices.' (111) Significantly, the Club members are most wrong-headed in their judgment of Squire Petrick, the character who as a middle-class male most resembles themselves. They recognize only Annetta Petrick's 'curious mental delusion' (163) and are quite blind to the degree to which the Squire repeats and compounds her self-deception by looking upon her alleged affair with a marquis as a means toward 'improving the blood and breed' of his family. In the other stories, the narrators project their own assumptions about the aristocracy onto figures they can never wholly understand. But Petrick is one of their own kind. Despite their professed cynicism they are, like him, men 'of good old beliefs in the divinity of kings and those about 'em' (158), betraying by their romantic fascination with title that they too simultaneously love and despise the men of whom they speak in such superior tones.

These shared assumptions make the narrators almost indistinguishable from one another. It is mildly interesting that 'Barbara' should be told by a surgeon and 'Anna' by a colonel, but none of the stories is linked in any functional way to the personality of its teller. Often Hardy is inconsistent in his use of the first-person narrator, only reminding the reader at isolated moments that the story is being uttered by a fictional character. At one point, the reader is told that the story is merely the 'substance' (133) of the original account, at another, that it is 'only an approximation' (149). It is obvious that Hardy's intention was not, like Chaucer's, to establish a close and complex relationship between his stories and their individual tellers – he devoted little attention to the narrative links between the stories when expanding the collection – but rather to create in the Wessex Field and Antiquarian Club a general narrative context for the volume as a whole. He described this technique in a letter to the *Pall Mall Gazette*: 'to guard against the infliction of "a hideous and hateful fantasy," . . . the action is thrown back into a second plane or middle distance, being described by a character to characters, and not point-blank by author to reader.'[54] The narrative setting is established, in other words, not so much by the single characters telling their stories but, more important, by their relationships to each other as storyteller and audience engaging in constant dialogue about their subject. John Bayley has criticized this narrative technique because he prefers Hardy's own presence to that of a persona,[55] but the use of these storytellers establishes both the meaning of the individual stories and the rich ambivalence of the whole volume. Not only do these narrators see their stories entirely from a male point of view, but this distortion is compounded by their antiquarian interest which leads them to see the dames only as historical figures, past and dead. The narrative setting suggests a constant contrasting between the passionate vitality of the women and the 'regulation papers on deformed butterflies, fossil ox-horns, prehistoric dung-mixens, and such like' for which their stories have been 'made to do duty' (48–9). The narrators perceive the dames as they do fossils, or stuffed birds 'murdered to extinction' (49).

This attitude on the part of the narrators makes the description of the Club, spoken at the beginning of the volume by a more enlightened narrative voice, ironically apt and thematically significant:

> This Club was of an inclusive and intersocial character; to a degree, indeed, remarkable for the part of England in which it had its being – dear, delightful Wessex, whose statuesque dynasties are even now only just beginning to feel the shaking of the new and strange spirit without, like

that which entered the lonely valley of Ezekiel's vision and
made the dry bones move: where the honest squires,
tradesmen, parsons, clerks, and people still praise the Lord
with one voice for His best of all possible worlds.   (49)

The conclusion of the volume, with its image of 'stuffed birds'
and 'varnished skulls' (236), makes abundantly clear that these
'benighted members of the Field-Club' (235) have still not
truly brought to life, even in their own imaginations, the 'dry
bones' of the noble dames – a fact demonstrated by their
self-satisfied judgments of these women and by the prejudicial
social barriers which arise even among themselves as they
depart for another year (235). The references in the quoted
passage to Ezekiel's vision and to *Candide* come together to
present the central issue which divides the reader from the
narrators. Like Voltaire's Dr Pangloss they cling to a complacent optimism that accepts the status quo without question or
self-examination. But the reader, who has presumably seen
the stories from a wider perspective, must judge the dames
differently, as though he has encountered 'the new and
strange spirit without' which sees persons in terms of their
humanity rather than their class, and some forms of suffering
as the effect of injustice and prejudice rather than as an
unalterable fact of life. It is this contradiction between the
narrow moral pronouncements of the narrators and the
probing moral questions inspired by the narratives which
makes it possible to invoke such a term as 'ambivalent
exempla' to describe them. Exempla supportive only of
conventional morals in the eyes of the 'benighted' narrators,
they challenge the reader to think with a more enlightened
point of view about the central moral issues which have led to
such suffering and stifling of human affections: questions of
birth, inheritance, class, family, and sex itself.

3 *Life's Little Ironies*: Tragedies of Circumstance

Life's Little Ironies at once departs from and develops the subject matter and technique of Hardy's earlier stories. While *Wessex Tales* and *A Group of Noble Dames* are historical and rural, the major events of these stories – with the significant exceptions of 'To Please His Wife', 'The Fiddler of the Reels', and the collection of sketches called 'A Few Crusted Characters' – take place in an unspecified present. The volume resembles the two preceding ones in differing ways: as in *Wessex Tales*, its narrative voice assumes a rhetorical stance – this time ironic rather than pastoral – which teaches the reader to interpret events from a particular perspective; as in *A Group of Noble Dames*, social conventions play an important part both in the formation of character and in the development of the action. But whereas in *A Group of Noble Dames* these conventions are linked to a particular period in history, in *Life's Little Ironies* they are seen as forces operating in the present, and among the respectable middle classes to which many of Hardy's readers belonged. This shift to an explicit concern with contemporary problems is an expression of Hardy's tendency at the end of his fiction-writing career to question outspokenly both the social conventions of the time and the literary conventions created by and supportive of them. Never, as H. E. Bates notes, did the conventions of social morality play a larger part in literature than in the course of Hardy's lifetime,[1] and it was during the late 1880s and early 1890s – when all of the *Life's Little Ironies* stories were composed – that he seems to have felt most strongly a frustration at the restrictive power of Victorian moral conventions over contemporary life and literary expression.

The entries in Hardy's notebooks between 1888 and 1894, the period when the stories were written, express his increasing vexation at the rigidity of 'social conventions and contrivances – the artificial forms of living' (*EL*, 279). A central issue in his mind, as *The Woodlanders* and *Jude the Obscure* reveal, was the failure of marriage to solve what he called 'the immortal puzzle – given the man and woman, how to find a basis for their sexual relation' (*TW*, vii). A large measure of his sympathy was for women, as this note of April 1891 demonstrates:

> A community of women, especially young women, inspires not reverence but protective tenderness in the breast of one who views them. Their belief in circumstances, in convention, in the rightness of things, which you know to be not only wrong but damnably wrong, makes the heart ache, even when they are waspish and hard.   (*EL*, 308)

In 1893, he reported a conversation he had at Lady Londonderry's about 'the difficulties of separation, of terminable marriages when there are children, and of the nervous strain of living with a man when you know he can throw you over at any moment' (*LY*, 23). The following year, he wrote a brief article for the *New Review* containing his advice on how to prepare one's daughters for marriage, and went on to question 'whether marriage, as we at present understand it, is such a desirable goal for all women as it is assumed to be'.[2] Chagrined also at the corresponding restrictions of convention over literature, Hardy complained that novelists were 'obliged to arrange situations and *dénouements*' which were 'indescribably unreal' and to 'make characters act unnaturally' in order to produce 'the spurious effect of their being in harmony with social forms and ordinances'. To his mind, the proper subject of literature was rather a frank treatment of 'the position of man and woman in nature'.[3]

Hardy defended the conclusion of *Tess* by saying that 'the optimistic "living happy ever after" always raises in me a greater horror by its ghastly unreality than the honest sadness that comes of a logical and inevitable tragedy'[4] – a statement which could also be made about the stories in *Life's Little*

Ironies. Hardy's conception of the tragic form is, indeed, important to an understanding of all his late fiction. In 'Candour in English Fiction', he recommended for the late nineteenth century a literary form like that of the tragedies 'formerly worked out with such force by the Periclean and Elizabethan dramatists', in which the basic 'collision between the individual and the general' receives

> enrichment by further truths – in other words, original treatment: treatment which seeks to show Nature's unconsciousness not of essential laws, but of those laws framed merely as social expedients by humanity, without a basis in the heart of things; treatment which expresses the triumph of the crowd over the hero, of the commonplace majority over the exceptional few.[5]

Hardy's view of contemporary fiction as a new form of tragedy contributes to the structure, tone, and narrative technique of the stories in *Life's Little Ironies*, in which small episodes are seen as tragic, and in which social conventions play a major role in working out the destiny of the characters. This is not to say that Hardy's stories are deterministic, but rather to point out that whereas in classical and Shakespearean tragedy character is the dominant mover of the tragic action, here the catastrophe is reached by the dramatic interaction of persons and society, of character and environment. As he set down in a notebook in 1889: 'That which, socially, is a great tragedy, may be in Nature no alarming circumstance' (*EL*, 286).

This concern with the social aspect of tragedy creates a unique combination of tragic and comic effects. Hardy wrote in 1888: 'If you look beneath the surface of any farce you see a tragedy; and, on the contrary, if you blind yourself to the deeper issues of a tragedy you see a farce.' (*EL*, 282) He explores this perception by pursuing the tragic dimensions of situations that contemporary literature was accustomed to treat in a satirical or sentimental vein. It is relevant that at the end of 1890 Hardy was reading 'mostly' satirists (*EL*, 301), for in *Life's Little Ironies* he, like the satirical writer, points to the vices and follies of men and to the contradictions inherent in their lives in society. But Hardy's ultimate purpose is different

from that of the satirist, who exposes inconsistencies in order
to evoke ridicule and contempt. Here a recognition of human
foibles inspires sympathy and a deepened understanding of
the tyranny of social conventions. As in the 'Satires of
Circumstance' poems, characters are the victims or perpe-
trators of absurd predicaments, but at the same time the
emphasis on the human suffering underlying 'Circumstance'
gives to the stories a tragic dimension. 'Tragedies of circumstance', they contain satirical plots which are inverted to
create tragic effects. Using the subject matter and situations of
comedy, they elicit from the reader pity and fear, the
emotions of tragedy. This effect is achieved by the use of a
narrative voice that looks at events not from the complacent
distance of the Antiquarian Club but from the compassionate
perspective of a philosopher who understands human nature
though he cannot change it. Guided by this humane point of
view, the reader learns to override customary Victorian
attitudes, discerning with intelligence the real moral issues
and judging them with a charity that transcends convention.

'An Imaginative Woman', moved to the beginning of *Life's
Little Ironies* in 1912, sets the keynote for Hardy's conception
of the volume as a whole. Its subject is the failure of a
nineteenth-century middle-class marriage, its theme the futility of imagining that life will conform to private dreams. Its
plot is a carefully wrought inversion of the conventions of
sentimental fiction and drama: the gradual building up of
romantic expectations is met not by happy fulfilment but by
disappointment and regret. Ella Marchmill,[6] the story's
heroine, is at once a victim of circumstances and the builder of
her own unhappy fate. Her inner life, like that of many of
Ibsen's heroines, is made up of conflicting forces: romantic
fantasizing and the practical business of living; intellectual
and physical passion; conjugal, maternal, and Platonic love.[7]
The story's original title was 'A Woman of Imagination',[8] but
Hardy's later choice rightly stresses Ella's hubris – not her
imagination but her imaginativeness.[9] Her chief fault, and the
cause for much of her unhappiness, is a tendency to draw only
'vague conclusions' about her position as a wife and mother
and to channel all her 'delicate and ethereal emotions' into
'imaginative occupations, day-dreams, and night-sighs'

(4).* Ella's poetry is an evasion of reality rather than a heightened engagement in it.

The 'commonplace' (7) vulgarity of Ella's husband stems from a want of sympathy or subtlety in his thinking, and his consequent reduction of all responses to crude and dismissive judgments: 'Bless his picturesque heart!' (18); 'What sly animals women are!' (27); 'Get away, you poor little brat! You are nothing to me!' (31) His supreme satisfaction 'with a condition of sublunary things which [makes] weapons a necessity' parallels his unthinking complacency toward Ella. Although 'usually kind and tolerant to her' (5), he is oblivious to her emotional needs. Ella, however, also contributes to the sterility of the marriage. Her evasive tactic of 'shrinking humanely from detailed knowledge of her husband's trade' (4) is part of her instinctive hesitancy in confronting problems, and she is as secretive about the events of her own inner life as Marchmill is about his social activities. A complete incompatibility of temperament makes Ella and William reciprocally indifferent.

Ella's attraction to Robert Trewe reflects both the incompleteness of her marriage and her failure to acquire a mature sense of her own worth. She is drawn to him by an adolescent self-absorption rather than a desire to love someone else. So one of Ella's first impulses upon taking over Trewe's room is to test 'the reflecting powers of the mirror in the wardrobe door' (6). As she tells her husband on her deathbed, 'I wanted a fuller appreciator, perhaps, rather than another lover – ' (30). Ella sees Robert Trewe only in terms of his role as a poet – a position to which she herself aspires. Much of the first-hand reporting about Trewe is done by Mrs Hooper, who has a romantic and stereotyped idea of a poet's character and physical appearance, but Ella's similarly naive adulation also includes jealousy. Her physical reaction to him is an aspect of her sense of intellectual inadequacy, inspiring a bizarre, one-sided rivalry with 'this circumambient, unapproachable master of hers' (11). In the scene in which she dons Trewe's mackintosh and cap before the mirror, Ella thrills at the sensation of wearing the poet's clothing and prays that it

---

*In this chapter only, page references to *Life's Little Ironies* appear without identifying initials.

might inspire her like the mantle of Elijah, but at the next moment a 'consciousness of her weakness beside him' makes her feel 'quite sick' (12). The same mixture of sexual fantasy, intellectual admiration, and professional envy emerges when Ella ceremoniously prepares, as if she were about to make love, to look at Trewe's picture. After 'first getting rid of superfluous garments and putting on her dressing-gown', she addresses the image 'in her lowest, richest, tenderest tone: "And it's *you* who've so cruelly eclipsed me these many times!" ' (16)

Ella's sexual feelings become still more explicit when she is contemplating the scraps of verse which Trewe has written on the wall behind his bed. Her most passionate fantasies are linked to Trewe's character as a poet, and to her intense yearning to assume that role herself. As in the scene with the poet's mackintosh, Ella attempts to assume Trewe's posture in the hope that this might inspire her creativity:

> He must often have put up his hand so – with the pencil in it. Yes, the writing was sideways, as it would be if executed by one who extended his arm thus.
>   These inscribed shapes of the poet's world,
>
>> 'Forms more real than living man,
>> Nurslings of immortality,'
>
> were, no doubt, the thoughts and spirit-strivings which had come to him in the dead of night, when he could let himself go and have no fear of the frost of criticism. No doubt they had often been written up hastily by the light of the moon, the rays of the lamp, in the blue-grey dawn, in full daylight perhaps never. And now her hair was dragging where his arm had lain when he secured the fugitive fancies; she was sleeping on a poet's lips, immersed in the very essence of him, permeated by his spirit as by an ether.   (17)

Here images of sexual desire and poetic inspiration are inextricably mixed, as if the two impulses were one in Ella's mind.

Not only does Ella link her erotic fantasies with Trewe's role as a poet, but she also thinks of him in peculiarly literary terms. The images of the quoted passage – as well as the two lines of poetry – are taken from the speech of a spirit in

Prometheus Unbound (I, 737–51). Shelley's spirit sees the poet as
an ethereal, almost supernatural being, occupying a level of
existence different from that of mortal men: 'Nor seeks nor
finds he mortal blisses,/ But feeds on the aërial kisses/ Of
shapes that haunt thought's wildernesses' (I, 740–2). In a
similar fashion, Ella thinks of Trewe as an imaginary figure
conjured up in a dream, likening her position to that of the
bride in the Song of Songs imagining in sleep the arrival of her
beloved. Ella's engagement in literature is deeply emotional,
but it is completely removed from actual experience. For this
reason, the jarring contrast of Ella's husband's 'heavy step'
(17), which interrupts her while she is looking at Trewe's
picture, has important symbolic and actual implications. His
arrival 'with the air of a man who had dined not badly', his kiss,
and the lovemaking which must surely have followed his
statement, 'I wanted to be with you to-night' (18), are for Ella
both a negation and a desecration of her love for the ethereal
poet. It is presumably at this moment – when Ella's vulgar
husband disturbs her erotic reverie – that the 'little brat' (31)
of the story's conclusion is conceived.

The complications ensuing from Ella's exclusively imaginative relationship with Robert Trewe and her exclusively
physical relationship with William Marchmill are most forci-
bly demonstrated in her attitude toward her children. When
the reader first sees Ella, she is reading a book while they are
'considerably further ahead with the nurse' (3). Throughout
the story, Ella's poetic fancies and her maternal responsibilities are opposed. The publication of her book of poetry is
described in language that might be applied to a miscarriage
or the birth of a stillborn child, and at this juncture in her
poetic career Ella again becomes pregnant in actual fact:

> a few reviews noticed her poor little volume; but nobody
> talked of it, nobody bought it, and it fell dead in a
> fortnight – if it had ever been alive.
>   The author's thoughts were diverted to another groove
> just then by the discovery that she was going to have a third
> child.   (9)

Coincidentally, but significantly, Marchmill pays 'the publisher's bill with the doctor's' (9), and Ella is left with still

another child 'to a commonplace father' (7). As her imagined relationship with Robert Trewe grows more intense, Ella's feelings about her children subtly conflict with her emotions about the rising poet. When he cancels his visit to Coburg House, she finds that she cares about the children only 'half as much as usual' (14), and when he fails to arrive at her Midland home at 'the pregnant day and hour' (22), she begins 'unnecessarily kissing the children', until she is overcome by 'a sudden sense of disgust at being reminded how plain-looking they [are], like their father' (24). Ella's children are actual and symbolic representations of her sexual relationship with a man who bears no connection with her emotional life. Her death in childbirth is the consequence of a pathetic discrepancy between the physical and the mental, a rejection – again both actual and symbolic – of a life in which her intellectual and emotional existence remains barren and unconsummated, while at a physical level her marriage is active and fertile.

The closing incidents of the story, in which Ella gives Marchmill the impression that she had an affair with Trewe, suggest that in her perfervid imagination she has begun to believe what before she had only imagined and desired. She hedges guiltily when Marchmill asks her about the lock of hair and never corrects him when he refers to Trewe as a 'dead lover' (28). Even in her unfinished deathbed speech, when she begins to tell Marchmill the 'entire circumstances' (30), there is no indication that Ella would finally have explained the real nature of her relationship with Trewe. But the greater irony is that Marchmill eventually begins out of his own jealous imagination to believe Ella's fantasies, becoming as much an imaginative man as she is an imaginative woman. This pattern, by which a wife's tendency to imaginative projection is transferred to her husband, resembles that of 'Squire Petrick's Lady'. As in the *Noble Dames* story, too, the victim is the child – orphaned by one parent, and rejected by the other.

But while the incidents in 'Squire Petrick's Lady' are explained by a preoccupation with class, 'An Imaginative Woman' addresses a more immediate contemporary problem: the frequency with which Victorian marriages in all classes were made with no consideration of 'tastes and fancies, those smallest, greatest particulars', but rather out of the compelling 'necessity', felt especially by women, 'of getting life-leased at all cost' (4). The Petrick marriage had originally been a love-match, and Annetta's delusion was temporary and linked with her deathbed delirium, but 'An Imaginative Woman' portrays unhappiness and self-deception at every stage of married life. The reader is left with an overwhelming sense of the futility and cruelty of an existence in which the conventions of marriage extinguish sexual passion, suppress the development to maturity of the partners, and taint as well the future of the offspring. The story's conclusion, heavy-handed as it is, can be justified as a logical extension of its basic irony, that imaginativeness – seemingly a harmless and even 'creative' escape from harsh realities – can itself become destructive.

The story's meaning is distorted, however, by the narrator's own willingness to believe in the 'known but inexplicable trick of Nature' (31) which causes Ella's child to look like Robert Trewe.[10] Although Hardy was familiar in 1891 with the hypothesis that inherited characteristics are determined by the germ plasm,[11] he seems to have clung to the belief, common both to folklore and to nineteenth-century medicine, that the unborn child can be influenced even in his physical characteristics by the past and present experiences of his parents. Treated as a folk belief, the idea was dramatized by Hardy in 'San Sebastian', a poem spoken by a man who sees a resemblance between the eyes of his daughter and those of a maiden he raped during the Napoleonic Wars. But such an acceptance of what is patently a superstition is less appropriate to the realistic mode of 'An Imaginative Woman' than to the ballad, and in a story critical of the propensity toward imaginativeness, it is disconcerting to find the storyteller himself engaging in such fanciful speculations. The narrator's acceptance of the notion that 'the dreamy and peculiar expression of the poet's face sat, as the transmitted idea, upon the child's' (31), distracts the reader from Marchmill's own turn to imaginativeness – surely the more important irony.

In its structure, however, 'An Imaginative Woman' embodies a flawless formal irony. At every turn, the reader's expectations are frustrated by Hardy's rejection of all the possible satisfactory endings. The story repeatedly provokes curiosity as to whether the 'imaginative woman' Ella

Marchmill and the 'imaginary woman' (25) projected by Robert Trewe are one and the same. If this were so, the story would have a conventionally happy ending, with the meeting of hero and heroine as a 'dream come true' (although this would be complicated, of course, by Ella's marriage). If, on the other hand, they were to discover that they were not suited to each other – it is quite possible that he would have considered her as looking, like her home, 'so new and monied' (24) – then at least the reader's curiosity, if not his romantic expectations, would have been satisfied. But Hardy deliberately denies to the reader, as he does to Ella, any sense of completeness in the story's conclusion. This refusal to resolve the questions and conflicts emerging from the narrative pattern is a statement in formal terms of what *Life's Little Ironies* consistently expresses: that there is an inevitable discrepancy between what is hoped for or expected, and what is to be. 'An Imaginative Woman' is a perfect introduction to a collection of stories in which imagined happiness always fails to be realized in conventionally sentimental terms.

'The Son's Veto' is again focused on a woman whose marriage has insufficiently satisfied her emotional needs and has an unconventionally unhappy ending, but in subject and tone the story is a striking contrast to 'An Imaginative Woman'. Ella Marchmill evades and at the same time creates her predicament by forming an imaginary world for herself, while Sophy Twycott, free of such self-absorption, suffers from a lack of self-esteem that prevents her acting, as naturally and morally she should, on behalf of her own happiness. Moreover, while Ella's child is an innocent victim of her self-indulgence, Sophy's son (even more than her husband) is the guilty perpetrator of her lonely isolation. The story invokes the pastoral contrast between urban and rural to represent a corresponding antithesis between the conventional values of the Twycott men and the 'pure instincts' (47) of Sophy. Removed from the 'pretty village' (37) of Gaymead when she marries a man who stands above her in class and education, Sophy is separated from all her former personal attachments and from the way of life to which she is suited. In departing from the country she loses not only its idyllic picturesqueness but also its dense complexity, both physical and imaginative: 'their pretty country home, with trees and shrubs and glebe' is replaced by 'a narrow, dusty house in a long, straight street, and their fine peal of bells' by 'the wretchedest one-tongued clangour that ever tortured mortal ears' (41).

The opening paragraphs of 'The Son's Veto' place the reader in the midst of the crowd admiring from behind Sophy's 'nut-brown hair' (35). The story is offered as a response to the reader's curiosity about this 'interesting woman' (36), an unravelling of the 'mystery' represented by this Rapunzel's 'long locks, braided and twisted and coiled like the rushes of a basket' (35). The first section supplies the reader with the details of the sad woman's 'little tragi-comedy', while also presenting in broad outline the story's main patterns of conflict. In the child who reprimands his mother 'with an impatient fastidiousness' (37), and who surreptitiously eats cake concealed in his pocket, is the seed of the gentleman clergyman who places his own pride above his mother's happiness. In Sophy's agreement to marry, like a childish Dorothea Brooke, out of 'veneration' (40), and in her uncomplaining submission to her son's correction, are the roots of her inability to act as an adult, from a position of equality with her husband and of authority over her child. Sam Hobson, seen first as 'the figure of a man standing in the hedge' (38) before the trees and western sky, is the person who later will represent not only closeness to nature but also a form of masculine assertiveness in which the older Twycott is seriously lacking. And in Twycott's proposal to Sophy – prompted by his liking for her as a 'kitten-like, flexuous, tender creature' (39) – is the basis of a marriage that takes 'Sophy the woman' (41) into little account.

The story's irony emerges from the relationship it portrays between mother and son, in which the normal roles of parent and child are repeatedly reversed. Randolph's ambitions, which cause him to 'blush for' and to dominate his mother, have thrown his personality off balance. While he has lost 'those wide infantine sympathies, extending as far as to the sun and moon themselves, with which he, like other children, had been born', he is none the less 'far from being man enough' (43) to estimate his mother at her true worth. His immaturity is transparent in his hyperbolically self-centred outburst about his mother's marriage to a grocer, degrading him 'in the eyes of all the gentlemen of England!' (50). Sophy, of course, shares in the blame for Randolph's ambiguous position between child and man. When, for example, he throws an infantile tantrum at the idea of her marrying Hobson, she assents to his orders as though he were properly in authority over her, and at the same time, in another inversion of roles, treats him as a child much younger than his years, kissing him 'as if he were still the baby he once had been' (50).

Randolph and his father are consistently associated with images of the city, where nature is fenced in oppressively by boundaries. Twycott's villa has a 'fragment of lawn in front' (42), the concert Sophy attends with Randolph is in 'a green enclosure' (35), and the cricket field is hedged in both by physical boundaries and by the complex rules associated with the game. The boy is frequently described in costumes that represent his social status. At the concert he wears a 'hat and jacket' which imply that he belongs 'to a well-known public school' (36); at the cricket-match he is among the boys grotesquely attired in 'broad white collars and dwarf hats' (49); and in the story's closing scene, as he travels in the funeral procession to his mother's grave, he is again a visible representation of his class and calling – 'a young smooth-shaven priest in a high waistcoat' (52). Randolph is a carica-ture, Hardy's purest embodiment of his own animus against the clergy – a hostility that he had expressed in his portrayal of the Clare brothers, and that he would realize in greater depth, though with more sympathy, in the Halboroughs of 'A Tragedy of Two Ambitions' and the youthful Jude Fawley. Randolph manifests too the characteristically fastidious social awareness of the rising man which Hardy had present-ed in as early a work as *Desperate Remedies*, where Owen Graye regards his sister's marital possibilities solely in the light of his own professional advancement. In Jude's words, Randolph is 'mundane ambition masquerading in a surplice' (*J*, 153).

In contrast to the ambitious young cleric is Sam Hobson, the one character who perceives the unnaturalness of Sophy's position and himself bridges the gap between the seclusion of the rural village and 'the rhythm and racket of the movements called progress in the world without' (39). Instead of abandoning his roots, Sam moves forward in the world by bringing the life-giving resources of the country into the city. A self-made man, he is more concerned with advancement than is the passive and reclusive middle-aged vicar Sophy marries, and, unlike Randolph, he improves his status by hard work rather than by a vigilant concern with appearances. His entrepreneurial skills are charted by his progression from managing the 'market-gardener's on the south side of London' (45) to running 'the largest fruiterer's shop in Aldbrickham' (52).

This sense of Sam as a transitional figure linking the values of the country and the city is communicated most vividly by the image of the early-morning procession toward Covent Garden, in which Sam's cart, among others, is laden with vegetables:

> She often saw them creeping along at this silent and dusky hour – waggon after waggon, bearing green bastions of cabbages nodding to their fall, yet never falling, walls of baskets enclosing masses of beans and peas, pyramids of snow-white turnips, swaying howdahs of mixed produce – creeping along behind aged night-horses, who seemed ever patiently wondering between their hollow coughs why they had always to work at that still hour when all other sentient creatures were privileged to rest. Wrapped in a cloak, it was soothing to watch and sympathize with them when depression and nervousness hindered sleep, and to see how the fresh green-stuff brightened to life as it came opposite the lamp, and how the sweating animals steamed and shone with their miles of travel. (44)

The seeds of this evocative image are to be found in Hardy's note of 7 July 1888: 'One o'clock A.M. I got out of bed, attracted by the never-ending procession [of market-carts to Covent Garden] as seen from our bedroom windows, Phillimore Place. Chains rattle, and each cart cracks under its weighty pyramid of vegetables.' (*EL*, 276) Hardy's manner of embellishing the original image is illuminating. The clichéd 'pyramid of vegetables' is expanded to include 'bastions' and 'swaying howdahs', giving the commonplace scene a curiously exotic quality. At the same time, the unspecified vegetables of the note are given a particularity which adds a striking visual clarity: in the light of the street-lamp, cabbages, beans, peas, and 'snow-white turnips' are 'brightened to life' in a vision that appears to Sophy's eyes like a transfiguration. The rich profusion of this early-morning procession is a striking contrast to the sterile image of the coaches standing immobile 'under the lurid July sun' (49) at Lord's cricket ground, surrounded by a wasteland of high-class refuse: 'the *débris* of luxurious luncheons; bones, pie-crusts, champagne-bottles, glasses, plates, napkins, and the family silver' (49).

Balancing the exotic and almost spiritual quality of the vegetable cart are the sweaty horses, who have drawn this burden from its source in the country. The emphasis on their suffering is significant because it brings to light Sophy's own capacity for sympathy. Just as the game-birds incident deepens the reader's feeling for Tess by pointing up her ability to suffer for others even in the midst of her own troubles, so too does Sophy gain dignity by virtue of her commiseration with these 'aged night-horses'. The compassion shown by Tess and Sophy puts even their weaknesses in a favourable light and distinguishes them from such figures as Ella Marchmill and Sue Bridehead, who lose stature on account of their intense self-absorption. While Sophy sympathizes with the horses, however, she also has an unexpressed admiration, and even envy, for these animals who 'steamed and shone with their miles of travel' because they provide, by the very physical nature of their fatigue, a contrast to the 'depression and nervousness' which accompany her own enforced idleness. In a sense even they, old and exhausted though they are, form part of the vitality that invests the entire scene.

Images of immobility and movement, linked to Sophy's physical disability, also define her state of mind. When she first moves to London, she lacks interest 'in travelling any-where' (43), but Sam Hobson – associated with the earth, work, and the idyllic Gaymead – is able to propel Sophy into movement. This process is subverted, however, by Randolph's wilfulness, and after her perverse avowal before his crucifix, Sophy's despairing inertia becomes the permanent condition of her mind and her body. While Sam advances his business in Aldbrickham (the county town is a successful compromise between country and city), Sophy's lameness becomes 'more confirmed as time [goes] on, and she seldom or never [leaves] the house in the long southern thoroughfare' (52). It is sadly ironic that the story's final image should be the funeral procession bringing Sophy's body back to Gaymead. In the confrontation between Randolph and Sam, the market-gardener's 'neat suit of black', expressive of true mourning, is matched by the vindictive Twycott's angry glance, 'black as a cloud' (52).

Added to the circumstantial irony of this scene is the formal irony of the story's plot. While 'An Imaginative Woman' is a sentimental story without a satisfactory conclusion, 'The Son's Veto' is a fairy tale gone wrong. Here the figure of crass ambition conquers the resouceful man of strength, vitality, and virtue; and while conventionally the goodness of the heroine is the force that prevents evil from triumphing, this attribute in the imprisoned Sophy prevents her finding happiness. The fairy-tale motif also enriches, by its incongruous linkages, the irony of the story's contemporary and social levels of interpretation: the 'princess' is a simple and uneducated woman married to a man twice her age; the figure of ambition is a clergyman, the princess's legitimate son; the virtuous knight is a market-gardener. By placing the reader in sympathy with the conventionally good figures of the fairy tale, Hardy forces him to make unconventional judgments – to champion the greengrocer and to detest the priest.

A similarly unorthodox inversion of conventional assumptions can be found in 'For Conscience' Sake', a story that undermines one of the most sacrosanct of Victorian tenets, the duty of a man to marry the woman he has wronged. The plot has a source in a story Hardy heard in 1882 about a woman who refused to be 'made respectable' by the lover who earlier had 'betrayed and deserted' her (*EL*, 203–4). *Early Life* reports that the 'eminently modern idea embodied in this example – of a woman's not becoming necessarily the chattel and slave of her seducer – impressed Hardy as being one of the first glimmers of woman's enfranchisement' (204). In 'For Conscience' Sake', the issue of 'respectability' in social and sexual relationships is based on a distinction postulated with careful conciseness in its first sentence between 'the utilitarian' and 'the intuitive theory of the moral sense' (55). Mr Millborne is a Victorian gentleman who, having abandoned his pregnant sweetheart twenty years earlier, has belatedly reached a sense of 'dissatisfaction' with himself at the recollection of his 'unfulfilled promise' (56). Characteristically, he describes his guilt only in terms of a business agreement that was never completed, betraying no awareness of having influenced for the worse the quality of two human lives. Although he has the judgment to know that he cannot 'rectify the past by money' (59), he finds it easiest to explain his compromised 'sense of self-respect' (58) by drawing a pecuniary analogy: 'If I were to ask you to lend me fifty pounds, which I would repay you next midsummer, and I did not repay you, I should consider myself a shabby sort of fellow, especially if you wanted the money badly. Yet I promised that girl just as distinctly.' (57) For the utilitarian Millborne the simple act of belatedly fulfilling a promise is the logical way to rectify the wrong done by the delay. 'For Conscience' Sake' depicts the blindness and failure of his scheme. Contrary to his expectations, the woman he seduced has long since ceased to need his help, and when he does coerce her into marriage, his conventional attempt to right a wrong leads not to happiness but to unhappiness, not to respectability but to the loss of it.

Leonora Frankland contradicts all that Victorian convention would expect the 'wronged' woman to be. Like Beethoven's Leonore, she capably performs male roles; like many of Shaw's self-sufficient heroines, she is well-dressed, moderately attractive, dignified in her manner, and 'of cheerful and excellent repute' (61) in the eyes of her neighbours. The traditional roles of seducer and seduced are, from a social standpoint at least, reversed. Millborne exists in self-enforced exile and anonymity in London, as though he were the one who has been disgraced. Living 'inside the door marked eleven', he is known best to the 'local crossing-sweeper' (55), and his acquaintances care little about him. At the same time, Leonora – the unwed mother – lives 'in a central and open place' in Exonbury with 'a well-burnished brass door-plate' displaying her name 'prominently' (60), and is quite 'a recognized townswoman' (61). While Millborne has retired 'somewhat early' (56) with the income he inherited from his father, she, in addition to teaching music and dancing, has 'made most of her income by letting out pianos on hire, and by selling them as agent for the makers' (61). Leonora's pragmatism and resourcefulness deprive Millborne of the 'expected scene of sad reproach' (63) between himself and his old fiancée he had so romantically envisioned. At a different level, however, Leonora is as profoundly conventional as Millborne. She is clear-headed in her initial refusal to marry the father of her child, but her hard-won respectability has led her to an unquestioning subservience to the expectations of the 'genteel' (61) society in which she lives. This is apparent not only in her social and philanthropic projects but also in her happy endorsement of the 'scantly-whiskered' (65) Reverend Percival Cope as a suitor for her daughter. Millborne's suit is successful when he convinces Leonora that their marriage would improve Frances's chances with the young clergyman.

The courtship of Percival Cope and Frances Frankland provides an ironic parallel to that twenty years earlier of Millborne and Leonora. Both the young Millborne and his prospective son-in-law regard marriage as a choice that will influence their respective reputations. Millborne had rejected Leonora because 'it was represented to me that it would be beneath my position to marry her' (58), while Cope has given a hearing to 'friends of his who object' to Frances's 'vocation' (65). It is an added irony that Cope's temporary forsaking of Frances results not from her professional status but from the questionable relation she bears to Millborne: 'it did not coincide with his judgment to marry into a family whose mystery was of the sort suggested' (69). A 'scrupulously correct clergyman and lover' (71), Cope is less moved by a natural attraction to Frances than by his 'natural dislike' for her origins. Hardly a 'passionate lover of the old-fashioned sort', this Victorian Percival seeks a Grail that is more secular than sacred and that is 'distinctly tempered with the alloys of the century's decadence' (69).

The sea journey, during which Frances's changed features reveal the physical relation she bears to Millborne,[12] uncovers both Cope's hypocrisy and the futility of Millborne's apparently corrective act. This incident ultimately drops the 'apple of discord' (69) into the Millborne marriage and brings about the real consequences of Millborne's tardy attempts to rid himself of the burden of his conscience: not respectability and happiness for his child but rather the 'discovery of her irregular birth' (71) and her ensuing disgrace. F. A. Hedgcock has observed that whereas in much of Hardy's fiction the forces of circumstance and change destroy happiness, in 'For Conscience' Sake' it is human meddling that unbalances the stable equilibrium achieved by the passage of time.[13] Millborne's desire to put his 'impulse to the test' (59) – this time a moral impulse rather than a sexual one – threatens Frances's prospects for the future.

The seasickness incident, with its emphasis on the 'spectral' (67) presences in Frances's face, leads naturally into the Gothic imagery in the third section of the story. At various points, Millborne is referred to as 'an enemy' to Leonora's house, her 'evil genius', her 'unmitigated curse' (71), an 'intrusive tell-tale presence' (73), and 'the man who had come as the spectre to their intended feast of Hymen, and turned its promise to ghastly failure' (71). But Millborne deviates from the prototypal spectre–bridegroom at the feast. Hardly an Alonzo the Brave, this ghost is not the rejected suitor seeking revenge on his unfaithful intended, but is himself the false one, seeking to purge his conscience of past wrongs. Nor is Leonora a 'false Imogine': she and Frances are doubly Millborne's victims, suffering first from his dishonourable absence, and later from his seemingly honourable appearance as an appeasing revenant. This ghost, indeed, seems to be based, not on Alonzo the Brave, but on the dead lover of Gottfried Augustus Bürger's 'Lenore' (translated as 'William and Helen' by Walter Scott in 1796), who returns from the Crusades to carry his faithful fiancée to their 'bridal bed' in the grave. Hardy's Leonora is also wedded to a corpse, for Millborne tries to pull her down with him into his moral death-in-life. This modern treatment of the ballad theme differs from Bürger's, however, in its conclusion. Millborne's efforts to set things right lead only to renewed and exacerbated suffering, but he restores his wife and daughter to their former life by retreating again into a death-like anonymity and losing himself in drink. This ghostly lover returns to his grave alone, while Leonora, Hardy's modern version of the ballad figure, survives and prospers.

The basic irony of 'For Conscience' Sake' can be found in its title. The phrase 'for conscience' sake' is spoken by several of Hardy's characters who try to justify what is not a moral but a conventional action. Lucetta tells Henchard, 'I thought I ought to marry you for conscience' sake, since you were free, even though I – did not like you so well' (*TMC*, 225); Grace Melbury's father rebukes himself for promising his daughter to Giles Winterbourne with the words, 'I am ruining her for conscience' sake!' (*TW*, 97); Angel Clare stops himself from kissing Tess's 'too tempting mouth . . . for tender conscience' sake' (*T*, 193); and Jude exclaims of Sue's return to Phillotson, 'And yet she did it for conscience' sake, poor little Sue!' (*J*, 455). This repeatedly ironic use of a common Victorian cliché points to the important place of the word 'conscience' in the propagation and enforcement of nineteenth-century social conventions. By invoking the word, Millborne gradually pulls Leonora, who at the outset has a clear sense of her own position, into the sphere of his own moral confusion: 'he kept on about his conscience and mine, till I was bewildered, and said Yes!' (71) Earlier in the story a sardonic and apparently tangential account is offered of Leonora's 'giving musical recitations in aid of funds for bewildering happy savages, and other such enthusiasms of this enlightened country' (61),[14] reminding us, perhaps, that a theme of 'For Conscience' Sake' is the moral 'bewilderment' that accompanies conventional life, in which 'intuitive' and 'utilitarian' judgments about matters of conscience are often confounded. Both Millborne's belated marriage to Leonora and the attempt to convert 'happy savages' to Christianity are symptomatic of moral short-sightedness. By depicting a situation in which an act of conscience leads to 'the reward of dishonourable laxity' (74), Hardy formulates a new and more complex moral for his Victorian audience: that past wrongs cannot be rectified by acts of formal morality in the present.

A still graver moral problem emerges in 'A Tragedy of Two Ambitions'. The story repeats the theme found in 'The Son's Veto' of the aspiring cleric embarrassed by an unrespectable parent, but explores with greater sympathy and subtlety the problems encountered by those who seek to improve their professional, and therefore social, status. The story treats ambition with both censure and compassion. Joshua Halborough is described as 'watching his own career with deeper and deeper interest' (80), and so repudiating Hardy's own maxim, which he wrote in a notebook during January 1888, the year in which 'A Tragedy of Two Ambitions' was composed:

> Be rather curious than anxious about your own career; for whatever result may accrue to its intellectual and social value, it will make little difference to your personal well-being. A naturalist's interest in the hatching of a queer egg or germ is the utmost introspective consideration you should allow yourself.   (*EL*, 267)

But despite Hardy's disapproval of what he calls in one poem those 'souls of Now, who would disjoint/ The mind from memory, making Life all aim' (*CP*, 16), he did have an instinctive understanding of persons who see life 'as a science of climbing' (*EL*, 70) and he inspires in the reader a measured sympathy for the basically unlikeable Halborough brothers by dramatizing their difficult position in life. They have been prodded on by an ambitious mother toward a desire to move beyond their father's class and way of life, but lack the means, on account of his profligacy, to do so. In wider historical terms, they, like Jude, were born at a time when limited possibilities for social mobility within the class system had begun to develop, especially 'in old-fashioned country places' where 'the Church conferred social prestige up to a certain point at a cheaper price than any other profession or pursuit' (94). A major theme of 'A Tragedy of Two Ambitions', as in *Jude*, is 'the tragedy of unfulfilled aims' (*J*, viii).

The opening scene of the story, in which the Halborough brothers are seen 'plodding away at the Greek Testament' (77), dramatizes the way in which their human affections have become subservient to their professional aspirations. Denying themselves all social contacts with the village outside, they feel warmly only toward their sister Rosa, whom they love 'more ambitiously than they [love] themselves' (82). Their drunken father is the obstacle to their success, and is seen from the outset as a nuisance and encumbrance. Helmut E. Gerber has noted that each character fits into an image pattern of light and dark colours – the 'sunny Rosa, the dark cloud of the father, and the gray (shading into black) of the brothers'[15] – but this rigid division of shades is not always sustained. Old Halborough, for instance, is pictured throughout 'in the light drab clothes of an old-fashioned country tradesman' (78), and only Joshua, who regards him as 'a squalid spot in the expanse of his life' (84) and 'the cloud no bigger than a man's hand' (92), sees him in images of darkness. It is more useful to observe the colour imagery as part of a wider range of metaphors contrasting images of life and impulse with those of sterility and intellectual death-in-life. Descriptions of richness and warmth are associated only with Rosa, who with her 'bright eyes, brown hair, flowery bonnet, lemon-coloured gloves, and flush beauty' seems 'like an irradiation into the apartment' (103) of her brothers. She arouses such feelings in Albert Fellmer that he resembles 'a sleeper who had awaked in a summer noon expecting to find it only dawn' (91). While Joshua is 'patiently boring the tunnel', Rosa's sexual vitality allows her 'to fly over the mountain' (92). At the same time, the 'dusty panes' of Cornelius's National School, the 'purple splendour' (84) of the glass reflections on the floor of Joshua's Theological College, and the humorously appropriate 'clump of laurel' (85) behind which Joshua intercepts his father and gypsy stepmother – all of these images speak only of the brothers' plodding ambition. The deadness of their lives is expressed in their faces, described as 'pale' (85), 'rather harsh' (82), and 'arid as a clinker' (84).

The imagery associated with Rosa can from another point of view be regarded as ironic, because of its correspondence with her position in the Halborough family. As her name suggests, she is their cultivated flower, and is loved by her brothers because their hopes for rising are dependent on her marital prospects. But in the story's conclusion, significantly set in spring, the image of new life represented by Rosa's child is displaced by the blossoming sapling that testifies, as in a ballad, to a murder. This symbol of her father's death by water, rather than Rosa's happy state, is the reward that has come out of the labours of Joshua and Cornelius. The benefits derived from their investment in Rosa's success (made with money borrowed from a farmer) are vicarious, but their guilt is personal and private. The story implies, moreover, that even Rosa's happiness will eventually be tainted by the knowledge of her brothers' crime.

It is not in the contrast between Rosa and her brothers, however, but in the less visible differences between Joshua and Cornelius that the central theme of the story is delineated. 'The anger of the elder was reflected as simple sadness in the face of the other' (79), the reader is told early in the story, and these different reactions characterize them at each point where the presence of their father threatens to shatter their ambitions. From the start, Joshua is always the calculating initiator who wants desperately to 'rise!' (79) while Cornelius is the half-willing, half-unwilling follower who would probably, without his brother's influence, be satisfied with life as a schoolmaster. This 'junior' (81) brother is warmer and more innocent than Joshua, and sees life more humanely and profoundly. To fulfil 'the vision of his career', Joshua has 'shouldered a body of doctrine' and is prepared 'to defend it tooth and nail, solely for the honour and glory that warriors win' (83). Cornelius, although less a scholar than Joshua, is concerned with the usefulness of Christianity for his own time. Cornelius's failings as a cleric are merely intellectual, while Joshua's are moral.

Joshua's hypocrisy emerges in his first sermon to the Narrobourne congregation, in which he demonstrates, like Hawthorne's Dimmesdale, a power to transfix the attention of his audience 'as by a fascination' (88), while failing to apply the lesson of his eloquent speech to his own situation. His text is taken from Psalm 30 (the song for the dedication for the house of David), in which the Psalmist praises the Lord for having hidden His face, forcing him to make the humble supplication, 'O Lord, be thou my helper' (Ps. 30:10). Privation, in other words, can be a means toward achieving holiness, submission a road to strength. The irony is obvious. What Joshua knows as a preacher does not touch him in his own life. The same point is demonstrated, but more sympathetically, by Joshua's letter to Cornelius, with its assessment (added in 1894) of the five desirable attributes of a minister. He makes a distinction, relevant to his grievance against his father, between what is humble and what is shameful (the story's alternate title had been 'The Shame of the Halboroughs'):[16]

> The case as it stands is maddening. For a successful painter, sculptor, musician, author, who takes society by storm, it is no drawback, it is sometimes even a romantic recommenda-

tion, to hail from outcasts and profligates. But for a clergyman of the Church of England! Cornelius, it is fatal! To succeed in the Church, people must believe in you, first of all, as a gentleman, secondly as a man of means, thirdly as a scholar, fourthly as a preacher, fifthly, perhaps, as a Christian, – but always first as a gentleman, with all their heart and soul and strength. I would have faced the fact of being a small machinist's son, and have taken my chance, if he'd been in any sense respectable and decent. The essence of Christianity is humility, and by the help of God I would have brazened it out. But this terrible vagabondage and disreputable connection! If he does not accept my terms and leave the country, it will extinguish us and kill me. For how can we live, and relinquish our high aim, and bring down our dear sister Rosa to the level of a gipsy's step-daughter? (87)

The analysis of Victorian society implicit in this complaint, however unedifying Joshua's unquestioning acceptance of it may sound, defines his difficult position: he and his brother are victims of circumstances that prevent their advancing, except by hypocrisy.

Their dilemma reaches its dramatic climax in the drowning scene, where Joshua holds Cornelius back from saving their father, and the younger brother becomes a willing accomplice in murder by negligence. (The incident may have a source in the drowning of Grandcourt in *Daniel Deronda*, where Gwendolyn Harleth hesitates in throwing a rope to the husband she has already killed in her thoughts.) Joshua sways Cornelius to his point of view by passionately invoking not only their own ambitions, but also those they maintain for Rosa: 'Her life and happiness, you know – Cornelius – and your reputation and mine – and our chance of rising together, all three – ' (99). Here as elsewhere Joshua fluctuates between 'we' and 'I', as though the success of his brother and sister are merely elements of his own. But the argument is his most convincing one, and has led Albert J. Guerard to call the deed 'a very plausible crime'.[17] A crime, nevertheless, it is. Hardy told Edmund Gosse in 1888 that the story was about 'a cold blooded murder',[18] and in order to emphasize the culpability of the two brothers added this sentence in 1912: 'In

their pause there had been time to save him twice over.'
(100)

But once these moments have passed, the brothers' respective perceptions of their own guilt differ considerably. Relevant here is the symbol of the 'straight little silver-poplar' (105) growing from the drowned man's walking stick, which serves to assimilate a whole range of allusions in the story. The detail of the budding tree was probably suggested to Hardy by the Dorset legend about the ash tree which grew from a whip stuck in the ground when a drunken mail-van driver was drowned in Heedless-William's Pond[19] (the place is mentioned in 'The Fiddler of the Reels' [178]). But the poplar sapling is also a focus for the Biblical symbolism running throughout 'A Tragedy of Two Ambitions'. The New Testament text the two brothers are translating in the opening scene is the Epistle to the Hebrews, which distinguishes between the priesthoods of the old and new covenants, and refers to 'Aaron's rod that budded' (9:4), the symbol of the House of Levi, the tribe chosen by God to assist the Jewish priests (Num. 17). So too Aaron's staff, by turning into a snake at command, proved to the Egyptian pharaoh that Moses and Aaron were priests of the true God (Exod. 7:8–13). With the 1894 addition of the sapling symbol to the story, Cornelius's exclamation, 'Ah, we read our *Hebrews* to little account, Jos!' (105)[20] comes all the more naturally: the flowering poplar reminds him of Aaron's rod and of what it symbolizes in the biblical text he had so painstakingly translated. This memory leads him to the Epistle's special praise of the New Testament priest who must distinguish himself, like Christ, by enduring the cross, while despising its shame. This, of course, is the Christian lesson of humility to which Joshua alluded in his letter, but which he only half understood. These repeated biblical references to priesthood point to a central irony: that Joshua – whose name is that of the successor of Moses and Aaron who led the Israelites into the Promised Land – has failed in his priestly vocation.

An additional irony lies in the fact that it is Cornelius, and not Joshua, who at last recognizes their guilt in refusing to suffer 'the sharp thorn of their crown' (78) by 'enduring' the 'shame' of their father and their background. Joshua's regrets are merely of a practical and superficial sort:

'She's all right,' said Joshua. 'But here are you doing journey-work, Cornelius, and likely to continue at it till the end of the day, as far as I can see. I, too, with my petty living – what am I after all? . . . To tell the truth, the Church is a poor forlorn hope for people without influence, particularly when their enthusiasm begins to flag. A social regenerator has a better chance outside, where he is unhampered by dogma and tradition. As for me, I would rather have gone on mending mills, with my crust of bread and liberty.'   (104–5)

Although the mention of 'dogma and tradition' may suggest that Joshua feels a measure of guilt, the petulance and self-indulgence of his regret, especially evident in the concluding rhetorical flourish about the 'crust of bread and liberty', show that he is disillusioned not with himself but with his expectations regarding the church. Each brother considers putting an end to his 'trouble' for profoundly different reasons: as they bend 'their steps homewards' – a distant echo of the closing lines of *Paradise Lost* – each has the same 'contingency to consider' (105), but a very different 'Fall' to look back upon. Joshua's sense of failure derives from his practical mistake of having chosen the church as a means of social advancement, but for Cornelius, there is the much heavier 'moral burden' (*EL*, 282) of genuine guilt. The 'Two Ambitions' of Joshua and Cornelius Halborough result in 'Tragedy' indeed, but the brothers experience tragic recognition from widely diverging levels of perception.

It is possible to think of the word 'tragedy' in the title of Hardy's story as ironic because the Halboroughs are not tragic heroes in the classical sense. But if one considers the differing characters of the two brothers – and especially their contrasting behaviour in the story's closing scene – it would seem truer to say that if there is 'irony' in the story's title, then it can be directed only at Joshua. Cornelius, though he has previously been overshadowed by his more charismatic brother, reaches a kind of tragic stature in the story's conclusion as he perceives the symbolism of the silver-poplar tree which 'turned white' at 'every puff of wind' (105). What is a transitory moment of moodiness for Joshua is for Cornelius the beginning of an abiding despair. By finally distinguishing so clearly between the two brothers, who in the first scene had seemed almost a clerical vision of Rosencrantz and Guildenstern, Hardy directs the reader's attention to the two levels of irony that can be perceived in the best of his *Life's Little Ironies* stories: the satirical irony of circumstance, and irony of form or meaning. Joshua is able to discern the irony of his situation – the fact that events have backfired on him – but fails to see, as Cornelius does, the wider pattern of which he is a part. Cornelius looks into his own heart, and sees that the greatest inconsistency was not in his decision to enter the church, but in himself. This insight represents Hardy's irony in its most profound, intense, and dramatically achieved configuration.

'On the Western Circuit' repeats certain themes about sex and marriage which emerge in the stories preceding it. Edith Harnham's reason for marrying recalls Ella Marchmill's need to become 'life-leased' (4), and her passion for Charles Bradford Raye 'by a species of telepathy' (132) is a form of imaginativeness (though the fact that she has held his hand makes him a more palpable object for fantasizing than Robert Trewe). Like Mr Millborne, Raye trifles with a woman's feelings 'for the sake of a passing desire' (119), and Edith sends copies of Raye's letters to Anna for 'conscience' sake' (129). The story perfectly integrates irony of circumstance with irony of form. Its plot typifies the sort of bizarre web of events and motives found in the well-made play,[21] but the conventional pattern of action is here a vehicle for exposing an unconventional idea – what Shaw called in reference to Ibsen's drama 'the endless recriminations of idealistic marriage'.[22] The theatre of Hardy's time often explored in a farcical manner the fallible aspects of marriage, but tended not to touch upon the toll in human suffering demanded by it. This allowed the audience to judge the characters only by their actions, and to laugh at their wretched plight. But in Hardy's story the reader's sympathies are constantly in tension with the laughter which the plot elicits: the funniest moments are also the most painful. Hardy blends these contrasting effects by linking – as Shaw and Ibsen were doing in the drama – the farcical situations of the well-made play with their practical consequences in the lives of its characters. This link is achieved by placing stereotyped characters in conventional situations, but then going on to examine in depth the motives and feelings of these supposed types. The cardboard figures of stage melodrama are given flesh and blood, and by this process the impact on the reader is significantly altered: laughter becomes compassion.

At the outset, the three main characters of 'On the Western Circuit' seem almost clichés. Raye is an 'end-of-the-age young man' (118); Anna is a 'pretty rural maiden' (119), innocent and illiterate; Edith, like Ella Marchmill, is an unhappy wife in the *Madame Bovary* tradition. Though handled with far less irony than Flaubert's Emma, she too is a 'lonely, impressionable creature' (118) watching life from her domestic windowsill. Within the bounds of these broad stereotypes, the story creates persons who, by their very representativeness, illuminate the manner in which instinctive sexual needs are modified, and even defined, by social and intellectual expectations. The characters regard each other as stereotypes. A connoisseur of country beauties, Raye is drawn to Anna on account of her rural origins, while both Anna and Edith admire Raye for what they conceive to be his urban sophistication. For Anna this means simply that he is 'so genteel that [he] must have plenty of money' (114), while for Edith he represents, in keeping with her deeper needs, the spiritual and physical rapport lacking in her relationship with her ageing and insensitive husband. Each character's image of the loved one is a distortion of fact. Instead of seeing Anna's frivolous conversation for what it is, Raye believes that her purported letters express her true character; Edith invests all of her emotional interest in Raye after his idle touch of her hand, and chooses to ignore that he has seduced Anna with no apparent intention of marrying her; both Edith and Anna have an inflated opinion of Raye's professional status, and Anna's adoration of him is so great that she approaches him 'as if he were a god' (137). One aspect of the story's complexity lies in the difference between the characters' appraisals of each other, and the more objective and comprehensive view which the reader has of each of them.

Seen in this wider perspective, Raye is a man who, though educated and full of professional expectations, finds himself of no consequence. As a result, he idealizes all that is different from himself – especially all that is rural – and plays imaginative roles, as his quick assumption of a sparkish posture in the story's opening scene demonstrates. His romanticism emerges in his attitude to Anna, to whom he is attracted because he conceives of her as a 'pink and breezy' (121) contrast to his dreary life in London. So his regard for her grows in proportion as her alleged letters present her as an ideal figure complementing his urban self-consciousness; where Raye must alter his costume to suit his various environments, Anna seems 'a young girl who felt her womanhood to be enough for her dignity' (121). Raye's choice of 'his select country beauty' (112) is linked to his sense of her, despite her expressed disdain for 'the lonely country' (113), as a beautiful 'product of nature' (112), but as soon as his image of her as an educated innocent has been shattered by his discovery of her illiteracy, his idealistic attitude toward her simple roots takes a sudden but predictable turnabout. In his self-dramatizing style, Raye compares his marriage to 'a galley, in which he, the fastidious urban, was chained to work for the remainder of his life, with her, the unlettered peasant, chained to his side' (136). Raye is probably right to assume that his marriage will prevent his advancing far professionally, but it is typical of his romantic sensibility that he continues to regard Anna as a stereotype. To see her either as a 'fascinating child of nature' (120) or as an 'unlettered peasant' is equally to reduce the woman – as Angel Clare does Tess – to an abstraction.

The characterization of 'the emotional Edith Harnham' (118) is given its depth in a different way: where the vacuum of Raye's life is professional and mental, hers is physical and emotional. From the beginning, she is presented as a woman of deep and unsatisfied passion: 'an interesting creature rather than a handsome woman; dark-eyed, thoughtful, and with sensitive lips' (115). The sterility of her marriage is dramatized in miniature in the scene where Harnham saunters into the room from which she is watching the fair; and the explicitly physical quality of her attraction to Raye, a result of this barren relationship with her husband, is baldly described in a sentence added to the story in 1894: 'That he had been able to seduce another woman in two days was his crowning though unrecognized fascination for her as the she-animal' (125).[23] But the depth of Edith's loneliness is shown by more than the 'vicarious intimacy' (128) she forms with 'the image of a man to whom she was hardly so much as a name' (125). Even before Raye (the symbolism of his name is obvious) penetrates the darkness of her life, Edith seeks desperately to fill an emotional void by befriending Anna: 'being without children [she] had wished to have her near her in preference to anybody else, though she had only lately come.' (113) Edith's interest in Anna is animated by more than responsible concern: she allots the girl a meagre ten minutes at the fair, and chooses to go out herself and find her despite the housemaid's offer to do it. Upon finding Anna, she behaves, almost as if she were jealous, with undue severity and possessiveness. Later, as the romance between Raye and the young girl develops, Edith literally projects herself into the girl's position.

Throughout the story, the 'mistress' and 'maiden' are constantly compared, and at several crucial moments, the one actually assumes the role of the other. In education, intellectual sophistication, and social standing, Edith is in every way Anna's 'mistress', but at a deeper level they are akin. Sharing their roots and childhood on the isolated Mid-Wessex Plain, these two women are united in their inexperience and vulnerability. Edith is more tactful, but 'little less impulsive than Anna herself' (117). Just when Anna is becoming 'quite fluent in the use of her mistress's phraseology' (123), Edith, without Anna's knowledge, forms a bond of intimacy with the girl which begins to blur the lines of their separateness. It is in the privacy of Edith's 'bed-chamber' (122)[24] that Anna first speaks of Raye's letter, and even at this early stage, the mistress knows to hide what will become a virtual appropriation of Anna's position and identity: 'Edith Harnham's large dark eyes expressed some interest in the contents, though, in her character of mere interpreter, she threw into her tone as much as she could of mechanical passiveness.' (123)

Edith's self-projection is more remarkable because she is to some extent aware of the moral danger of her position. Textual changes made in 1894 for the first edition emphasize her transgression. In the manuscript and in the periodical publications, Edith explains to Anna that she is hesitant to continue ghosting the letters 'Because of its possible effect upon me'; in 1894, the word 'possible' was deleted.[25] The earlier versions read, for the question put to the reader about the ghost-writing, 'Why was it a pleasure?'; the first edition has it, 'Why was it a luxury?' – a word hinting more strongly at self-indulgence.²⁶ The 1894 printing also contains the first mention of the detail that 'many letters on both sides were not sent on at all' after Anna returned to the Plain.²⁷ This is the story's firmest suggestion of Edith's guilt.

The more Edith withholds from Anna, the more she projects herself into the girl's youth and position. The substance of Edith's letters to Raye is never set down, but the mention of 'the sympathies' she develops 'in playing this part' (128) of seduced maiden suggests that she is attempting to forsake her own identity and to become Anna – the mistress of Charles Raye, and the mother of his child. It is as though Edith were trying vicariously to restore in herself the youth she has lost in her marriage to an elderly wine-merchant. Her letter-writing involves self-deceit as well as an effort to deceive Raye – a delusive attempt to transfer her emotional sensibility onto the person and circumstances of her young maid. This whole range of motives, coupled with her altruistic attempt to save Anna's reputation, lies behind Edith's behaviour as she returns to her empty, silent, and dark house after the marriage:

> Entering, she could not bear the silence of the house, and went up in the dark to where Anna had slept, where she remained thinking awhile. She then returned to the drawing-room, and not knowing what she did, crouched down upon the floor.
> 'I have ruined him!' she kept repeating. 'I have ruined him; because I would not deal treacherously towards her!'
> (136–7)

Edith's visit to Anna's empty bed-chamber is the mute gesture that speaks most eloquently of the emotional identification she has formed with the young girl. Anna's marriage to Charles Raye is for Edith a double loss.

Even when the reader's sympathy for Edith is strongest, however, the story does not allow him to forget the concerns of the other characters. In addition to Edith and Raye, there are also their respective spouses to consider – the 'worthy merchant' (137) and the young wife soon to bear a child. Because the story ends not with the kiss between Edith and Raye but with two vignettes displaying the two married couples, the reader is compelled to stand back and juggle all the variables in the situation. The very title 'On the Western Circuit'[28] and the unobtrusive but deliberate use of legal language throughout the narrative invites the reader to analyse events as though in a court room. This style may result from Hardy's experiences dating from 1884 as a Justice of the Peace[29] and from his observations made while attending the London police courts in 1890 'to get novel padding' (*EL*, 297). Many of the story's descriptions of human situations have a legal tone: Anna's courtship with Raye leads to 'her sense of a claim upon him'; his letter to her is a 'document' (122) and her tactful response to him is inspired by 'Mrs. Harnham's counsel' (126), whose 'judgment had ruled' (127) in their discussion of Anna's feelings. Edith Harnham plays the part of counsel to Anna quite literally. Because of 'the girl's inability to continue personally what had been begun in her name' (128), Edith not only advises her but also represents her in her suit against (and for) Charles Raye. Raye's decision to marry the girl is also the result of a consultation: 'The upshot of the discussion [with his sister] was that though he had not been directly advised to do it, Raye wrote, in his real name, what he would never have decided to write on his own responsibility' (129). Both Edith's and Anna's marriages are called contracts (125, 133), Raye's proposal to Anna is followed by 'a statement of his position and prospects' (130), and the 'formalities' of their marriage are called the 'ratification of a previous union' (133). All these legal phrases are of course clichés, and their use in isolation is not particularly unusual or striking, but the sterile precision of this official language serves to objectify the reader's feelings. At the same time, its very insufficiency in portraying human problems heightens the story's drama and poignancy.

The legal theme of 'On the Western Circuit' reaches a dramatic climax in the recognition scene where Anna's illiteracy is disclosed and the real writer of the letters unveiled. By cross-examination, Raye elicits the facts from Edith as though she were a defendant reluctantly called to the witness-box:

> 'Do I guess rightly?' he asked, with wan quietude. '*You* were her scribe through all this?'

'It was necessary,' said Edith.

'Did she dictate every word you ever wrote to me?'

'Not every word.'

'In fact, very little?'

'Very little.'

'You wrote a great part of those pages every week from your own conceptions, though in her name!'

'Yes.'

'Perhaps you wrote many of the letters when you were alone, without communication with her?'

'I did.' (134–5)

At this point, Raye accuses Edith of 'Delighting me deceptively!' (135) – precisely the crime he has committed in seducing Anna, and which Anna, by allowing Edith to ghost her letters, has committed against Raye. But although Raye is unaware of this irony, he knows the limitations of the law in administering over human problems:

'Why, you and I are friends – lovers – devoted lovers – by correspondence!'

'Yes; I suppose.'

'More.'

'More?'

'Plainly more. It is no use blinking that. Legally I have married her – God help us both! – in soul and spirit I have married you, and no other woman in the world!'

'Hush!'

'But I will not hush! Why should you try to disguise the full truth, when you have already owned half of it? Yes, it is between you and me that the bond is – not between me and her! Now I'll say no more. But, O my cruel one, I think I have one claim upon you!'

She did not say what, and he drew her towards him, and bent over her. 'If it was all pure invention in those letters,' he said emphatically, 'give me your cheek only. If you meant what you said, let it be lips. It is for the first and last time, remember!'

She put up her mouth, and he kissed her long. (135–6)

Raye's analysis comes out of his recognition of the conflicting legal and spiritual allegiances that shape their existence, and Edith's kiss (in keeping with the form of the cross-examination, it is the answer to a carefully formulated question) symbolizes her acceptance of the 'bond' between herself and Raye, the 'claim' he has upon her – despite the existence of formal contracts which bind each to another.

The pattern of images set up in the story's opening scene provides a framework for the focus on legal contracts. Charles Raye is distracted from contemplating the cathedral by 'a roar of sound' (109) from Melchester Fair, a place like 'the eighth chasm of the Inferno as to colour and flame' (110) – the chasm set aside for those who have committed fraud. In this 'lurid light' (109), the marriage that perpetuates the story's unhappiness can be seen as growing quite naturally out of a triangular network of fraud and deception: Raye idly seduces Anna with no intention of marrying her,[30] Anna calls on Edith to represent (and misrepresent) her, and Edith's actions move beyond the needs of the one she is defending to become a private 'luxury'. It is appropriate that Edith's marriage, too, has been the result of fraudulent advice: 'Influenced by the belief of the British parent that a bad marriage with its aversions is better than free womanhood with its interests, dignity, and leisure, she had consented to marry the elderly wine-merchant as a *pis aller*.' (125) Edith knows well, therefore, that Anna's deception of Raye might 'lead to dissension and recriminations' (131).

'On the Western Circuit' invites the reader to consider it either from an ethical standpoint, seeking a root cause for the misery found in the conclusion, or from a psychological standpoint, never imputing blame but seeing the story as the poignant depiction of a particular aspect of human experience. But the incompatibility of the story's ethical and human levels of interpretation is a statement of the very irony that the story is dramatizing: the inability of men and women when making sexual choices to act with full self-knowledge and without deception toward each other – and the resulting inadequacy of the legal contracts which give formal expression to these choices. This theme is given dramatic force by the ostensible conventionality of the story's characterization, plot, and language – features which led James Joyce to complain of its 'copybook talk',[31] and Ford Madox Ford to cite it as an example of the way Hardy's 'anecdotes' are 'merely glanced at and not treated at all'.[32] But to have internalized the story in a Joycean manner, or to have 'treated' it in the technical sense that Ford uses the word, would only have upset the carefully balanced opposition of the impulses for judgment and for pity which 'On the Western Circuit' so effectively preserves. By the manner in which the story's emotional content undermines the comic conventions which give it shape, the reader is prevented from allowing his laughter to supersede his pity, or his rational faculties to supplant his compassion. Here the human foibles which the comic plot uncovers are, by virtue of the story's sympathetic characterization of its stereotyped figures, the subject for commiseration as well as for censure. Indeed the very agony of the story's conclusion lies in what usually makes the structure of comedy pleasing and satisfying: the fact that the plot has worked itself out so neatly and inexorably, meting out to everyone his just deserts.

A similar mixture of judgment and pity is elicited by 'To Please His Wife', but in other respects this story is different from the rest of *Life's Little Ironies*. The preceding five narratives are set at approximately the time in which they were written and their characters are distinctly Victorian, while this piece represents a significant leap backwards in time. H. F. V. Johnstone sets the story at 'about 1840',[33] but internal evidence suggests only that its date is at some indefinite point in the past. The gold guineas which Shadrach Jolliffe puts before Joanna were not coined after 1813,[34] but her mention of 'rumours of war' (155) is never made more specific, and the conversation about education implies that the story is taking place somewhat later in the nineteenth century. In any case, the story's subject – ambition, and its capacity for destruction of the self and family – is a central theme in *Life's Little Ironies*, and Joanna Phippard has a strong kinship with Randolph Twycott, Percival Cope, and Joshua Halborough in that her natural 'instincts' are 'choked' (152) by the ambition that is her master passion. Because she is a woman living in the nineteenth century, however, Joanna's ambition takes a different form: her hopes for 'rising' are pinned not on her own professional achievements but on 'mating considerably above her' (144). As a result her female ambitiousness is intricately meshed with feelings of sexual envy, and she can only define her own happiness and success by measuring it against that of her closest peer. Emily Hanning, however, does not share her friend's ambitiousness – her love for Shadrach has no connection with his class or financial assets – and so, ironically, a triumph over Emily in the sexual arena prevents Joanna's advancing socially. Joanna then projects her expectations onto her sons, hoping that 'they will perhaps be as near to gentlemen as Emmy Lester's precious two, with their algebra and their Latin!' (152). In this Joanna is prefigured by the deceased Mrs Halborough of 'A Tragedy of Two Ambitions', who died of 'too keen a strain' (79) toward advancing the education of her sons. By placing Joanna in an earlier period, Hardy studies a type common in late Victorian times as she would appear in a somewhat different era. Like the seemingly anachronistic presence of 'The Honourable Laura' in *A Group of Noble Dames*, the position of 'To Please His Wife' in *Life's Little Ironies* serves to demonstrate that the human problems portrayed throughout the volume are not indigenous only to a single historical period. Again, past and present have common themes.

Joanna's perception of the changing positions of herself and 'her gentler and younger rival' (144) are presented in terms of the topography of Havenpool. At first Joanna lives in 'an elevated suburb where the more fashionable houses stood' (144), while Emily's stationery shop is 'below the pavement level' (145) in Sloop Lane. But after Emily has married the wealthy Mr Lester the contrast is reversed: she lives in 'one of those large, substantial brick mansions frequently jammed up in old fashioned towns', and looks 'down from her position of comparative wealth' upon Joanna's 'humble shop-window' (149). Emily's 'big brick house' reflects 'the oppressive sun's heat' (150) into Joanna's shop, and the size of Emily's mansion with its 'large and carpeted staircase' (161) is everywhere emphasized, while Joanna is forced after the departure of her husband and sons to maintain a shop 'which now consisted of little more than a window and a counter'. The claustrophobic smallness of Joanna's quarters causes Emily's silk dress to rustle 'arrogantly' (157) as she squeezes her way into Joanna's parlour. In all of these instances, it is as if the reader were seeing the scene through Joanna's envious and distorting eyes.

In direct opposition to Joanna's ambitiousness stand Emily and Shadrach, who, by their lack of concern for social advancement, find a measure of happiness. Emily is presented as a foil to Joanna. Without attempting to rise in class, she faces the vicissitudes of her life with resourcefulness, flexibility, and resilience. When she is living with her father, she keeps a stationery shop to fill in the 'gaps of his somewhat uncertain business' (143), and, unlike Joanna with her grocery shop, makes the best of her straitened circumstances by 'tastefully' setting out on display 'articles in themselves of slight value, so as to obscure the meagreness of the stock-in-trade' (145). In her romantic attachments, too, Emily shows an ability to survive by riding with the tide. Despite her disappointment at losing Shadrach, she is able to make a good and prosperous marriage, and declares 'that she had never supposed that she could live to be so happy' (149).

Shadrach too has a nature utterly unlike Joanna's, but here the contrast is depicted differently, by descriptions of him that have an almost mythical quality in their outlining of his heroic contours. His surname is that of Captain Peter Jolliffe, of Poole, who in 1694 attacked a French privateer, three times as strong as his own craft, which had captured a Weymouth fishing boat; as a reward, Hutchins reports, he was presented with 'a magnificent gold chain and medal' by the king.[35] The fictional character also has affinities with his biblical counterpart, who survived the fire because of his faith in God: this latter-day Shadrach is saved 'providentially' from death at sea, and has an unquestioning belief in the forces of goodness. The image of him as an 'isolated form . . . in the precise middle of the chancel-step, . . . fixed on his knees, facing the east, his hat beside him, his hands joined' (142) is a visual emblem of Shadrach's trust in, and submission to, the workings of Providence. A 'religious and scrupulous man' (148), Shadrach follows form to the letter, and is as true to his own word as he is to the words of prescribed ritual.

Shadrach's compliance with his fate, however, is characterized by a directness and a literalness that can only be called naive. In his sincere effort to do the 'proper thing' at the church, he manifests an obliviousness to all reasonable and 'usual' (142) procedure. Jolliffe's integrity and rigid adherence to principle make him but malleable stuff in the hands of the world – and of worldly women like Joanna. Because he had 'early gone to sea' (142), his awareness of the ways of men on land is neither thorough nor profound, and upon arriving in Havenpool he soon finds himself – despite his initial preference for Emily – being towed along 'in the wake of Joanna Phippard' (144), as though he were a disabled vessel and she the strong and capable craft leading him toward port. This same tendency toward compliance makes Shadrach, 'not endowed with the narrow shrewdness necessary for developing a retail business in the face of many competitors' (150), a failure in the grocery business. His purity and simplicity are inappropriate for life in the small nineteenth-century town of Havenpool, with its wealthy merchants and genteel society. He is an unsophisticated hero marooned in a complex and competitive world.

Shadrach's naivety is especially apparent when he arrives home after his first sea journey. To his mind, he is carrying a fortune in gold: 'an enormous canvas bag, full and rotund as the moneybag of the giant whom Jack slew' (153). The reference to Jack the Giant Killer emphasizes the differences between the worlds Joanna and her husband inhabit. For Shadrach the visibility and palpability of the gold are enough to warrant excitement: he has brought to his wife a hero's booty, which falls 'into her lap with a sudden thud, weighing down her gown to the floor' (153). But, like the insatiable Ilsabel of Grimm's 'The Fisherman and His Wife', Joanna is a more acquisitive and ambitious spirit than her husband – she desires a university education for her sons, as well as a carriage and pair – and the spoils of Shadrach's conquest are hardly sufficient for the investments she has in mind. The marriage of Shadrach and Joanna is a union not only of unlike temperaments but of sharply contrasting world-views – the naively heroic and the ambitiously competitive. It is symbolic, therefore, that it is the adventuring vessel bearing Joanna's name which drags her loved ones to the bottom of the sea, and her own hopes and sanity with them: her competitive spirit destroys her natural human affections. Ironically, it is only after Joanna has lost the husband and sons she had so thoughtlessly and selfishly squandered that she expresses a faith, now futile, in those powers of Providence to which Shadrach had earlier bowed in submission and gratitude. In her mad grief, Joanna finally becomes the kind of wife one might have expected Shadrach to have.

Appropriately, the replacement of Joanna's ambition by her grief alters the narrative mode used to describe her. The woman who had subordinated her intense love for her children to a jealous desire to exceed her neighbour in social standing is suddenly transformed into the sailor's widow of the ballad, lamenting the treachery of the sea and haunting the scenes of happier days. This shift in the imagery describing Joanna contributes to the formal irony of the story's structure. At first virtually a personification of ambition, she suddenly acquires in her grief some of the human qualities she previously lacked. This is true despite the fact (perhaps because of it) that Joanna's madness diminishes her possible tragic stature. Her final state is heart-rending, but it allows her to escape from any recognition of her own contribution to the working-out of her destiny. So she irrationally pins blame on forces outside herself, on Emily, Providence, and the sea. But it is precisely in this weakness that Joanna, reduced almost literally to a skeleton, becomes most human. As a personification of ambition, she comes to her deserved end, but as a woman she is the object only of pity.

A theme of 'To Please His Wife', and of all the earlier stories in *Life's Little Ironies*, is the suppression by convention and ambition of the fundamental impulse for happiness. Basically iconoclastic and ironic in their intentions, these stories attempt to undermine the reader's respect for social advancement, his trust in the inviolability of the marriage contract, and his belief in a conventional ideal of romantic love. But 'The Fiddler of the Reels' concludes *Life's Little Ironies* on a predominantly conservative note. The sexual instinct itself is seen, much as Schopenhauer viewed it,[36] as a potentially dangerous force which, even more than social laws, can tyrannize over men's lives. The story's historical framework, which begins during the late 1840s and extends into the England and America of the 1890s, offers a disturbing suggestion. Despite the fact that the narrator sees the Crystal Palace as representing 'an era of great hope and activity among the nations and industries' (171), Mop Ollamoor's presence reflected in its mirror, and his later reported appearance in America, are neither incongruous nor anachronistic events. His wizardry moves beyond the confines of the rural folk tale to become an emblem of the irrational instincts that will always drive men, even in the most prosperous and civilized of societies. By the conclusion of the story, the 'sense of novelty' perceived by the 'old gentleman' of the opening paragraphs in the Exhibition's 'sudden bringing of ancient and modern into absolute contact' (165) has become for the reader a 'sense' of the perennially unchanging pattern of life. 'The Fiddler of the Reels' portrays the essential sameness of 'ancient' and 'modern', of past and present.

This double dimension in the story has its source in the integration of its folkloric and modern elements, achieved by a narrative point of view which, as in several of the *Wessex Tales*, carefully balances nostalgic recollection with objectivity and judgment. The story is told not by the 'old gentleman' (165) whose words open the story, nor even by one of his contemporaries, but rather by a younger member of the old gentleman's group, who has derived his information from the 'seniors in our party' who had known Mop Ollamoor well (166). This narrative technique combines not only nostalgia with hindsight, but also these attitudes with the more objective point of view of the somewhat younger man who, fascinated by the past of his native locality, gathers the various pieces of information he can glean from tradition, and tries to make sense of them from the vantage point of his own place in history. This perspective accounts for the narrator's use of scientific imagery to describe Car'line Aspent's 'compelled capers' – she jumps 'as if she had received a galvanic shock' (169) – and for his invocation of contemporary medical authority to interpret her condition: 'The next evidences of his influence over her were singular enough, and it would require a neurologist to fully explain them.' (169)

This co-presence in 'The Fiddler of the Reels' of folk and legendary elements with contemporary ways of explaining experience is part of the story's essential method and complexity. As in many of Hawthorne's romances, a dynamic opposition is set up between new and old, and between the scientific and the magical interpretations of events. The double point of view permits the reader to apply mythical concepts to realistic scenes. Car'line is first charmed by the Orphic 'fascination' of Mop's music while she is simply pausing for a rest on a bridge in Lower Mellstock (168). The mystifying reflection of Mop in the glass at the Great Exhibition – which recalls traditional beliefs in demonic appearances viewed through a reflected image – is seen by Car'line, logically and prosaically enough, as she is 'standing near a large mirror in one of the courts devoted to furniture' (177). Car'line's final subjection to Mop in the Quiet Woman can also be explained on two levels. Realistically speaking, it is too much 'gin-and-beer hot' (180) which causes her to lose control of herself, but on the deeper mythical level she has defied two taboos of folklore: she has 'crossed the threshold' (179) of a charmed place and accepted the nourishment offered there. Actually or symbolically, Car'line's willingness to enter the inn and drink the liquor, 'though she did not exactly want this beverage' (179), are imprudent acts for a person of her hysterical temperament. Similarly, her vomiting of 'the sperrits' (184)[37] after the dance is a purgation that is both physical and spiritual. Throughout 'The Fiddler of the Reels' actual and symbolic action follow identical patterns.

The story's potential for double interpretation leads the reader to a recognition that the underside of all human experience, even the most mundane, has its mysterious and uncontrollable aspects. The repeated motif of the 'direct contact' of technological and natural forces is emblematic of the fact that human nature cannot be overcome by scientific advancement. Images of progress are defeated by the forces of nature: the women arriving in London on the ' "excursion-train" – an absolutely new departure in the history of travel', are 'blue-faced, stiff-necked, sneezing, rain-beaten, chilled to the marrow' by nature's 'wind and rain' (174); after the Exhibition, the park trees 'that had been enclosed for six months [are] again exposed to the winds and storms, and the sod [grows] green anew' (177); and neither the civilizing influences of 'London life' nor the veil which Car'line has worn 'to keep off the wind' (179) can shield her from the glance or the music of Mop Ollamoor.[38]

The story's major characters can similarly be seen from two points of view. Figures in the rural world of the Froom Valley, they can also be interpreted as forces within, or aspects of, human nature. In the delineation of Mop Ollamoor, at once a 'nominal horse-doctor' (170) and a diabolical embodiment of sexual potency, the supernatural aspects of his character are emphasized. He is linked to Dionysian rites and able, like Orpheus, to move by his music even inanimate objects; like the Pied Piper he is capable of leading children where he wills; like Eros he is not susceptible to the emotions he inflicts on others (he laughs while the children cry at his music); he is, in short, the quasi-mythical figure who gives 'The Fiddler of the Reels' its symbolic dimension. Of 'un-English' complexion, 'coming from nobody [knows] where', smelling suggestively of '"boy's-love" . . . steeped in lamp-oil', and possessing 'weird and wizardly' powers (166), Mop is a kind of demon lover with an uncanny knowledge of the physical and mental state of his victims – hence his otherwise coincidental appearances in London and at the Quiet Woman on the evening of Car'line's return to the Froom Valley, and his immediate recognition of her behind her veil. The aura of supernaturalism surrounding Mop is suggested not by Gothic trappings or by a ghost-like appearance but by the sheer potency of his physical and psychic presence, inseparable, it seems, from his music – an impression confirmed by the fact that Mop never speaks, but expresses himself only with the 'lingual character' (167) of his fiddle-playing and his 'gimlet-like gaze' (182).

A disturbing combination of the primitive and the decadently civilized, Ollamoor is at once foreign and indigenous to the world of Wessex. His powers of fascination are linked both with the 'Italian or German city' (182) from which his fiddle came and with the 'mass of dark heath-land' (183) into which he disappears with Carry, a 'place of Dantesque gloom' (184) suggesting the chthonic powers associated with uncultivated nature. The suffix 'moor' or 'more' is common enough in Dorset/Wessex place names, but his surname may also derive from the word 'blackamoor' (a term that can refer figuratively to the devil)[39] and seems to suggest 'olive Moor' or 'oily Moor'. In any case, Mop functions in the story both as a mystifying demonic presence and as the actual human being who fathered little Carry. As a man and as a symbol, he is a sexual force which can move women to act irresponsibly, and in a manner destructive not only of their own independence but also of the order of society as a whole. Without ever losing his human aspect, Mop possesses deeply mythical dimensions.

Car'line Aspent and Ned Hipcroft can also be seen from a

double perspective, but in an altogether different manner. Human and finite in every sense, they represent particular forms of sexual imbalance in the human psyche. Car'line is a woman 'of fragile and responsive organization' who, of all adults, is 'the most influenced by Mop Ollamoor's heart-stealing melodies' (168). Her essential characteristic is immaturity. Even at the conclusion of the story, hers continues to be a child's mind in a woman's body, and she never moves beyond 'unsophisticated maidenhood' to become, by learning from her past experiences, one of those 'girls whose love for [Mop has] turned to hatred' (166). Her infantile nature betrays itself above all in her utter lack of self-knowledge. Considering her pregnancy a matter of simple bad luck, she fails to understand the nature of the force that seduced her in the first place; she thinks that she can confront Mop 'quite calmly – mistress of herself in the dignity her London life [has] given her' (179), and that her veil will protect her from his penetrating eye. But like Barbara Grebe, Car'line is 'limp as withywind', always yearning for 'something to cling to' (170),[40] a frail vessel enclosing only vanity and passion. When her demon lover has departed from her, Car'line is left a child again, her will 'shattered' (184), content merely to get her share of 'rest' (185). As sex was for her a forsaking of the conscious self, so now is sleep. Car'line's sexuality never develops to embrace the social responsibilities of marriage and motherhood, and her complete lack of interest in the fate of her own child indicates most forcefully that she is a hollow vessel, a child herself who never achieves womanhood or comes to possess the mature qualities of individuality and selfhood.

Car'line's 'manly and simple wooer Edward' (170), whose name means guardian or protector, has affinities with Gabriel Oak and Giles Winterbourne, faithful and patient lovers of women who are attracted to flashier and bolder sexual types. But just as Car'line is a weak personality in comparison with Bathsheba and Grace, so Ned suffers from being measured against his precursors. Although a 'respectable mechanic' (170) – unlike Mop who is only a 'veterinary surgeon in theory' (166) – Ned seems locked in time, both in a physical and a professional sense. His mind and body are confined too much to the conscious world that Car'line, in a different form of weakness, forsakes. Accepting Car'line's refusal of his marriage proposal, Ned derives from it 'a new start in life' (170).[41] In London, however, he is content to improve 'as a workman' without shifting 'one jot in social position'. He is also complacent about his personal life:

> In his quiet lodging in Lambeth he moved about after working-hours with the facility of a woman, doing his own cooking, attending to his stocking-heels, and shaping himself by degrees to a life-long bachelorhood. For this conduct one is bound to advance the canonical reason that time could not efface from his heart the image of little Car'line Aspent – and it may be in part true; but there was also the inference that his was a nature not greatly dependent upon the ministrations of the other sex for its comforts.   (171)

The real 'inference' of this passage is that Ned is seriously lacking in sexual energy. Never once (the same is not true of the presentations of Oak and Winterbourne) is Ned's physical attraction to Car'line described. His sexual indifference is also suggested by the fact that, unlike Mop, he 'had not the slightest ear for music; could not sing two notes in tune, much less play them' (170). Even Ned's marriage is described in words suggesting passivity: 'without any definite agreement to forgive her, he tacitly acquiesced in the fate that Heaven had sent him.' (177)

Despite his obvious weaknesses, however, Ned is an attractive character, especially in the scene where he warms to Car'line and her child as they stand before him, pathetically drenched with rain, in Waterloo station. His quick assumption of a 'paternal' role (the conjugal role seems quite secondary to him) is Ned's most definitive effort to break out of his locked position in time. Childless, he embraces young Carry at just the point when the Exhibition is about to close down and become 'a thing of the past' (177). As Eppie is for Silas Marner, so the child is Ned's only investment in the future, and all of his energy is channeled toward her. This accounts for his insistence that Carry is his child, despite her paternity: 'But she *is* mine, all the same! Ha'n't I nussed her? Ha'n't I fed her and teached her? Ha'n't I played wi' her? O, little Carry – gone with that rogue – gone!' Ned's readiness to assume what were conventionally considered to be maternal roles explains his open indifference to Car'line: 'She's not so particular much to me, especially now she's lost the little maid! But Carry's the whole world to me!' (184) It may also account for Ned's 'sudden hatred toward his native district' (185), for him now a place with only a past and not a future, and his lifelong obsession (rather like that of Mr Peggotty in *David Copperfield*) with recovering the lost child. Just at the point when, through the disappearance of Mop Ollamoor, Car'line is abandoned by the life-force, it takes possession of Ned in a completely different way, as a 'passionate paternal love for a child not his own' (184).

If 'The Fiddler of the Reels' presents any vision of balanced sexuality, it can be found in the narrator's remarks about the Mellstock Quire. Mop, significantly, 'did not rise above the horizon thereabout till those well-known musicians were disbanded as ecclesiastical functionaries' (167). This fact suggests that until the parish of Mellstock had lost the harmonious and communal music of its local choir, it was immune to the disturbing charms of a Mop Ollamoor. The presentation of music and dancing in *Under the Greenwood Tree* is indeed strikingly different from that in 'The Fiddler of the Reels'. In the world of the Mellstock Quire, images of sexual union are wholesome, leading to 'the palpable confederacy of man and wife' (*UGT*, 56) and to the creation of families. As Mr Spinks observes: 'Dancing . . . is a most strengthening, livening, and courting movement, 'specially with a little beverage added! And dancing is good.' (*UGT*, 47) The difference between Mop's music and the choir's is not simply that the latter play sacred music, while Mop has 'never bowed a note of church-music from his birth' (167). The Mellstock musicians are perfectly capable of a lively reel and are even aware of the potentially diabolical power of string music. As Reuben Dewy remarks: 'There's always a rakish, scampish twist about a fiddle's looks that seems to say the Wicked One had a hand in making o'en' (*UGT*, 25). But in the world of *Under the Greenwood Tree*, the 'rakish' music is always kept in its place and incorporated into the wider realm of the community's music-making, which also includes church-music and carolling. The 'jigging' part of the tranter's Christmas Eve party is postponed, upon the authority of Grandfather William, until after midnight. The irrational urges are not, in short, repressed but rather are integrated into the wider communal way of life. In the context of the balanced and stable world represented in *Under the Greenwood Tree*,[42] the judgment of Mop's music by the Mellstock Quire takes on special significance: 'In their honest love of thoroughness they despised the new man's style. Theophilus Dewy (Reuben the tranter's younger brother) used to say there was no 'plumness' in it – no bowing, no solidity – it was all fantastical.' (167) It is precisely the qualities of 'thoroughness' and 'solidity' in the music and in the lives of the Mellstock Quire which make their dancing harmonious and 'good', and it is the 'fantastical' quality of Mop's music which, in the absence of any communal band of musicians in Mellstock, makes Car'line's jig hysterical and convulsive.

Hardy wrote 'The Fiddler of the Reels' soon after his father's death, an event which led him to set down in his notebook his mother's memory of 'the three Hardys as they used to appear passing over the brow of the hill to Stinsford Church on a Sunday morning, three or four years before my birth ... their fiddles and violoncello in green-baize bags under their left arms' (*LY*, 10). This revival in Hardy of the nostalgic memories of his local past, coming at a time when he was preoccupied with contemporary problems, may account for the persistent juxtaposition in 'The Fiddler of the Reels' of past and present. The theme of progress, represented by the railroad and the Exhibition, is framed by the story's rural setting in 'those outlying shades of the world, Stickleford, Mellstock, and Egdon' (166). The motif of music, so closely linked with Hardy's childhood and ancestry, may also have been suggested to him by the death of his father. Several critics have noted the significance of music in Hardy's writing and its relationship, when used as a metaphor, to sexual love and to Hardy's own 'ecstatic temperament' (*EL*, 18).[43] It is unlikely that Hardy ever read Soren Kierkegaard's essay on Mozart's *Don Giovanni*, but its ideas provide a suggestive philosophical basis for Hardy's close identification of sexual desire with love of music in 'The Fiddler of the Reels':[44]

From this it by no means follows that one needs to regard music as the work of the devil, even if our age does offer many horrible proofs of the daemonic power with which music may lay hold upon an individual, and this individual in turn, grip and capture a multitude, especially women, in the seductive snare of fear, by means of the all-disturbing power of voluptuousness. It by no means follows that one needs to regard music as the work of the devil, even though one notices with a certain secret horror that this art, more than any other, frequently harrows its votaries in a terrible manner, a phenomenon which strangely enough seems to have escaped the attention of psychologists and the multitude, except at the single moment when they are startled by the wild shriek of some despairing individual. However, it is noticeable enough that in legends, hence in the popular consciousness which finds its expression in legends, the musical is again the daemonic.[45]

In 'The Fiddler of the Reels', Hardy explores the demonic dimension of music and of sex in a form that is at once legendary and modern in its frame of reference and hence embodies a truth not only about the past, but also about the present. This extension of the story's meaning into a contemporary context is confirmed by the concluding image of Car'line's child as a middle-aged woman accompanying Mop in his fiddling. Like Syrinx, who was metamorphosed into Pan's pipe, Carry is dehumanized and made into a passive instrument. An emblem of the future generation, she represents in her subservience to Mop the extension of his powers into the present and into the new world. In this context, the vision of Mop and Carry 'performing in some capacity now' (185) in America (the audience for which the story was first written) becomes the most disturbing image in the whole story, and the year 1851, which the old gentleman had referred to as 'an extraordinary chronological frontier' (165), is seen for what it truly is: one of many chapters in the endless and repetitive history of man's struggle, even as the technological achievements of civilization become more sophisticated, with his own primitive psyche.

It may seem inconsistent with the implicit judgments offered by the other stories in *Life's Little Ironies* that 'The Fiddler of the Reels' should place a communal ideal above the force of instinct in the single human being. Its invocation of the pastoral world of *Under the Greenwood Tree* suggests, indeed, that the integration into the whole person of man's irrational side can best be achieved in a milieu where marriage and stability contribute to a communal way of life. But if one looks closely at the earlier stories, it becomes clear that it is not society itself that Hardy finds repressive, but rather the inability of certain social laws and conventions to perform the stabilizing function for which they were originally designed. Laws had become, as he told Edmund Gosse in 1907, 'artificial, clumsy, and ineffectual',[46] and had begun to destroy the very happiness they were created to preserve. In Hardy the 'little ironies' of life emerge from the incompatibility of instinct and law, but also from man's essential need for social order. 'Tragedy', he had said, 'may be created by an opposing environment either of things inherent in the universe, or of human institutions' (*LY*, 44). Hardy's endorsement in *Life's Little Ironies* of both the revolutionary and the conservative views about social institutions is not an inconsistency, but rather a startling recognition of the basis for man's unhappiness – the fact that he is both a solitary and a social being.

On the title page of *Life's Little Ironies*, Hardy makes a distinction between the 'Tales' of the first part of the volume and the 'Colloquial Sketches' which fall under the heading of 'A Few Crusted Characters'. The term 'sketch' apparently refers to the limited scope and length of the narratives, while 'colloquial' points both to the presence of first-person narrators and to the casual tone in which they speak. Ernest Baker has called 'A Few Crusted Characters' a comic 'antidote' to the sombreness of the first half of *Life's Little Ironies*,[47] but comedy is an inadequate term for these anecdotes. Their predominant tone is humorous but mixed in with the laughable is, as Douglas Brown has phrased it, 'an elegiac framework'[48] that both undercuts and encloses their more farcical aspects. There is, moreover, a serious underside to the farce. Hunting, the hanging of petty criminals, and the lifehold occupancy of property are all subjects about which Hardy wrote more gravely elsewhere, and the sketches remain gently humorous only because of the unquestioning acceptance by their narrators of things as they are: except for the old groceress's outcry about 'cruel times' (246) in 'The Winters and the Palmleys', a protesting tone is absent from these narratives. None of the speakers doubts, for example, the authority of the Squire to put Andrey Satchel and Netty Sargent out of their homes, or to abolish the church choir. As Samuel Hynes has said, the humour of 'A Few Crusted Characters' is 'not a form of entertainment', but 'a way of enduring the inevitable'.[49]

Critics have categorized the narratives in 'A Few Crusted Characters' as fabliaux or ballads,[50] but neither of these forms by itself explains the special quality of their genre, their blending of the personal concern of John Lackland for the 'ordinary' with the bias of his fellow travellers toward 'their own opinion that the remarkable [is] better worth telling than the ordinary' (251). A central subject of 'A Few Crusted Characters' is, indeed, this disparity between private and communal memory, dramatized in Lackland's moonlit visit to the local cemetery where he finally discovers 'the village community that he had left behind him five-and-thirty years before' (259). The sketches have three audiences: the local people in Burthen's waggon, John Lackland, and the reader, whose vantage point is ostensibly at an even greater remove than Lackland's. To the travellers of Longpuddle, these anecdotes have a particular insular significance, like those landscape paintings of Mr Day's which are 'world-ignored', but admired and even owned by 'every dwelling in the parish' (190). So these narratives are known and remembered by all the village, but different persons have unique rights to tell them, depending on the directness of their access to the original events. Burthen's knowledge of Tony Kytes's exact route; the clerk's memory of the wedding-randy where the Hardcomes changed partners; the curate's account 'almost word for word' (215) of the way James Hardcome explained his story to him; the knowledge about William Privett's death which the seedsman's father got from a series of witnesses; Mr Profitt's first-hand observations as a choir-boy of old Andrey's embarrassing experience at the Squire's; the aged groceress's recollections of Jack Winter's funeral which she watched as a child 'by [her] mother's side' (245); the registrar's less direct knowledge of George Crookhill's tale from stories he had heard 'as a boy at school' (246); and Mr Day's memory of Netty Sargent's 'black hair and dancing eyes . . . and her sly way of screwing up her mouth when she meant to tease ye!' (252) – all of these personal experiences create a special entitlement to tell a tale.

As the names 'Burthen' and 'Lackland' suggest, there is a Bunyanesque quality to this journey from the market town to the small village, from a public into a private world, far 'from the view of gazing burghers' (191). But here as elsewhere in *Life's Little Ironies*, the conventional form is used ironically. Lackland's Celestial City is a vision not of a happy eternity, but of his unreclaimable past in a place where old faces 'have dropped out o' their frames, so to speak it, and new ones have been put in their places' (193). He returns to Longpuddle with 'magnified expectations from infantine memories', but his connection with the 'local life', once as personal as that of the inhabitants, has been irremediably interrupted, and he must disappear, 'ghost-like' (259), from its environs. For the reader, however, there can be a satisfactory conclusion to the journey in that it can lead him to a reasonably coherent impression of this small and self-contained universe. While as an 'absolute foreigner' he can appreciate the 'peculiar charm attaching to an old village in an old country' (259), he also becomes familiar, like the reader of *Wessex Tales*, with some of the complex substance of rural life. The subject matter of 'A Few Crusted Characters' covers the main events of life – birth, marriage, and death; its time span stretches from the hanging many decades earlier of Jack Winter to the recent marriage of young Andrey Satchel; its range of classes extends from a simple carrier to 'small farmers' (204) and on to the aristocratic Lord and Lady Baxby who are guests of the local Squire. As a unit, it forms a frozen image of a world actually both static and fluid, lost in the past yet constantly changing and always present to the minds of its local narrators.

An important element in the cycle is the process of courtship and marriage which, by its altering of emotional and financial alliances from one generation to the next, constitutes a central drama of rural life. 'Tony Kytes, the Arch-Deceiver' is a farcical foreshortening of the process of courtship. In the brief span of an afternoon, a country lad accepts and rejects three women as marriage partners and finally settles upon one by a process of elimination which, though hardly logical, is not untrue to life – except, perhaps, in the speed with which different choices follow upon each other. The characters in the sketch are comic stereotypes. In addition to the intrusive fathers are three distinct types of woman, the forward Unity Sallet, the 'dashing' (196) but 'backward' (199) Hannah Jolliver, and the demure and faithful Milly Richards. As so often in Hardy's work, the women are interested in Tony not only because they find him sexually attractive, but also because they are anxious to 'throw over' each other. For his part, Tony is both the perpetrator and the victim of sexual coercion. His reactions to the advances of each of the three girls are natural enough, but made irresponsible by their thoughtless spontaneity. Tony is deceptive, but the title 'Arch-Deceiver' is humorously excessive when applied to a man who is as much a fool as a knave. Hardly a vice-figure, or even a Don Juan, the round-faced Tony is an everyman of sorts, at one moment naively succumbing to flirtation, at the next engaging in blatant deception. His 'nunnywatch' (200) is a result partly of his male simplicity. Absurdly unaware of the pride, anger, and jealously which move the three girls, he thinks preposterously that he can preserve 'peace and good-will' (197) by kissing them 'all round . . . fair and square' (202). His story is a farcical summation of two conflicting attitudes toward sex: a male desire to have all women with no complications, and a female inclination to competition and exclusiveness. The sketch points up the potential absurdity of both these points of view while at the same time emphasizing their truth to human nature. Tony's marriage to the faithful Milly is at once an indication of the arbitrariness of such decisions (if Hannah's father had not turned up, things might have developed differently) and a demonstration of what Tony finds so hard to acknowledge: that limitation and compromise are inevitable components of a sexual choice.

A more sober look at marriage, 'The History of the Hardcomes' presents two pairs of lovers who despite their higher social standing are not unlike Tony in their fluctuating sexual preferences. It is suggested, indeed, that Tony's 'fickle nature' had 'infected' (210) them all on the night of the wedding-randy. The consequences of a frivolous marital choice, avoided by the narrator of 'Tony Kytes', are the subject of this anecdote. The lively sexual atmosphere of the country dance leads to an impulsive changing of partners between two engaged couples. After marrying the new partners, the members of the original couples are again drawn to each other. Like Maggie Tulliver and Stephen Guest in *The Mill on the Floss*, Stephen Hardcome and his cousin's wife drift into an irrational state of sexual oblivion, carried by the tide of emotion into a forgetfulness of all their previous commitments and responsibilities, even of self-preservation. The narrators refer repeatedly to what 'was planned by nature' (207) for these pairs of lovers, but the irony of such a point of view is that it is fickle 'nature' which distracts these lovers and later, when it is too late to reconcile matters simply, draws them together again. As much as Tony Kytes, but with more serious effects, the Hardcomes live and marry by momentary whims.

'The Superstitious Man's Story' links William Privett's sudden death with five apparently supernatural occurrences. Hardy himself half-believed in ghosts,[51] and his motive in writing 'The Superstitious Man's Story' seems at least in part to have been documentary. He wrote to Edward Clodd in 1894 that the association of the miller-moth with the human soul 'is, or was until lately, an actual belief down here. It was told me years ago by an old woman. I may say, once for all, that every superstition, custom, etc., described in my novels may be depended on as true records of the same, whatever merit in folklorists' eyes they may have as such, and are not inventions of mine.'[52] What is inventive about 'The Superstitious Man's Story', however, and what distinguishes it from a simple footnote on folklore, is the personality of its teller and his mode of expression. The very title of the sketch directs the reader to the unreliability of its narrator and thus to the true substance of its subject matter: not the isolated anecdotes by themselves, but the manner in which they are believed. For this rural narrator, who has assembled and coordinated his information from five separate first-hand witnesses, the details associated with the death gratify that yearning for significance which Freud says characterizes the superstitious mind.[53] So although Lackland calls 'The Superstititous Man's Story' 'rather melancholy' (219), the attitude of the seedsman's father toward his tale is one of satisfaction at the perfect correspondence of the supernatural occurrences with the copious circumstantial details surrounding them. He is a spokesman for a particular rural attitude, eager to see a pattern in the mystifying course of life and to replace an instinctive fear of death by a fascination with its inevitable but always startling suddenness.

The next three sketches, beginning with 'Andrey Satchel and the Parson and Clerk', represent a shift in tone and emphasis. While the first three narratives portray various rural attitudes toward marriage and death, these have a more specific theme: the simultaneous opposition and interdependence, especially strong in the feudal society of a rural village, existing between the common people and those authorities of church and property who formalize and organize their lives. These sketches, two of which are told by Christopher Twink the master-thatcher, are the most inventive and 'colloquial' in 'A Few Crusted Characters', not only for the hilarity of their content, but also for the richness of their hyperbolic language and metaphor. They contain a wealth of local dialect, in both their expository accounts and their quoted dialogues, and the liveliness of the thatcher's own mind is apparent in his descriptions of the parson slapping the Bible together 'like a rat-trap' (222) and of the young couple bursting out of the tower 'like starved mice from a cupboard' (228).

Hardy probably conceived the plot of 'Andrey Satchel and the Parson and Clerk' from an idea for a story he jotted down in 1878 about an 'honest Earl' who out of honour married a blacksmith's daughter after having been 'accidentally shut up in a tower' with her,[54] and from a story he heard at Lord Portsmouth's about a hunted fox that ran up an old woman's clock-case (*EL*, 240). Parson Billy Toogood is based on the Reverend William Butler, rector of Frampton in the early decades of the nineteenth century, described in the 1896 preface to *Life's Little Ironies* as a 'truly delightful personage' who followed the 'composite calling of sportsman and divine'.[55] In Hardy's assembling of these disparate details, the farcical humour resides not only in the embarrassing plight of the couple locked in the tower during the hunt, but, more dramatically, in the contrast between the forthright passions of Andrey and the sublimated ones of Toogood. Satchel's drunkenness after the christening is matched, we learn, by the parson himself, who at the same ceremonies 'never failed to christen the chiel over again in a bottle of port wine' (224); the sexual exploits of young Andrey, though not themselves repeated by the clergyman, have a kind of counterpart in the latter's passionate obsession with fox-hunting. Hardy's disapproval of hunting is submerged here beneath the farcical account of the chase, and several broad touches having to do with Toogood were added in 1894, including the paragraph describing him as a 'bachelor man' who 'every time he went to bed in summer . . . used to open the bed at bottom and crawl up head foremost, to mind en of the coming winter and the good sport he'd have, and the foxes going to earth' (224). The account of the hunt itself, full of conventionally romantic images of gentlemen and horses and hounds moving 'up hill and down dale, like the very wind' (225), is deflated at a stroke by the ridiculous conclusion, an image of frustrated passion, of the fox trapped up the old woman's clock-case.

The utter single-mindedness of both the parson and his clerk, brought home by their forgetfulness of Andrey's and Jane's predicament, raises some questions about the position of the clergy in village life, as does the prologue to 'A Few Crusted Characters', in which the curate is late in catching Burthen's van, projecting an image of ridiculous ineptitude. 'Old Andrey's Experience as a Musician' makes a similar point about the place of the gentry in the rural community. The initial impression is one of cordiality and generosity between classes, but the values of the two groups begin to clash when the Squire's mother refuses to support the choir's kind tolerance of Andrey. Told as the childhood memory of Mr Profitt, who had been a choir-boy at the time, the story's principal mode is that of comedy verging on caricature, especially in the descriptions of the Squire's mother, who is seen by the young boy as a 'tall gruff' and 'hook-nosed old lady' (231), a figure of superior age, class, education, stature, and authority. The confrontation between this woman and the absurd old Andrey, whose face when scrutinized by her looks 'as if it were made of rotten apple' (231) is a purely comic scene, made all the more absurd because of Andrey's male silliness and awkwardness in the face of female authority. But the farce is muted in the story's conclusion, with its sense that disaster has only just been averted. Old Andrey's fate is determined by a triangular power structure including the Squire, his mother, and his wife. Each wields authority differently: the old woman, who has Andrey 'turned out of the house as a vile impostor' (232), the Squire himself, who in a fit of anger threatens to give him notice to leave his cottage, and – the merciful stroke that preserves the farce – the Squire's wife, whose charity toward Andrey transcends the orders of both and at the same time reinforces the position of the Squire's family as a paternalistic preserver of order.

Both 'Old Andrey's Experience as a Musician' and the next sketch, 'Absent-Mindedness in a Parish Choir', are based on the sort of choir for which Hardy's father and grandfather played in the early decades of the nineteenth century, the model for the Mellstock Quire of *Under the Greenwood Tree*. Hardy said in his 1912 preface to that early novel that his portrayal of such church officials was 'penned . . . lightly, even . . . farcically and flippantly at times', and fell short of the 'deeper, more essential, more transcendent handling' (*UGT*, x) he would have liked to give it. Though such a comment would also be applicable to 'Absent-Mindedness', the sketch does possess a special elegiac quality that lends a seriousness and pathos to the farce. Like the members of the Mellstock Quire, these local musicians appear foolish in the presence of authority, and yet have a dignity of their own – an impression reinforced by the insensitivity of those in power to their position in the parish as an 'important union of interests' (*UGT*, viii), religious, social, and artistic. At the same time the Squire is described frankly as a 'wickedish man' who cannot 'rule his passion' (235) any more successfully than the men he dismisses. At the centre of one of the most comical sketches in 'A Few Crusted Characters' is a profound and irretrievable loss, created by a Squire's ignorance.

Jack Winter, a much more dignified figure than the buffoonish Satchels, represents another loss – this time of a particular kind of innocence and rural pride. The subject of 'The Winters and the Palmleys', as of 'To Please His Wife', is sexual jealousy between two women. It portrays the strong tie that can exist between a widow and her only son – evident also in Widow Jethway of *A Pair of Blue Eyes* and Susan Nunsuch in *The Return of the Native* – and the insatiable sense of grievance that can accompany the loss of such a child. This alone can explain the horrible retaliation of Mrs Palmley on Mrs Winter, reminiscent of Miss Havisham's revenge in *Great Expectations*. But the pattern of personal reprisal here takes on a form that has a wider significance for the rural village: Jack is destroyed not only by the anger of Mrs Palmley, but also by the insidious intrusion of sophistication and pretension into the not 'very large world' (238) of Longpuddle. Harriet Palmley, possessing the accomplishments but not the charms of Fancy Day, represents urban vanity at its most 'heartless' (242). Esteeming the visible elegance of the written word above its meaning, she can break the integrity of honest Jack Winter, 'the pride of that day in being able to write with beautiful flourishes, and the sorrow at not being able to do so, raging so high' (240). The image of this rural youth hanged in 'the heaviest fetters kept in the jail' (245)[56] is a tragic illustration of the failure of law to judge accurately the motives of those who transgress its limits. He is the helpless victim of a tripartite force undermining the vitality of the rural community: combined with the personal revenge of his mother's rival is the cold gentility of Harriet's urban values and the uncomprehending power of an authority that can hang a man for petty burglary.

The last two sketches in 'A Few Crusted Characters' present a rural trait that can be seen both as a vice and a virtue: cunning resourcefulness. 'Incident in the Life of Mr. George Crookhill' is a straightforward comic exemplum, demonstrating 'a case of the biter bit' (246). Hardy may have got the idea for the anecdote from a story he jotted down in his 'Facts' notebook about a deserting soldier who killed a drunken man he had befriended in order to steal his clothes and escape.[57] But Hardy's version, in keeping with its farcical tone, steers clear of any real violence, and the irony lies entirely in the humorous turn of the plot, whereby Crookhill is almost convicted not only of the theft of which he is guilty but of the more serious crime of desertion as well. The sketch is comic throughout, but beneath the absurdity of Crookhill's situation is the threat of hanging for another man's offence – something the deserting Dragoon would happily have allowed.

A less harmful deception is that performed by Netty Sargent, a far more attractive representative of the rural spirit than George Crookhill. In 'Netty Sargent's Copyhold', Hardy treats in a comic vein a subject about which he writes seriously in *The Woodlanders* and in *Early Life*, where his old neighbourhood of Higher Bockhampton is described nostalgically as

mainly occupied by lifeholders of substantial footing like
the Hardys themselves. . . . But the lifeholds fell into hand,
and the quaint residences with their trees, clipped hedges,
orchards, white gatepost-balls, the naval officer's masts and
weather-cocks, have now perished every one, and have been
replaced by labourers' brick cottages and other new farm-
buildings, a convenient pump occupying the site of the
mossy well and bucket.   (*EL*, 3–4)

In this sketch the Squire is portrayed as a villain who
'constitutionally hated these tiny copyholds and leaseholds
and freeholds, which made islands of independence in the
fair, smooth ocean of his estates' (255); but the more direct
threats to Netty's well-being are the dilatoriness of her uncle,
and the whimsicality of Fate which snatches away old Sargent
a mere 'few hours' (254) before he is to sign the renewal of his
copyhold. In these circumstances, the reader's sympathies are
entirely with Netty, who by an 'ingenious contrivance' (258) is
able to defeat the law and the selfish Squire it protects. By her
pragmatism and 'nerve' (258), Netty triumphs over the very
forces that defeat old Andrey, the church choir, and Jack
Winter. But in keeping with the ironic mode of *Life's Little
Ironies*, she fails to overcome the less definable and control-
lable tyranny of life itself, which had caused the Hardcomes
and Jane Satchel to choose the mates they did. Netty's final
fate is a gently sardonic combination of good and bad fortune,
as she finds herself secure both of her cottage and of a less-
than-perfect husband.

Seen as a whole, 'A Few Crusted Characters' is miscellaneous in subject matter and unchronological in its transitions
from one narrative to the next. The first three sketches, very
different from each other, are followed by a second three that
are more uniform in content and manner because they are
drawn together by two generations of the Satchel family and
by the Longpuddle Church choir. The last three, finally,
return the reader to his impression of haphazardness: a truly
appalling story of revenge is followed by a farcical anecdote
and then by a grimly humorous tale which has, like life itself,
both a satisfying and a disappointing conclusion. Yet despite
their random arrangement, the sketches achieve a kind of
thematic coherence. They are unified by their setting (the

carrier's van travelling to Longpuddle), by their context (the shared memories of the local people), and even by the turnpike road itself, which most of the characters in the narrative either travel along or intersect at some point. As a group, the sketches in 'A Few Crusted Characters' form a small composite picture of village life, bringing together diverse experiences and encompassing several decades of local history – the remembered past of old and young alike.

The original title for the 1891 periodical printing of 'A Few Crusted Characters' was 'Wessex Folk', a term suggestive both of the folk-tale aspect of these anecdotes and of the rural background of their narrators and characters. As a title, 'A Few Crusted Characters' preserves the impression that one is being exposed to a specific set of personalities, but it conveys in addition the sense that these 'Crusted Characters' come from a different era, ancient and almost inaccessible. Hardy is never specific as to whether the 'Characters' are the subjects of the sketches or the people telling them, but in a sense both the travellers in Burthen's van and the people they talk about inhabit the same plane in the reader's mind, remote from the present and from the urban world. It is this impression of lost time and place, dramatized in the deracination of John Lackland, which gives to 'A Few Crusted Characters' its elegiac unity of tone. The journey to Longpuddle begins on a 'Saturday afternoon of blue and yellow autumn-time' (189), a point in the year when nature is vividly alive for a few final moments. It is this fragile, 'Crusted' instant which Hardy preserves in the little world of 'A Few Crusted Characters'.

It may seem inappropriate for this collection of rural anecdotes to follow such a sombre and contemporary set of stories as *Life's Little Ironies*, but a close scrutiny reveals that both sections of the volume are treating the same fundamental human problems. Shadrach Jolliffe's confusion about which woman to marry anticipates that of Tony Kytes; deception in love is a theme both of 'On the Western Circuit' and of 'Tony Kytes'; clerical hypocrisy is a subject of 'The Son's Veto', 'A Tragedy of Two Ambitions', and 'Andrey Satchel and the Parson and Clerk'; female jealousy produces tragedy in both 'To Please His Wife' and 'The Winters and the Palmleys'; and the irrational side of the sexual instinct allures Car'line Aspent and the Hardcomes alike away from domestic happiness. These links make the sketches in 'A Few Crusted Characters' a fitting conclusion to the whole volume. Just as the longer 'Tales' of *Life's Little Ironies* expose the tragedies that can underlie a comically absurd sequence of events, so these small narratives portray the same phenomenon, by embodying the peculiar combination found in oral village culture of the burlesque and the pathetic, the humane and the cruel. These 'Colloquial Sketches' are life's little ironies writ smaller.

In both the 'Tales' of *Life's Little Ironies* and the 'Sketches' of 'A Few Crusted Characters', there is an important correlation between character and environment, but in the 'Tales' this relationship is dramatized even in their formal structure. Instead of departing completely from the conventional plots of the day – an approach which surely would have inspired disapproval in a Victorian audience – Hardy uses those familiar plots for his own purposes, twisting and playing with them so that the differences between good and evil, so strongly delineated in the conventional plots, are less definite. By presenting to his audiences familiar scenarios, mostly of the sort found in current sentimental fiction and stage comedy, and then defying their expectations by altering or inverting the morals of these plots, Hardy, like Ibsen (and Shaw after him), is able to jar his audience into questioning the very conventions of which the literature of the time was so supportive. Hardy's 'villains' (Randolph Twycott, Joshua Halborough) are respectable professional men of whom his readers in other circumstances would approve, and his 'heroines' (Ella Marchmill, Leonora Frankland) are women whose unconventional sexual behaviour might otherwise inspire indignation.

During the period when *Life's Little Ironies* was being written, Hardy saw several of Ibsen's plays and read accounts of others (*EL*, 307; *LY*, 20).[58] Significantly, he called them 'tragic productions' (*LY*, 20–1) with 'situations' not unlike those in *The Woodlanders* (*EL*, 289), for Ibsen quintessentially exemplifies the form of 'tragedy' which Hardy saw as peculiar to his own time: the treatment of the individual's struggle with social conventions. In Ibsen, as in the later Hardy, there is frankness in sexual matters and a willingness to portray even disastrous *dénouements* when they are appropriate to the pattern of action. In both writers too the relationship between character and environment is richly complex. The tragedy emerges, not because people are repressed from outside by conventions, but because they themselves have been conditioned by their environments and social expectations to such an extent that they have internalized artificial social laws. Many of Ibsen's characters – Hedda Gabler, Nora in *The Doll's House*, Rebecca in *Rosmersholm*, and Ellida in *The Lady from the Sea* – manage in various ways to escape or transcend the social conventions that circumscribe their lives. But Hardy's characters, with the possible exception of Ella Marchmill, remain imprisoned in themselves and in the environments that created them. Their tragic hubris lies in the degree to which conventional beliefs, customs, and desires govern the ways they regard each other, construct their visions of happiness, make their sexual choices, and live their respective lives – trapped in the very cages of respectability that they have built for themselves.

The tragic lives of these characters are brought to life by the complex mode of irony that informs both the structure of the stories' events and the tone in which they are reported. A prodigious number of critics have attempted to analyse and define the function of irony in Hardy's fiction, as well as the relation it has to his 'philosophy of life',[59] and it is possible here only to summarize those ideas that apply directly to the distinctive ironic mode of the stories in *Life's Little Ironies*. In the same year as the publication of the short story volume, Annie Macdonnell was careful to separate Hardy's 'satire and bitter irony' from 'cynicism', of which, she contended, he 'utters not a word'.[60] More recently, Jean R. Brooks has noted that Hardy's 'ironic mode is the reverse face of his compassion', a fact which results in the '"if only" structure of Hardeian irony'.[61] Mary Caroline Richards discerns 'two trends of irony in Hardy: the contradiction between *seems* and *is* which exhibits itself in traditional modes of dramatic irony; and the contradiction between *is* and *ought to be*'.[62] This second type of irony – that of satire – allows Hardy's unusual situations to transcend the level of the farcical, but it does not account for the fact that the stories never become, as the poems in his 'Satires of Circumstance' do, purely satirical.

This is true because none of the contradictions – neither those between appearance and reality, nor those between the real and the ideal – is attributed to any single character who could be considered a comic butt or a vice figure. Even the young clerics of 'The Son's Veto' and 'A Tragedy of Two Ambitions' – surely the most blameworthy characters in the volume – are portrayed in the context of the circumstances and environment that formed them. As David Daiches has noted, 'Hardy's irony is not directed at human egotism or at the disparity between real and assumed worth, but at the very conditions of human existence'.[63] Hardy's particular brand of irony in this volume of short stories derives from a tension between the desire for a better world and the contradicting sense that life can be no different.

The atmosphere of stoic acceptance counterbalancing the didactic quality of the stories' subject matter is produced by the rhetorical tone in which they are recounted. Assuming a posture of worldly wisdom and philosophical distance, the narrator of these stories – with an objectivity at once rational and compassionate – frequently invokes the wider patterns of behaviour to which the story's events correspond. Ella Marchmill is described analytically as moved by 'the instinct to specialize a waiting emotion on the first fit thing that came to hand' (11) and as 'entering on that tract of life in which emotional women begin to suspect that last love may be stronger than first love' (15). Randolph Twycott, it is said, once possessed the 'infantine sympathies' (43) of a child, but 'education' then 'ousted his humanity' (51). Mr Millborne is explained by the maxim that 'there are a few subtle-souled persons with whom the absolute gratuitousness of an act of reparation is an inducement to perform it; while exhortation as to its necessity would breed excuses for leaving it undone' (55). Joshua Halborough is seen as 'persuading himself that it was ardour for Christianity which spurred him on, and not pride of place' (83), while Charles Raye is classified, in terms of his position in history, as an 'end-of-the-age young man' (118) belonging to 'the classes that live on expectation' (121).

In certain respects, the rhetorical stance of this narrator resembles that of the 'Manager of the Performance' in *Vanity Fair*, who with the satirist's sharp eye sees into the heart of a situation, but whose 'general impression' of things, unlike that of the satirist, is 'more melancholy than mirthful'.[64] In the role of an 'observer of human nature',[65] both Thackeray's and Hardy's narrators sometimes stop the flow of the narrative in order to make a general comment. In the following passages from *Vanity Fair* and 'On the Western Circuit', the narrators turn the reader from the particular to the general and from a critical to a 'melancholy' stance:

> Her heart was dead long before her body. She had sold it to become Sir Pitt Crawley's wife. Mothers and daughters are making the same bargain every day in Vanity Fair.[66]
>
> Each time that she approached the half of her orbit that lay nearest him they gazed at each other with smiles, and with that unmistakable expression which means so little at the moment, yet so often leads up to passion, heartache, union, disunion, devotion, overpopulation, drudgery, content, resignation, despair.   (113–14)

Although these intrusions may seem awkward, they serve an important function, that of restoring the reader, especially at points where he might be judgmental, to the 'sober, contemplative, not uncharitable frame of mind'[67] with which Thackeray hoped his reader would regard the life of Vanity Fair. This rhetorical device can be compared to the reminiscent and stoically accepting tone of the rustics in Hardy's Wessex novels – a parallel that can be supported by the mention in *The Hand of Ethelberta* of 'the usual law by which the emotion that takes the form of humour in country workmen becomes transmuted to irony among the same order in town' (203). The rustic voice and the ironic voice serve to balance the introspection and self-involvement of the characters within the narratives themselves, and at the same time keep the reader mindful of the wider context in which the stories must be viewed.

Directly or indirectly, the general themes of all the stories in *Life's Little Ironies* involve the failure of modern marriage as an institution for formalizing and stabilizing sexual relationships, and the insidious effects of social ambition on family life. In most of the stories, these concerns are merged. Charles Raye, for example, will suffer professionally because of his marriage to an illiterate woman, while sexual desire and social ambition are inextricably linked in the personality of Joanna Phippard. Even those figures who do not marry – Randolph Twycott and the Halborough brothers – reflect their position as children of a marriage between one spouse who is socially ambitious and one who is not.[68] In these cases, the aspiring parent has planted in the child the seeds of his or her own desire for wealth and respectability, and the child in turn must, to achieve this aim, repudiate and destroy the other, surviving parent. But *Life's Little Ironies* is neither a didactic tract seeking to inspire a reform of the marriage laws, nor a satirical work directed at the follies of social ambition, though the stories have moments suggesting each of these descriptions. Seen as a whole – and including therefore not only the contemporary narratives but also those set in earlier periods – the volume can best be described as an impassioned depiction of man's inevitable failure to impose order upon the chaos of his being. Only the ironic perspective, with its simultaneous muted acceptance and compassionate regret, can accommodate what is both farcical and tragic about this perennial contradiction in the nature of life.

4 Miscellaneous Stories: Reflections on a Career

When *Life's Little Ironies* was published in 1894, Hardy had almost reached the end of his fiction-writing career. After the appearance of *Jude the Obscure* in 1895, he composed five short stories: 'A Committee-Man of "The Terror" ' (1896), 'The Duke's Reappearance' (1896), 'The Grave by the Handpost' (1897), 'Enter a Dragoon' (1900), and 'A Changed Man' (1900).[1] These, as well as 'Master John Horseleigh, Knight' (1893), were collected for Hardy's last short-story volume in 1913, along with six stories which had appeared in periodicals before 1891, when the International Copyright Law was passed: 'What the Shepherd Saw' (1881), 'The Romantic Adventures of a Milkmaid' (1883), 'A Tryst at an Ancient Earthwork' (1885), 'A Mere Interlude' (1885), 'Alicia's Diary' (1887), and 'The Waiting Supper' (1888). The volume's complete title – *A Changed Man, The Waiting Supper, and Other Tales, Concluding with The Romantic Adventures of a Milkmaid* – reveals not only Hardy's three presumable favourites among the twelve stories but also, by the absence of any thematic concept, his admission that the book has no coherent unifying principle. Unlike *Wessex Tales, A Group of Noble Dames*, and *Life's Little Ironies, A Changed Man* is uninteresting when considered as a volume.

But because Hardy made few substantial revisions for their volume publication, the stories in *A Changed Man* are significant as examples of his style and concerns at particular points in his development. The same could be said of Hardy's uncollected stories: 'How I Built Myself a House' (1865), 'Destiny and a Blue Cloak' (1874), 'The Thieves Who Couldn't Help Sneezing' (1877), 'An Indiscretion in the Life of an Heiress' (1878), 'Our Exploits at West Poley' (written in 1883, published in 1893),[2] 'Old Mrs. Chundle' (never pub-

157

lished in Hardy's lifetime, composed between 1888 and 1890),[3] and 'The Doctor's Legend' (1891). Among all of these works – collected and uncollected – some are weak examples of a characteristic mode, others failed attempts at a new one, while still others contain a mixture of the different techniques used with greater success in isolation in the first three short-story volumes. A few of the stories – most notably 'The Romantic Adventures of a Milkmaid' and 'The Waiting Supper' – are of a high quality and important in their own right. Seen in chronological sequence, the uncollected stories and those assembled in *A Changed Man* form a convenient framework for supporting a discussion of Hardy's whole career in writing short fiction, from his first efforts in prose and verse during the 1860s to the publication of his last short story in 1900.

Many of Hardy's earliest literary projects, produced before he thought of himself as a novelist or even a fiction writer, were conceived in an assortment of forms. In addition to the prize-winning essay, 'On the Application of Coloured Bricks and Terra Cotta to Modern Architecture', which he wrote while working for Arthur Blomfield in London,[4] Hardy considered writing architectural and art reviews for London magazines (*EL*, 61–2), and 'formed an idea of writing plays in blank verse' (*EL*, 71). Consistent with his effort in the late 1860s to bridge two careers, Hardy's first published work was a short sketch which reflected both his literary interests and his architectural experience. 'How I Built Myself a House', which appeared in *Chambers's Journal* in March 1865,[5] had as its original intention the amusement of the pupils in Blomfield's office, to whom Hardy gave 'mixed lessons in architecture and literature'.[6] Such a limited and specialized audience naturally influenced the sketch's style and tone, which displays continually the self-consciousness of a youthful writer trying to impress his peers. As fiction, it is anecdotal and casually told, with more emphasis on the single turn of phrase than on the overall effect – a style which imitates, as Robert Gittings has noted, the satirical writing of Thackeray and Dickens.[7]

This 'trifle', as Hardy was later to call it,[8] is basically a gentle satire on the mid-nineteenth-century building boom.[9] Its humour lies in the ironic euphemisms and comic incongruities of its language, as spoken by a narrator who provides the human focus for all the absurd inefficiencies which are part of the house-building process. The irony is at everyone's expense, but in the end it is directed back to the narrator, who sees himself as a victim of all the other characters – the architect, the builder, the surveyor, and even his own wife. This easily dominated man represents Hardy's first effort to use the first-person narrator for satirical purposes – a technique which he abandoned soon after in response to George Meredith's criticism of the more hostile satire in *The Poor Man and the Lady*. But although the sketch is in technique utterly different from anything Hardy later published, it anticipates his subsequent work in its perception that life is intrinsically unsatisfactory. The imperfections of the narrator's house result not only from the misunderstandings, omissions, and petty corruptions that mark the business arrangements, but also from the simple nature of things as they are. In Hardy's later years, a similar recognition shapes the tragicomic form of the stories in *Life's Little Ironies*.

The disappointment expressed in the light satire of 'How I Built Myself a House' exists in a more acute form in the disenchanted moods of the deeply personal poetry Hardy was writing during his apprenticeship in London. Between 1865 and his return to Dorset in 1867, he produced a considerable number of poems, many of which are in a broad sense narrative, but their main subject is more the language and cadence expressive of the speaker's emotion than the story being told. There is plot, for example, behind 'Amabel', 'Her Dilemma', and 'Neutral Tones', but their emphasis is rather the poetic representation of an emotion than the sequential presentation of action. 'The Two Men', written in 1866 and spoken by an omniscient narrator, is closer to pure narrative and, by its symmetrical building up to a single irony, has structural affinities with some of the *Life's Little Ironies* stories.

The poem of this period which most closely approximates Hardy's short fiction in its scope and narrative technique is 'The Bride-Night Fire', composed in 1866 and called 'The Fire at Tranter Sweatley's' for its publication in two periodicals during November 1875.[10] Like several of Hardy's stories, especially those collected in *Wessex Tales*, the poem is described as a 'Tradition' (*CP*, 71) and is told by a reminiscent and specifically rural voice. The earliest instance in Hardy of a deliberately plotted piece of fiction, it contains several situations used more seriously in his later work: the bone left after the fire anticipates the false evidence of Eunice Manston's death in *Desperate Remedies*; Barbree's donning of Tim's clothes (omitted in the periodical publications)[11] is paralleled in *Jude the Obscure*; the potentially scandalous sheltering of a woman recurs in *Jude*, and in *The Woodlanders* it is the cause for Giles Winterbourne's tragic death. In this poem, however – the humour of which Hardy was later to insist upon[12] – the reader's attention is diverted from tragic contingencies by the fast-paced language and the rapid accumulation of visual and social detail (perhaps evidence of William Barnes's influence).[13] By its frequent allusion to the village's customs and terrain and its preservation of local language, metaphors, and opinions, 'The Bride-Night Fire' presents a cameo portrait of a place and its culture. Just such a narrative strategy characterizes the most successful stories in *Wessex Tales*.

Early Life reports that the publication of 'How I Built Myself a House' was fortunate for Hardy because it turned his mind 'in the direction of prose' (62). But it was not until 1874, after he had become a widely recognized writer of novel-length fiction, that Hardy began to write prose stories with the same limited scope and conception as 'How I Built Myself a House' and 'The Bride-Night Fire'. One of Hardy's projected plots for a story is dated 1871,[14] but he never developed it beyond a summary, and the complexity of the outline suggests it may have been the skeleton of a novel or of a long poem. The plot might on the other hand be the basis for a short story Hardy mentioned in 1872. According to *Early Life*, he remarked to Tinsley 'that he had written a short story some time before, but didn't know what had become of the MS., and did not care' (116). There is also evidence that as early as 1873 Hardy received a request 'as to a short story' from Tinsley, but at that point he was too engaged with writing *Far from the Madding Crowd* to respond with more than a suggestion that he might do something 'in that way in the future'.[15] It was the popularity of this novel, however, which finally led to the publication of Hardy's first short story. Because *Far from the Madding Crowd* had been well received in the United States,

'Destiny and a Blue Cloak' was solicited by the *New York Times* and published in October 1874.[16]

Hardy's decision to publish a short story at this point in his career seems to have been an entirely practical one. *Early Life* describes his sentiments in 1875 when beginning *The Hand of Ethelberta*: 'For mere popularity he cared little, as little as he did for large payments; but having now to live by the pen – or, as he would quote, "to keep base life afoot" – he had to consider popularity.' (134–5) The remark, like his earlier statement to Tinsley 'that unless writing fiction paid him well, he should not go on with it',[17] seems to stem from his recent decisions, first, to give up architecture, which had guaranteed him a steady income, and then to marry, thus assuming more burdensome financial responsibilities. Clearly it was important for Hardy at this point in his development as a writer to make as much money as he could, and to get exposure in major periodicals.

The period of time Hardy spent on 'Destiny' is not mentioned in *Early Life*, but if it is not the 'lost' short story he described to Tinsley it was probably composed during the interval of approximately a month, between posting the final corrected manuscript of *Far from the Madding Crowd* to the *Cornhill* in early August of 1874 (*EL*, 132), and sending off 'Destiny and a Blue Cloak' on 12 September.[18] In any case, the story was mailed a mere five days before Hardy's marriage, and the fact that he later called it 'an impromptu' suggests that it was produced somewhat extemporaneously.[19] By its very bareness, 'Destiny' exemplifies the kinds of scaffolding on which Hardy's greatest effects are built. The relationship between Agatha Pollin and Frances Lovill, for instance, is an early example of that peculiar bond of fascinated obsession which pulls together many of Hardy's sexual rivals. Structurally, the counterpoising of the jealous emotions of the two women leads to a symmetrical pattern in the plot, by which Agatha and Frances rise and decline in position and beauty like figures on a wheel of fortune – a paradigm for the later and more successful uses of the same technique in 'Fellow-Townsmen' and 'The Withered Arm'. In 'Destiny', however, as in *Desperate Remedies*, Hardy's first published novel, the methodical working out of the story's action creates an impression of contrivance extreme even for Hardy. This is the case not because the events are implausible but because other factors usually important for Hardy – characterization, setting, and dramatically realized scenes – are here subordinated to a puzzle-like plot.

'Destiny and a Blue Cloak' was never collected in any of Hardy's four volumes of short stories, surely as a result of his own negative judgment on the work. Just months before his death, when a reprinting of the story was suggested to him, he labelled it as 'trivial' and of 'no literary value'.[20] But Hardy's reluctance to republish the story may initially have had something to do with its similarities to *The Hand of Ethelberta*, written shortly after the publication of 'Destiny'. Farmer Lovill, as Purdy has noted, 'might be called a first crude sketch for Lord Mountclere';[21] Agatha is like Ethelberta in her resolve to marry a man she does not love for the sake of her family; and the melodramatic climax of each narrative is the intercepted attempt of the young heroine to escape the ancient bridegroom, reminiscent of the frenzied ploys of many a Gothic heroine trying to avoid imprisonment.

Within a year of publishing 'Destiny and a Blue Cloak', Hardy was again conceiving of narratives on the small scale of the short story, but, as with 'The Bride-Night Fire', he chose to express them in ballad form rather than as prose fiction. It is impossible to determine the exact dates of composition for 'San Sebastian', 'Leipzig', and 'The Alarm', but Hardy wrote both 'The Sergeant's Song' and 'Valenciennes' in 1878,[22] and it seems reasonable to assume, as Purdy has suggested, that all of these Napoleonic poems 'may possibly be a portion of that ballad-sequence projected in June 1875 in a note foreshadowing *The Dynasts*'.[23] The narrative poems bore some relation in Hardy's mind to his prose fiction. 'Valenciennes', as its subtitle indicates, is told by Corporal Tullidge of *The Trumpet-Major* and 'The Alarm' arises from the same historical situation as that which causes the flight of Anne Garland and her family. 'San Sebastian', 'Her Death and After', and 'The Dance at the Phoenix' contain thematic resemblances to, respectively, 'An Imaginative Woman', 'Squire Petrick's Lady', and 'The Fiddler of the Reels'. These ballads and short stories can be linked in terms not only of their overlapping content and theme, but also of the limited range and self-contained quality of their plots, most of which contain a single anecdote or 'tradition', and demonstrate one corresponding irony. Where stories of such a scope occur within the novels, they tend to be tales within tales, told by a narrator who is also a character, like Tullidge's yarn in *The Trumpet-Major* and the reminiscences of Dairyman Crick in *Tess*. As in Scott, whose 'Wandering Willie's Tale' is both a story in its own right and an integral part of *Redgauntlet*, there is implicit in Hardy's novels a recognition of a shorter narrative form, the spoken tale.

After the publication of 'Destiny and a Blue Cloak', Hardy produced no short stories for three years. Then, in December 1877, 'The Thieves Who Couldn't Help Sneezing' appeared in *Father Christmas*, a children's annual.[24] 'Thieves' has affinities with such fairy tales as 'Jack the Giant Killer' and 'Jack and the Beanstalk', in which a seemingly invincible foe is defeated by the skill and guile of a young boy. In this tradition, the hero himself has no moral choice to make, except to oppose an externalized evil. 'Thieves' includes Hardy's first description of the Vale of Blackmoor, which became familiar to him during his stay at Sturminster Newton in the late 1870s, but which was only to figure largely in his fiction fourteen years later in *Tess*. Here, however, Hardy does not make much of the physical setting, and fails even to give a name to the great house 'which had been occupied by Queen Elizabeth and King Charles successively when on their visits to this part of the country'[25] – perhaps because any more specific use of local nomenclature would mar the romance-like atmosphere of a story which took place, as we are told in the opening words, 'Any years ago'.[26]

During 1878, Hardy returned to the social theme he had first explored in *The Poor Man and the Lady*. 'The Impulsive Lady of Croome Castle' (1878); republished in 1884 as 'Emmeline; or Passion versus Principle' and collected in *A Group of Noble Dames* as 'The Duchess of Hamptonshire' involves a marriage based entirely on the social and financial ambitions of the heroine's father. Hardy may have conceived of such a story at this point because he was resurrecting and reworking for publication those parts of *The Poor Man and the Lady* that he had not already adapted for segments of his novels. Presumably because it is made up of remnants of a longer piece, 'An Indiscretion in the Life of an Heiress' approximates in length neither to the short story nor to the novel, but rather to the *nouvelle*. The story is told chiefly from the perspective of the 'Poor Man', but it also contains a considerable measure of compassion for the heiress, who complains: 'To be woven and tied in with the world by blood, acquaintance, tradition, and external habit, is to a woman to be utterly at the beck of that world's customs.'[27] It is chiefly in terms of this perspective, which recognizes the lady's plight as well as the poor man's, that the later *Group of Noble Dames* takes its shape.

After the appearance of 'An Indiscretion', Hardy began composing tales with greater frequency and confidence. His developing sense of himself as a writer of short stories is reflected in a letter of March 1879, presumably to Harper's, saying that he could not respond to their request for a 'serial story', but might possibly send them a 'short sketch or story' within the year.[28] At this point, Hardy may merely have offered short stories to publishers when he was too busy to send a novel, but it is significant that at such an early stage he was already lining up periodicals to print his short fiction. The piece that Hardy subsequently sent to Harper's was probably 'The Distracted Young Preacher', published in the *New Quarterly* in April 1879 and simultaneously in *Harper's Weekly*, in instalments, during April and May.[29] One of his most successful short stories, it demonstrated for the first time the assimilation of his complex conception of Wessex within a short narrative form.

'The Distracted Young Preacher' (Hardy deleted the 'Young' for its publication in *Wessex Tales*) was followed in 1880 by 'Fellow-Townsmen' but the quality of these two pastoral histories was not sustained in his next story, 'What the Shepherd Saw'. Written in the autumn of 1881 soon after the illness which interfered with the completion of *A Laodicean*,[30] the story reveals Hardy's fictional preoccupations at a point when he was experimenting with the theatrical configurations of characters and the melodramatic effects in setting which characterized the stage productions of the time. So the shepherd boy is an unseen observer watching a procession of 'actors on the scene' (193),* and the 'Devil's Door' on the

---

* In this chapter only, page references to *A Changed Man* appear without identifying initials.

barren plain at night provides an eerie background for the action. The story has the familiar Gothic theme – found also in *Caleb Williams* and *The Marble Faun* – that the witness of a murder can somehow share the guilt of the actual criminal. Hardy's use of these conventions, however, is ineffective. The story's contrived plot is unduly complicated by the need to sustain the unseen observer device beyond the first two nights on the downs, and for this reason, the real symptoms of guilt which emerge in the story's conclusion – the Duke's thinness and sleepwalking, Bill Wills's 'pallor' (205), and his death 'somewhat under forty-nine years of age' (210) – are only perfunctorily presented. As in 'Destiny and a Blue Cloak', Hardy fails to see beyond plot and technique to the human emotions they are meant to dramatize.

This flaw is repeated in the weaknesses of 'Benighted Travellers' (1881; collected in *A Group of Noble Dames* as 'The Honourable Laura'), written during the same period. But the next story Hardy published represents a significant development and improvement of the same conventional techniques. Whereas in 'What the Shepherd Saw' the reader is forced to accept as truth what Bill Wills has seen and heard, in 'A Tradition of Eighteen Hundred and Four', as we have seen, an interesting ambiguity is created by the story's presentation as a 'Tradition' that is highly questionable in origin. Here the melodramatic elements – the desolate downs, the isolation, and darkness – serve not to heighten the reader's sense of terror, but rather to undermine his belief in the authenticity of the story by obscuring the judgment of its sole witness.

For different reasons, 'What the Shepherd Saw' is also a precursor of 'The Three Strangers', published soon after 'A Tradition of Eighteen Hundred and Four'. Here again a desolate place is the setting, characters arrive on the scene and depart as though in a theatrical production, and the plot has the ingenious contrivance of a stage melodrama. 'What the Shepherd Saw' includes a number of local particulars of the kind which function as important aspects of the pastoralism in 'The Three Strangers'. The detailed description in the opening paragraphs of the shepherd's hut anticipates the same sort of attention to specifics in the later 'Wessex tale', and the plot hinges on social assumptions unique to the rural world – here the attitude of the shepherds toward the Duke.

No one questions the nobleman's right to commit a murder 'on his own lands' (197) because, as the narrator says in the instructive tones of the pastoral voice, 'the Duke was Jove himself to the rural population, whom to offend was starvation, homelessness, and death, and whom to look at was to be mentally scathed and dumbfoundered' (195). Such information is a hallmark of Hardy's pastoral histories. Though mediocre by itself, 'What the Shepherd Saw' anticipates some of Hardy's best 'Wessex tales'.

'The Romantic Adventures of a Milkmaid' also uses conventions from melodrama and romance to serve the larger purpose of presenting an accurate picture of the rural way of life. Although the story has rightly been described as the most unrealistic prose narrative Hardy ever wrote,[31] it has close links with 'The Three Strangers'. Both narratives are shaped by the idea Hardy was almost simultaneously expressing in 'The Dorsetshire Labourer', where Dorset is described as a place with a distinct and living culture often misinterpreted by outsiders 'through inability to see below the surface of things'.[32] In these stories, Hardy helps his readers to see below the superficial by grounding the romance elements firmly in the real. Wessex life is presented in detail and, where necessary, it is interpreted for the reader. 'The Romantic Adventures' sets up a romance-like contrast of characters as a metaphor for an explicit comparison between the rural and urban worlds. The Baron appears mysterious to Margery Tucker because she has never encountered his type before, while she seems to him 'Nature's own image' (305) because he is not familiar with milkmaids. The story embodies a wide range of motifs from fairy tale and romance, each of which illuminates this basically realistic opposition between the Baron and the milkmaid, and the ways in which they – like Angel and Tess – misunderstand and romanticize each other.

The 'dark-mustachioed' (303) Baron is a mixture of stereotypes: the villain from melodramatic drama and fiction who keeps innocent maidens captive; the melancholy Jaques of a Wessex Arden, predisposed by temperament to indulge 'wayward emotions' (347); the demon lover of the ballad, who can lure a woman away from her simple and devoted husband (in this he prefigures Mop Ollamoor);[33] and the Byronic hero in his repentant stage, regretting past sins. But as this passage demonstrates, romantic images are subordinated to a pastoral contrast between rural and urban:

> 'You sent for me, and I have come,' she answered humbly, like an obedient familiar in the employ of some great enchanter. Indeed, the Baron's power over this innocent girl was curiously like enchantment, or mesmeric influence. It was so masterful that the sexual element was almost eliminated. It was that of Prospero over the gentle Ariel. And yet it was probably only that of the cosmopolite over the recluse, of the experienced man over the simple maid. (348–9)

The Baron is presented in deliberately stylized terms. An explicitly literary creation, he has a name that can only be expressed 'by pen-and-ink and good scholarship' (309), and his 'dark hair and heavy black moustache' appear 'like dashes of ink on a clean page' (363). A character with theatrical analogues, his mystery is dependent on contrived effects: 'for a man, no less than a landscape, who awakens an interest under uncertain lights and touches of unfathomable shade, may cut but a poor figure in a garish noontide shine' (399).

Margery is also portrayed in conventional romantic terms, even while being more fully understood by the narrator as a perfectly natural product of her environment. Like Red Riding Hood she travels through a danger-fraught terrain to take a basket of food to her grandmother; like Cinderella she is transformed for a single night into a princess at a ball; like the maiden of ballad and romance she is drawn from the safety of simple domesticity by a demon lover. But, as her 'keen appreciativeness of nature's moods and peculiarities' (301) reveals, Margery is also a functioning part of the 'bustling' (299) social and economic life in the Valley of the Exe, presented in the story's opening paragraphs in all its palpable and practical reality. In the style of the pastoral history, the 'noises that ascended through the pallid coverlid' of the fog – perhaps a metaphor for the realistic facts emerging from the mist of romance – are explained to the reader as they would be understood by a local viewer, 'any inhabitant of the district' (299). It is Margery's complete immersion in this rural world which gives a strangeness to her encounter with

the Baron, whose moustache, name, language, and knowledge of the polka are as much novelties to her as her own
'fresh face,... candid eyes, unpractised manner, country
dress' (305), and peasant dances are to him.

Margery's dangerous submission to the Baron's power is
presented in the scene in which she crosses the stile – a
symbolic gesture like passing over a threshold – to learn from
him 'the elements of modern dancing' (314–15). A similarly
emblematic moment is the transformation inside the tree-
trunk, a rebirth from which she emerges, Venus-like, out of
her 'wooden shell' (320), as a different woman with new and
impossible expectations for her future. At the ball, she is
drawn even deeper into her enchanter's 'mysterious
influence' (324) not only by the music and dancing but also by
her exposure to the more tangible emblems of wealth and
urban sophistication: 'work-tables that would set you in
amaze; silver candlesticks, tea and coffee pots that would
dazzle your eyes; tea-cups and saucers, gilded all over with
guinea-gold; heavy velvet curtains, gold clocks, pictures, and
looking-glasses beyond your very dreams.' (333)

In the latter parts of the story, the romance elements are set
aside for the comic subplot involving Jim Hayward and Mrs
Peach, a tiresome interlude reminiscent of Paula Power's
pursuit of George Somerset at the end of *A Laodicean*. But in
the final scenes, repeating even in the detail of the moored
yacht the action of the traditional ballad called 'The Demon
Lover', there is a return to the enchantment theme. Here the
disaster to which the plot has been moving – the Baron's loss
of rational control and Margery's complete submission to his
fascination – is only averted at the last minute, as she 'on a
sudden ... seem[s] to see all contingencies', and he simultaneously realizes the danger of his own 'lover's bad impulse'
(397). This recognition, out of character for Margery, was not
part of Hardy's original conception of the story. In 1927, he
wrote in the margin of his copy of *A Changed Man*:

Note: the foregoing finish of the Milkmaid's Adventures
by a re-union with her husband was adopted to suit the
requirements of the summer number of a periodical in
which the story was first printed. But it is well to inform
readers that the ending originally sketched was a different

one, Margery, instead of returning to Jim, disappearing with the Baron in his yacht at Idmouth after his final proposal to her, & being no more heard of in England.[34]

Hardy never restored this ending to 'The Romantic Adventures', but for the first edition of *A Changed Man* he did attribute greater responsibility to Margery in her momentary decision to flee with the Baron. In the *Graphic* version, the flight had been entirely the Baron's idea, and she had staunchly resisted it; her confession in the closing dialogue with Jim about being 'disappointed that he did not press me' was added in 1913.[35]

'The Romantic Adventures' anticipates the emphasis in *Life's Little Ironies* on sexual attraction and romantic illusions as potentially destructive forces. Margery's enchantment by the Baron looks forward to Car'line Aspent's more explicitly sexual submission to Mop Ollamoor in 'The Fiddler of the Reels', and the mutual attraction between the rural innocent and urban sophisticate prefigures the same sort of emotional magnetism in 'On the Western Circuit'. It is even possible that Hardy considered including 'The Romantic Adventures' in *Life's Little Ironies*. Although he had earlier called it a 'short hastily written novel' (*EL*, 205) which he did not think 'worth reprinting',[36] he expressed the hope in January 1893 that he would soon 'reprint it, correct from the original MS'.[37] What may have prevented his publishing it either in *Life's Little Ironies* or in a volume by itself is the story's unusual length, and its resulting failure to fit neatly into either of the conventional Victorian categories for fiction, the short story and the novel (James's defence of the *nouvelle* in his preface to 'The Lesson of the Master' did not appear until 1909). In any case, the prominence of 'The Romantic Adventures' in the complete title of *A Changed Man* suggests that Hardy did consider it to be, at least in comparison with most of the other narratives in the collection, of some interest and importance.

'Our Exploits at West Poley', written for the *Youth's Companion* in summer 1883,[38] is a more sophisticated children's story than 'The Thieves Who Couldn't Help Sneezing'. The story has, as Hardy phrased it, an 'apparent moral'[39] and resembles *The Adventures of Tom Sawyer* (published seven years earlier) in its contrasting of an impressionable and morally sensitive boy with one who is less thoughtful, but older and more 'master-ful'.[40] The continual references to Leonard's aunt and the adventures in the caves are also reminiscent of Twain's novel, while Steve's scheme to impersonate magicians is worthy of Tom Sawyer himself. But the moral issue here, in addition to Twain's subject of the destructive aspects of romanticism, is the danger of tampering with the 'most fragile' order of nature.[41] The diversion of the river is potentially a form of original sin – involving serious consequences not only in the present but also, by the transmission of this knowledge from one generation to the next, for the future. Still another theme is represented by the presence at the story's beginning and end of the Man who had Failed for want of 'energy'[42] – a contrast to Steve, who, though he lacks 'intellectual power', has 'the courage and faculty to do'.[43] This opposition between the sins of indolence and energy anticipates Michael Henchard, whose tragedy lies in his fluctuation between evasion of responsibility and extraordinary initiative. Considering that Hardy began work on *The Mayor of Casterbridge* soon after completing 'Our Exploits', it is appropriate that the tale should conclude by expressing in concrete financial and professional terms the moral lesson Steve has learned. Just as Henchard's rise and fall are identical with his position in the community, so Steve's achieved maturity is reflected in his situation as 'the largest gentleman-farmer of those parts, remarkable for his avoidance of anything like speculative exploits'.[44]

'A Tryst at an Ancient Earthwork', like 'Interlopers at the Knap' published a year earlier, reflects Hardy's continued interest in portentous settings. But unlike 'Interlopers', in which the pictorial and the dramatic are meshed, 'Tryst' demonstrates the comparative ineffectiveness of descriptive writing when it is not associated with a significant pattern of action. The piece is essentially a picture in words rather than a short story, and its skeletal plot, inserted only in the latter half, is anecdotal rather than dramatic. The sketchy narrative content is based on the same Gothic subject that often attracted Hawthorne: the scientist who in his eager quest for knowledge loses his moral sense. Hardy's particular handling of the theme reveals, however, more than any insight into such a personality type, his own suspicion of people with the credentials of education. According to Purdy, this character was based on a Dorchester antiquary of Hardy's acquaintance,[45] and it was presumably this fact which prevented his publishing the piece in England until 1893. Even then, Hardy only sent it to the *English Illustrated Magazine* because Clement K. Shorter had requested a story from him and he had 'nothing else' to send.[46] And Hardy was distressed at the title the British periodical gave it – 'Ancient Earthworks at Casterbridge' – because, as he told Mrs Henniker, 'it is just possible that a character who appears in the narrative may be said to be drawn from a local man, still living, though it is really meant for nobody in particular'.[47]

The hostility in Hardy's portrayal of the archaeologist limits the characterization in 'Tryst' to crude caricature, but the story's earlier portions, comprising most of its length, afford a striking example of Hardy's methods in descriptive writing. The narrative voice, one of his few experiments in a sustained use of the first persons, is almost a disembodied presence – like the implied spectators invoked in his pastoral histories – perceiving sights and sounds, and interpreting them for the reader. The descriptive passages set up, as Julian Moynahan has suggested, an implicit contrast between the narrator and the archaeologist – the one able to unearth the past with his imagination, the other interested in its present form as 'portable property' and a proof for his private theory.[48] This distinction makes the story's original title, 'Ancient Earthworks and What Two Enthusiastic Scientists Found Therein',[49] especially apt in its couched reference to the different enthusiasms of the two men. Neither this contrast between the two characters, however, nor the rich density of Hardy's prose, makes 'Tryst' continually interesting. The vignette at its conclusion seems merely a device to justify the descriptive passages, which look forward to the visually dramatic scenes at The Ring in *The Mayor of Casterbridge* and at Stonehenge in *Tess*. But perhaps because such places are more impressive as backgrounds for climactic moments within the longer rhythm of the novel, Hardy did not attempt again to create grandiose settings for his short stories.

'A Mere Interlude', published in the same year as 'Tryst', prefigures some of the situations and themes of the *Noble Dames* and *Life's Little Ironies* stories. Like the noble dames,

Baptista Trewthen is a common woman who finds herself in uncommon circumstances, and as in 'An Imaginative Woman', 'The Son's Veto', and 'On the Western Circuit', a central concern of the story is the difficult position of a woman forced into marriage by social and economic pressures. In the details of its plot, 'A Mere Interlude' recalls 'Fellow-Townsmen', the most ironic of the *Wessex Tales*. The 'decayed glazier' (289) who blackmails Baptista has the menacing qualities of Barnet's friend Charlson, and the drowning of Charles Stowe recalls that of Mrs Downe – as well as anticipating the same sort of event in 'The Waiting Supper', 'A Tragedy of Two Ambitions', and 'The History of the Hardcomes'. All of these drownings reflect Hardy's increasing interest during the late 1880s and early 1890s in surprising and even implausible plot elements as metaphors for the strange unpredictability of life.[50] Sudden deaths operate as catalysts of new moral dilemmas, usually by changing a character's sexual and marital alternatives. 'A Mere Interlude' also demonstrates Hardy's special fascination with the impulsive quality of human nature: Baptista's quick submission to Charles Stowe may be based on two true reports in the 'Facts' notebook of sudden decisions to marry, including one concerning a woman who eloped with her fiancé's cousin after a secret courtship of only ten days.[51]

As a 'life's little irony', 'A Mere Interlude' is interesting for its portrayal of Baptista, a woman with no unusual qualities who demonstrates that even the most nondescript people can act in surprising ways when faced with a 'crisis' (259). Baptista's Christian name suggests that her 'interlude' will be a 'baptism' of some sort, and her surname – blending the words 'truth' and 'burthen' – implies that these two things are somehow linked. Because Baptista is unable to articulate her own feelings even to herself, the reader must rely only on her actions as indicators of her emotional state. Her mood of 'passivity' (263) at missing the boat expresses her disinclination to marry Mr Heddegan, her marriage to Stowe is carried out with little discussion or forethought, and her 'trance-like state' (275) after his death is a manifestation of her fear or inability to comprehend fully what has happened to her. The 'hideous contiguity' (285) of her two husbands, the most improbable aspect of the story's plot, is an external representation of something which she must in any case face internally – an idea articulated explicitly in *Two on a Tower*, where the final confirmation of Sir Blount Constantine's death leads Lady Constantine to feel 'as though her first husband had died that moment, and she was keeping an appointment with another in the presence of his corpse' (243).

Baptista's whole experience, despite its complicated pattern of coincidences, is a cathartic progression from the 'terror' of being haunted by the 'spectre' of her past (274), through the 'Horror' (285) of that fear's fulfilment in the discovery of Stowe's corpse, to the private recognition of her widowhood implied in her attendance at his funeral, and to the public admission of her 'tragedy' (292) before Hedeggan. The irony which promises to emerge from all of this is that Baptista will be doomed, because of Hedeggan's own 'four tragedies' (294), to the very calling she had married him in order to avoid. In this early treatment of a *Life's Little Ironies* theme, however, Hardy does not pursue the irony relentlessly to its end, but rather turns the 'tragedy' into a 'tragi-comedy' (296) with a happy ending – perhaps, as George Wing has suggested, because he felt compelled to provide 'sentimental fodder for the magazine-readers'.[52] But this ending is not sentimental in every sense. Baptista's happiness, like that of Elizabeth-Jane in the conclusion of *The Mayor of Casterbridge* published the following year, is based on the experience and knowledge of human suffering. Despite its optimistic conclusion, 'A Mere Interlude' is an important precursor of the *Life's Little Ironies* stories, for here the *deus ex machina* that transforms disillusionment into fulfilment is the very perception that lends poignancy to the later narratives: 'That in humanity . . . there [is] nothing to dislike, but infinitely much to pity.' (296)

'Alicia's Diary', published two years after 'A Mere Interlude', also anticipates the themes of *Life's Little Ironies*, but fails to achieve an interesting or effective quality of irony. This is because Hardy allows a superficial plot to overtake the initially interesting focus on characterization. Like 'A Tryst at an Ancient Earthwork', the story is one of Hardy's few experiments in sustained first-person narration and here, as in the early 'How I Built Myself a House', the personality of the speaker is an essential aspect of the narrative tone and meaning. The story's diary form recalls the epistolary technique of Richardson's narrators who write down their adventures almost while they are happening, but it also repeats the device in Browning's dramatic monologues of making characters indirectly disclose far more of themselves than they intend, or even can comprehend. Beneath her expressed affection for her younger sister, Alicia reveals a disturbing jealousy and possessiveness. To allay her envy, she thinks of herself as Caroline's mother and protectress, and tries to preserve the girl's 'childlike simplicity and gentleness' (87) – in effect, to prevent her developing into adulthood. Caroline's trip to the Continent and her sexual relationship with a man undermine both Alicia's sense of her own maturity – she marvels to think that a sister 'so childlike as to be five years [her] junior in nature' (91) should marry before her – and her feeling of pre-eminence in Caroline's affections: 'This simple prattle is very sweet to me, my dear sister, but I cannot help feeling sad at the occasion of it. In the nature of things it is obvious that I shall never be to you again what I hitherto have been: your guide, counsellor, and most familiar friend.' (92)

An aspect of Alicia's envy is a voyeuristic desire to live through her sister's private experiences. Long before she has met Caroline's suitor, Charles de la Feste, she imagines in his influence 'some sort of glamour or fascinating power' (95), and dreams of herself and her sister as 'two women beloved by one man' (94). Then, merely from seeing his picture, she thinks of Charles as possessing 'the romantic disposition of a true lover and painter of Nature' (96). Her preoccupation emerges even in her attitude toward her mother's death, which she views more as a deterrent to Caroline's plans than as a personal loss: 'I cannot even divine how poor Caroline's marriage is to be carried out if mother dies.' (94)

Alicia's impassioned solitude makes her a precursor of two important figures in *Life's Little Ironies*. In her imaginative infatuation with the unseen de la Feste she is like Ella Marchmill of 'An Imaginative Woman'; in her jealous possessiveness toward Caroline and simultaneous appropriation of the younger woman's lover, she is like Edith Harnham of 'On the Western Circuit'. Indeed, as the quotation from *Marmion* suggests – 'O what a tangled web we weave/ When first we practise to deceive!' (111) – Hardy is pursuing here the same theme of deceit in love which forms an important motif in the imagery, language, and plot of 'On the Western Circuit'. But the story's handling of all these subjects is seriously flawed in the second half, after Charles's love for Alicia has been established. At this point characterization is obscured by an excessive concern with plot and scenic description (based on observations Hardy had made during a recent trip to the Continent) and the result is trivial melodrama. 'Alicia's Diary' presents an ironic theme but falls short of blending simple situational irony with irony of form. In 'An Imaginative Woman' and 'On the Western Circuit', the subjects of imaginativeness and deceitfulness in sexual love are presented more profoundly, in large part because the melodramatic plots are there an aspect of, rather than a distraction from, the central meaning.

'The Waiting Supper' was written during a period when Hardy was also working on 'The Withered Arm', 'The Melancholy Hussar', and 'A Tragedy of Two Ambitions'.[53] At this point he was producing narratives typical of each of his three short-story volumes. 'The Withered Arm' and 'The Melancholy Hussar' are emphatically 'Wessex tales', 'A Tragedy of Two Ambitions' belongs unquestionably to *Life's Little Ironies*, and 'The Waiting Supper' contains a mixture of familiar elements. In its setting it is a 'Wessex tale', in its plot it is a 'life's little irony', and in its comments on 'chronicled families' (34) and its emphasis on the destructiveness of class consciousness it has affinities with the *Noble Dames* stories. Nic Long's promise to make himself worthy of Christine Everard by education and travel foreshadows quite specifically Edmond Willowes's resolution to improve himself in 'Barbara of the House of Grebe'.

Although Hardy published a version of the last two sections of 'The Waiting Supper' in the *Dorset County Chronicle* in 1890, he never chose to reprint the complete story until 1913 – perhaps because it repeats so many of the situations found in his other works. The abortive marriage of Christine and Nic hearkens back to that of Stephen Smith and Elfride Swancourt in *A Pair of Blue Eyes*, and Christine's tenuous widowhood closely resembles the positions of Bathsheba Everdene in *Far from the Madding Crowd* and Lady Constantine in *Two on a Tower*. The rural lover of a woman who has been educated in more sophisticated circles, Nic is like Giles Winterbourne, and his perception on his return to the Froom Valley that the older population 'had moved house in mass' (65) to the graveyard makes him a precursor of John Lackland. It is probably this direct correlation with 'A Few Crusted Characters', as well as the similarity with the drowning in 'A Tragedy of Two Ambitions' which prevented Hardy's collecting the story until the appearance of *A Changed Man*.

The *Dorset County Chronicle* version of 'The Waiting Supper', called 'The Intruder: A Legend of the Chronicle Office', contains the actual supper scene and its aftermath with minor revisions which alter and simplify the past of the three main figures. Here the ominous crash of the old clock is omitted, and, as in the first periodical publications of the story, it is Bellston himself (here called Belland) who arrives at Christine's door, not his messenger and his portmanteau. Perhaps to remove the similarity in plot to 'A Tragedy of Two Ambitions' (published the previous year), there is no discovery of a skeleton at the conclusion of this version, and it is simply asserted that Bellston 'never re-appeared'[54] after he left Christine on the night of the planned wedding. As there are no extent manuscripts of 'The Waiting Supper', it is impossible to say whether the composition of 'The Intruder' came before or after the story's magazine version[55] (the apparent deletions of similarities to 'A Tragedy of Two Ambitions' would suggest the latter), but in any event the shorter version is a distillation of the legendary and anecdotal elements which comprise only a part of the longer form. It includes all the striking and surprising aspects of the climactic dinner scene, but does not devote any space to the procrastination which precedes this dramatic confrontation, an important theme of the more complicated version. It is ironic in the longer form, for example, that Christine should quote Browning's 'The Statue and the Bust' – a poem which imputes to its frustrated lovers the 'sin' of 'the unlit lamp' and 'the ungirt loin' (11. 246–7) and about which Hardy himself had said, 'there's nothing about procrastination that is not in that poem'.[56] 'The Waiting Supper' is also about habitual postponement, and one of its central ironies is that the behaviour of Nic and Christine in the final scene is perfectly consistent with that of their first meeting on the lawn of Froom-Everard House more than three decades earlier.

The recurrent pattern of evasion and delay is part of the story's concern with class prejudice. Nic's lower social status and lack of sophistication are an embarrassment to Christine, but this artificial disparity between them 'in little things' (47) is made to seem insignificant by the fact that there is little real financial difference in their family assets. Squire Everard, Christine's father, is the head of 'a countrified household of the smaller gentry, without much wealth or ambition – formerly a numerous class, but now in great part ousted by the territorial landlords' (27). The wealth of Nic's family, on the other hand, has considerable ambition and entrepreneurial skill behind it, and is described in solid mathematical terms: his uncle rents an impressive total of 1100 acres of land. In the story's 1913 version, Nic's relation to Christine is made somewhat less servile, moreover, by the removal of his uncle's farm – originally called Homeston Farm rather than the more splendid 'Elsenford'[57] – from Everard's own parish to a neighbouring one. The supposed difference in status between Christine and Nic – presented metaphorically in the opening scene by the expanse of lawn between her dining room and the tree beside which he is posted – is undercut by the fact that Nic, as a 'yeoman' (27) and the nephew of a tenant farmer, represents a small contingent of the very forces beginning to overtake the Squire's world. In economic terms, even James Bellston cannot compete with Nic: no mention is made of his wealth, and the existence of the 'son and heir' at the christening feast discounts the possibility that he will inherit the estate of his aunt and uncle, the 'queer and primitive couple' (39) of Athelhall.

The differences between Christine and Nic exist more in their own expectations about each other than in their actual circumstances. When they try to elope they are constantly at cross-purposes. Nic hopes to have 'absolute possession' of Christine so that he might 'work with spirit and purpose', while she wants to give 'substantiality' to a 'vague dream' (33) because she is annoyed at Nic's reproachful allusion to her position as a 'superior'. Her challenge to Nic – 'Take me whilst I am in the humour' (34) – is spoken in a spirit utterly different from that of Rosalind in *As You Like It*, whose words she is (probably consciously) echoing: 'Come, woo me, woo me; for now I am in a holiday humour and like enough to consent' (IV.i.64–65). Shakespeare's heroine speaks in playful seriousness, but Christine only expresses petulance. The combination of Christine's rashness with Nic's submissiveness leads to the postponements and evasions which repeatedly interfere with their marriage. The failed elopement, despite Christine's shifting of all the blame onto Nic, is the outcome of shared irresponsibility.

The unsuccessful consummation of this three-year courtship is further complicated for Christine by the appearance of James Bellston, a contrast to Nic in every detail: he has aristocratic blood, speaks 'proper' English rather than local dialect, and is well travelled. But Bellston is not 'particularly good-looking' (40), and his brazen remark about his uncle – he calls him a 'rough old buffer' (42) – places Nic's complaints in a more flattering light: 'And I did not know that my stingy uncle – heaven forgive me for calling him so! – would so flatly refuse to advance me money for my purpose' (31–2).[58] A comparison between Christine's two suitors is suggested again in the dance scene, where with Bellston she has 'the greatest difficulty in steering her partner through the maze, on account of his self-will', while with Nic she feels a 'perfect responsiveness' based on 'their tender acquaintance' (44). She must choose, like many of the noble dames, between a social 'harmony' with one suitor 'in the sun of afternoon', and her sexual and romantic affinities with another one 'idealized by moonlight' (42).

The second half of the story is at once a reversal and a repetition of the first half. The reversal lies in the social positions of the lovers: Christine lives in relative poverty and is the 'homely' partner (61), while Nic has amassed a 'fortune' (63) and is a 'man of the world' (61). The repetition lies in the pattern of their relationship: as of old, Nic crosses the meads to meet his sweetheart in Froom-Everard House, and once again Christine promises her hand and then recants, leaving Nic excluded from the dinner feast. The intrusive appearance of Bellston's portmanteau effectively prevents the marriage of Christine and Nic, but even when she is proven a widow seventeen years later, they are still hesitant to act:

'Is it worth while, after so many years?' she said to him. 'We are fairly happy as we are – perhaps happier than we should be in any other relation, seeing what old people we have grown. The weight is gone from our lives; the shadow no longer divides us: then let us be joyful together as we are, dearest Nic, in the days of our vanity; and

> With mirth and laughter let old wrinkles come.'

He fell in with these views of hers to some extent. But occasionally he ventured to urge her to reconsider the case, though he spoke not with the fervour of his earlier years. (82–3)

H. E. Bates objects to the 'wooden words' of this conclusion, questioning whether 'women ever speak to men like that',[59] but in view of Christine's previous characterization, the very stiltedness of her language is appropriate. As earlier, she placates Nic by poeticizing their situation, and again she misinterprets the meaning of the text. Here her use of biblical phrases mixes incongruously with Gratiano's speech in *The Merchant of Venice*, a passage which declares that one ought to live life to the fullest, even in old age:

> Let me play the fool!
> With mirth and laughter let old wrinkles come,
> And let my liver rather heat with wine
> Than my heart cool with mortifying groans.
> Why should a man whose blood is warm within,
> Sit like his grandsire cut in alabaster?   (I.i.79–84)

Although the 'shadows' of class and of Christine's husband no longer divide the lovers, they remain when they reach their fifties – too old to have children, but surely not for marriage – at the same psychological impasse as they did at the beginning, with Christine eager to live a romantic dream and Nic reluctantly assenting to the whims of his 'superior' (34).

The idea for 'The Waiting Supper' may have come to Hardy from a *Dorset County Chronicle* article which he had copied into his 'Facts' notebook: 'Long engagemt. Scotch youth & damsel (Elgin) – attachment – 1794. Separated, & marriage forbidden by their relations. Ten years passed;

union again nearly achieved, when doomed to disappt. Twenty more years mutually constant, & in uninterrupted correspce. Then married. Wd. it not have been better to wait till death, &c.—'[60] Hardy's query at the end of the note suggests that the extended friendship between Nic and Christine – 'in close communion, yet not indissolubly united; lovers, yet never growing cured of love' (79) – was to his mind the happiest ending achievable. But the story's consistent portrayal of evasive behaviour in the lovers – similar to Crabbe's handling of the same theme in such tales as 'The Parting Hour' and 'Procrastination' – intimates that Hardy also intended to imply some criticism of his characters in this conclusion. In any case, in keeping with the structure of a 'life's little irony', the narrative defies any romantic expectations the reader may have for Nic and Christine. In *The Well-Beloved*, published in periodical form four years after 'The Waiting Supper' first appeared, Jocelyn Pierston says to Marcia Bencomb in their shared old age: 'It is extraordinary what an interest our neighbours take in our affairs. . . . They say "those old folk ought to marry; better late than never." That's how people are – wanting to round off other people's histories in the best machine-made conventional manner.' (214–15) Hardy's refusal in 'The Waiting Supper' to 'round off' the 'histories' of Christine and Nic anticipates the formal irony of his best *Life's Little Ironies* stories, which refuse to resolve conflicts in 'the best machine-made conventional manner'.

Soon after the publication of 'The Waiting Supper', Hardy wrote a letter to Macmillan suggesting that they publish a group of his short stories as a collection. He recommended the project by mentioning that some 'well-known critics have often advised me to reprint them, informing me that they are as good as anything I have written (however good that may be)'.[61] Hardy may have been referring to Leslie Stephen's suggestion, made several years earlier, 'that you might write an exceedingly pleasant series of stories upon your special topic: I mean prose-idyls of country life – short sketches of Hodge & his ways, wh. might be made very attractive & would have a certain continuity, so as to make a volume or more at some future date.'[62] Hardy's delayed response to Stephen's advice probably results from the fact that in 1880, when the letter was written, the short story was not a popular form in England and Hardy may have lacked the confidence to approach a publisher with such a project. But at the end of 1887, with such achievements as *Far from the Madding Crowd, The Return of the Native*, and *The Mayor of Casterbridge* behind him, Hardy wrote in his notebook that the year 'enabled me to hold my own in fiction, whatever that may be worth, by the completion of *The Woodlanders*' (*EL*, 267). This sense of success finally allowed Hardy to overlook the Victorian prejudice in favour of the three-volume novel and to consider the collection of short stories as a legitimate fictional genre, worthy of book publication. Between 1888 (the date for the publication of *Wessex Tales*) and 1891 Hardy wrote more short fiction than at any other point in his career and assembled these works quite readily into coherent volumes. Both of Hardy's story cycles – *A Group of Noble Dames* and 'A Few Crusted Characters' – were written during this time, and four of the stories in *Life's Little Ironies* were composed in 1891 alone. Among Hardy's seven last volumes of prose fiction, four are his collections of short stories.

The publication of *Wessex Tales* also has a significant place in Hardy's career because it represents a step in his appropriation of 'Wessex' as the exclusive precinct for his fiction. As he wrote to one publisher: 'Could you, whenever advertising my books, use the words "Wessex novels" at the head of the list? I mean, instead of "By T. H.", "T. H.'s Wessex novels", or something of the sort? I find that the name *Wessex*, wh. I was the first to use in fiction, is getting to be taken up everywhere: & it would be a pity for us to lose the right to it for want of asserting it.'[63] By using 'Wessex' in a title for the first time Hardy asserted his 'right' to the name as an identifying term for his work. The five stories he selected for *Wessex Tales* represent not only some of the best stories he had written up to that date, but also those most closely related to the Wessex setting: 'The Three Strangers', 'The Withered Arm', 'Fellow-Townsmen', 'Interlopers at the Knap', and 'The Distracted Preacher'. Macmillan brought out the two-volume first edition of *Wessex Tales* in May 1888, it was published in America at the end of that month by Harper & Brothers, and in late 1889 Macmillan produced it in a one-volume edition.[64]

Between the publication of *Wessex Tales* and *Tess*, Hardy

wrote several short historical narratives, chiefly about the
figures who had lived in the great houses of Dorset and its
neighbouring counties during the seventeenth and
eighteenth centuries. In September 1888 he began working
on 'The First Countess of Wessex' (again he puts 'Wessex' in a
title) for publication as a Christmas story for *Harper's New
Monthly Magazine*[65] and asked the periodical in December of
that year for illustrations showing 'old English manor-house
architecture, & woodland scenery, with large gnarled oaks
&c., beside, of course, figures, in the costume of George the
Second's reign – the date of the story being about 1740'.[66] The
story, set earlier in time than any prose narrative Hardy had
written so far, was published in December 1889.[67] The
following January, 'The Lady Penelope', set in the early
seventeenth century, appeared in *Longman's Magazine*.[68]
Both of these stories were later collected in the book form of *A
Group of Noble Dames*, the expanded version of the cycle of six
stories which Hardy composed in the winter of 1889–90.[69]
Although the manuscript of this early form of *A Group of Noble
Dames* was not sent to the *Graphic* until May 1890, Hardy had
negotiated with them as early as March 1889 for its publication, carefully preserving the right not only 'to issue it
simultaneously in periodicals throughout the world',[70] but
also to publish it 'in book form at any time not less than a
month after its appearance in the *Graphic*'.[71]

The strategy of serial publication followed by volume
publication was as necessary, financially, to short stories as to
novels. As Hardy wrote to Mrs Henniker in 1893:

> You must remember that in England there is very little to
> be made commercially out of short tales – and that pub-
> lishers are as a rule shy of them, except those that are
> written by people who cannot write long ones
> successfully – an odd exception! – and have established a
> specialty in that line. You must not *waste* the stories for the
> mere sake of getting them printed quickly.[72]

This situation may have prompted Hardy in his communica-
tions with the *Graphic* to emphasize the length of *A Group of
Noble Dames*, calling it in one letter a 'story – same length as the
"Romantic Adventures of a Milkmaid"',[73] and at another

point a 'short novel'.[74] When there seemed to be confusion in his negotiations with the *Graphic*, Hardy even offered to send them 'a serial story for the short one'[75] – hoping, it seems, that a longer piece would satisfy the British periodical. Only for the American publishers did Hardy describe the form of the collection accurately, as 'a Tale of Tales – a series of linked stories'.[76]

Hardy also encountered problems in publishing the contents of *A Group of Noble Dames*. In June 1890 he received a letter from Arthur Locker, editor of the *Graphic*, requiring that he either write 'an entirely fresh story' or make significant alterations 'to suit our taste'.[77] In July Hardy wrote letters both to his wife and to Locker which suggest that changes to the collection were in the end 'rendered unnecessary',[78] but many of the tales in *A Group of Noble Dames* were none the less extensively bowdlerized for the *Graphic* publication in December 1890. This version was considerably different from the simultaneous American serialization, which, as Purdy notes, presented the stories as they were originally written.[79]

Soon after these periodical publications of *A Group of Noble Dames*, and upon finishing work on the serial issue of *Tess*, Hardy began in January 1891 'arranging *A Group of Noble Dames* for publication in a volume' (*EL*, 304). This work included restoring and revising the original manuscript, and altering and expanding the story-links in order to accommodate its four additional tales. 'The First Countess of Wessex' was inserted at the beginning, while 'The Lady Penelope' and the two tales which Hardy had published several years earlier were added at the end – 'The Impulsive Lady of Croome Castle' now becoming 'The Duchess of Hamptonshire', and 'Benighted Travellers' becoming 'The Honourable Laura'. Two titles of the original story cycle were changed: 'Barbara (Daughter of Sir John Grebe)' became 'Barbara of the House of Grebe', and 'The Lady Caroline (Afterwards Marchioness of Stonehenge)' was simplified to 'The Marchioness of Stonehenge'. The sequence of these six tales remained the same, except that 'Lady Mottisfont' and 'Anna, Lady Baxby' exchanged positions. In this altered and enlarged form, *A Group of Noble Dames* was published in May 1891 by Osgood, McIlvaine, the British agent of Harper & Brothers, who in June published it in America.[80]

'Master John Horseleigh, Knight', completed two years after *A Group of Noble Dames* was published, is written much in the style of that volume.[81] Its setting is in a past century (1539 is the earliest date in Hardy's prose fiction), its narrator, a 'thin-faced gentleman' (231), could easily have been a member of the Wessex Field and Antiquarian Club, and its plot is based on information found in the pedigrees and records of Hutchins's *History* of Dorset.[82] The story may also have been broadly founded on the tale Hardy heard of Mrs Carlyle's 'witch neighbour' who discovered she was married to a bigamist (*EL*, 158–9), and on the incident he wrote down in his 'Facts' notebook about the woman who married Lord Erskine 'without knowing anything of his rank & circums.' and lived in poverty after his death.[83] In any case, as Hardy himself admitted to Florence Henniker, 'Master John Horseleigh' is one of his 'slightest' works,[84] and it lacks the moral content complementing the heavy documentary quality of the best of the *Noble Dames* stories. The long description of Horseleigh's mansion, taken straight from Hutchins,[85] serves no important purpose, and the attention paid to Oozewood past and present has none of the significance or interest that such comparisons possess in Hardy's pastoral histories. The story's style is generally awkward and cumbersome – demonstrating more than anything else the fundamental weakness of many of Hardy's characteristic techniques when they are used perfunctorily, with no essential relation to the story's subject matter or meaning.

Even before Hardy began working on *A Group of Noble Dames*, he was also writing stories of a rather different sort, set neither in the Dorset of his childhood (as are many of *Wessex Tales*), nor in the two centuries before his birth (like most of *A Group of Noble Dames*), but rather in his own contemporary England. This transition from traditional and historical tales to stories of a more modern sort began in July 1888, when Hardy was working simultaneously on 'The Melancholy Hussar of the German Legion' and 'A Tragedy of Two Ambitions'. Hardy composed a considerable portion of 'The Melancholy Hussar' first, but stopped mid-stream and turned to the other story. He described in a letter to the *Universal Review* the 'period' flavour and 'picturesque' quality of 'The Melancholy Hussar', but wondered whether the editor would find such a story appropriate to its needs:

> Now the question has occurred to me: – suppose you do not want a tale of that sort for your very modern review? I have in my head a story of a different character – embodying present day aspirations – i.e., concerning the ambitions of two men, their struggles for education, a position in the Church, & so on, ending tragically. If you much prefer the latter sort of thing I will abandon the first – though that is the most advanced, & could be sent in a week or ten days. The other would take a little more time, as it exists at present only in the form of half a dozen notes.[86]

It appears that the *Universal Review* took up Hardy's suggestion: 'A Tragedy of Two Ambitions' was printed in the magazine the following December, while 'The Melancholy Hussar' was published elsewhere in January 1890.[87]

In 1891, a year in which Hardy mentioned to one publisher his recently acquired 'sureness of method',[88] three more stories with contemporary settings were published: 'For Conscience' Sake', 'On the Western Circuit', and 'The Son's Veto'.[89] In the following year, Hardy spent most of his time working on the serialized *Pursuit of the Well-Beloved*,[90] but in the closing months of 1892 he wrote 'The Fiddler of the Reels',[91] a story which begins in about 1851 and extends in its conclusion to the 'now' (*LLI*, 185) of the 1890s, the time of the story's narrator. Soon after Hardy had written these modern short stories, he told Mrs Henniker that he was 'more inclined' to write short stories than long ones,[92] and *Jude the Obscure* may have been originally conceived in 1888 as a short story (*EL*, 272). In 1894, Hardy gathered his contemporary stories into *Life's Little Ironies, A Set of Tales with Some Colloquial Sketches Entitled A Few Crusted Characters*. This volume included all of the 'modern' stories Hardy had written up to the beginning of 1893: 'The Son's Veto' (1891), 'For Conscience' Sake' (1891), 'A Tragedy of Two Ambitions' (1888), 'On the Western Circuit' (1891), and 'The Fiddler of the Reels' (1893). It also contained some of the more successful tales set in the past which still remained uncollected: 'A Tradition of Eighteen Hundred and Four' (1882), 'The Melancholy Hussar of the German Legion' (1890), and 'To Please His Wife' (1891). The collection concluded with a cycle of nine brief narratives entitled 'A Few Crusted Characters', which had been serialized in 1891 under the title 'Wessex Folk'. The volume went through five impressions within three months of its publication by Osgood, McIlvaine, and was also printed by Harper & Brothers in America.[93]

In 1895, Osgood, McIlvaine began to issue the first collected edition of Hardy's works; all three of the short-story volumes were included and published in 1896.[94] Hardy made extensive textual revisions to each collection,[95] wrote prefaces explaining the historical sources of some of the stories, and added 'An Imaginative Woman' (first published in April 1894)[96] to the beginning of *Wessex Tales*. Obviously more typical of *Life's Little Ironies*, the story most likely was included in *Wessex Tales* for a practical reason. *Life's Little Ironies* was produced from Osgood, McIlvaine's own first edition plates, but since they had not previously published *Wessex Tales*, new plates had to be made for that volume[97] – thus making it possible to add an entire story at the beginning without much additional work.

Perhaps because Hardy was no longer seriously devoting himself to prose fiction, the stories published after *Jude the Obscure* – with the exception of 'Enter a Dragoon' – are superficial treatments of old settings and themes. For the most part, they are attempts to get a complicated plot down on paper rather than to create a narrative with a coherent and significant pattern of meaning. 'A Committee-Man of "The Terror" ', as Purdy has discovered, is based on a letter of 1797, printed in *The Journal of Mary Frampton*, in which Lady Elizabeth Talbot reported from London on an incident in which a member 'of the Directory was seen . . . in the Strand and recognized by a French lady whose father, mother, and brother he had murdered. She fainted away in the street, and before she recovered enough to speak he had escaped in the crowd.'[98] Hardy heightens the drama of this actual situation by having his heroine fall in love with this man, and moves the scene from the London of the 1790s to the Budmouth of the early 1800s – thus recalling as a colourful background to his story the 'grand gathering' (214) of the king's court which had also figured in *The Trumpet-Major*.

Such a return to familiar fictional territory demonstrates

Hardy's reliance in the final stages of his fiction-writing career on earlier inspiration, and the results in 'A Committee-Man' reflect this lack of immediate engagement in his subject. The portrayal of the topography of Budmouth is unnecessarily detailed, and the attention to minor particulars which provide a certain period flavour does not so much supplement as replace a treatment of the serious issues underlying the story's situation. M. B——'s rationalistic separation of 'intent' and 'consequence' (217) identifies him as a common type among revolutionaries of the period, but the story itself passes too lightly over the premises of his logic and the immorality of his past. Instead of exploring the human problems inherent in the plot, Hardy focuses on the insignificant and implausible coincidence that the lovers 'had left the town by the same conveyance'. Mlle V——'s judgment that 'He, the greater, persevered' (227), romanticizes M. B——, and obscures even further the moral issues the story initially had raised. Mlle V——'s 'divinely sent vision' (225) of her headless relatives, the single scene which reminds the reader of the atrocities for which M. B—— was responsible, was added to the story for its publication in *A Changed Man* in 1913.

By refusing to portray the lovers as happily and romantically married, however, the conclusion of 'The Committee-Man' is faithful to the emotional implications of its situation. Hardy wrote to Florence Henniker that he did not think this ending 'a sad one' because the marriage 'w[oul]d have resulted in unhappiness for certain'. The same letter, none the less, betrays Hardy's uneasiness concerning the quality of the piece. After calling it a 'story', he qualified the term by suggesting it might rather be called a 'sketch'[99] – an amendment which pinpoints the basic frailty of 'A Committee-Man' as a narrative: it 'sketches' the outlines of an interesting story, but fails to present the subtler shades of meaning that might have emerged from it.

'The Duke's Reappearance' is also a superficial presentation of an ingenious plot, but here Hardy's affection for his own 'Family Tradition' (247) gives the writing a vitality unusual in his short-story writing at this late date. The references to 'Swetman's one-handed clock . . . that is still preserved in the family', to the 'original homestead . . . on the outskirts of King's-Hintock village' (247), and to the 'usual breakfast' there of 'ham 'and cider' (249), all reveal Hardy's fondness, reminiscent of his pastoral histories of the 1880s, for a past way of life. The actual 'Tradition' draws together elements from two stories that had come down to Hardy from his mother: the 'indubitably true' one that two of his maternal ancestors narrowly escaped assault by the victorious loyalist soldiers after the Battle of Sedgemoor; and the one 'of more doubtful authenticity', that Christopher Swetman was visited by a 'mysterious man' who may have been 'one of Monmouth's defeated officers' (*EL*, 7–8). Presumably because the latter is more interesting, Hardy chose to fictionalize that less substantiated tradition, and worked in the more plausible one only by transforming it into the incident in which the stranger tries to kiss Leonard Swetman. The story portrays a romantic attitude common in Dorset toward the Monmouth Rebellion.[100] Like the female speaker of 'At Shag's Heath', Christopher is 'not unfriendly' to the Duke's cause 'in his secret heart' (249), and feels guilty at the thought that he may have betrayed him.

The descendant of Christopher who tells the story gives it two possible interpretations, one romantic and the other realistic. Swetman remains convinced that the mysterious stranger on both occasions was the Duke himself – a version that can only be believed if one considers the second visitor to have been Monmouth's ghost, or if one accepts the rumour 'spread abroad in the West that the man beheaded in the Tower was not indeed the Duke' (255). But internal evidence suggests that the visitor was only one of Monmouth's officers (as Hardy himself believed), or that the second visitor was 'a friend of the Duke's, whom the Duke had asked to fetch the things in a last request' (255). By offering a story susceptible to these different interpretations, Hardy repeats the technique of 'A Tradition of Eighteen Hundred and Four' – implying that there might be an explanation for an unusual event, while at the same time portraying vividly the less probable version that was generally believed. As the narrator remarks, Swetman shared with 'thousands of others' a 'belief in the rumour that Monmouth lived' (255–6). 'The Duke's Reappearance' is Hardy's last pure version of a 'Wessex tale'. His three final stories portray traditional subject matter, but include as well in their form and narrative technique characteristics of the later work.

'The Grave by the Handpost', for example, is like a 'Wessex tale' in its setting and content (its subtitle for the periodical publication was 'A Christmas Reminiscence'),[101] but its plot has affinities with a 'life's little irony', or even a 'satire of circumstance'. The story is based on the custom, abolished in about 1830, of burying suicides at a crossroads, and driving a stake through their bodies.[102] A contrast is set up between the neighbouring towns of Broad Sidlinch, which still follows the 'barbarous' (136) custom of isolating and desecrating the bodies of suicides, and of Chalk-Newton, whose choir sings a hymn over Samuel Holway's grave, and whose parson is willing to grant him Christian burial. But this interesting geographical contiguity of two opposing attitudes – one primitive and superstitious, the other more modern and humane – is not presented in any depth, and in the end becomes merely an element in the 'satire of circumstance' which prevents Luke Holway from being buried next to his father because he has moved to Chalk-Newton.[103] The cruel twist at the conclusion, in which Luke's burial instructions are 'accidentally swept to the floor' (141), shifts the story's emphasis completely to circumstance. Seen in its entirety, 'The Grave by the Handpost' fails to achieve either the regional and historical depth of a 'Wessex tale' or the psychological and sociological complexity of a 'life's little irony'.

'Enter a Dragoon' is a more successful blending of such elements. Its setting in the Mellstock of the 1850s suggests that it might be considered a 'Wessex tale', and this impression is strengthened by the mention of 'old Owlett's' (160) liquor under the stairs (an explicit reference to 'The Distracted Preacher'), by the narrator's close attention to details of the local way of life, and especially by the dramatic opposition, frequent in Hardy's pastoral, between two suitors – one a familiar inhabitant of the area, the other glamorous and romantic because he is an outsider. In its structure and its treatment of social themes, the story is like a 'life's little irony'. Selina Paddock's 'odd' predicament (150) elicits from herself and others a typical spectrum of Victorian attitudes toward sex and marriage. Like Miss Havisham, she keeps her mummified wedding cake, but out of an entirely different motive: not as a reminder of a past disappointment or an effort to make time stand still, but 'as a testimony to her intentional respectability' (149) despite the illegitimacy of her child. She consents to marry Bartholomew Miller in order to have a 'comfortable home' (150) for her son, but as soon as Clark returns she automatically assumes, despite his unexplained tardiness, that she is rightly his, and even Miller shares this conventional view: 'You do belong to the child's father since he's alive.' (153) Selina's re-engagement satisfies both 'her heart, and her sense of womanly virtue' (155).

The sergeant-major's sudden death reveals the absurdity of Selina's logic. Despite medical evidence to the contrary, she remains convinced that Clark's heart failure is a direct result of his discovery that she had been engaged to Miller. Her quick assumption of widowhood is a refusal to sacrifice a 'melancholy luxury of dreaming what might have been her future in New Zealand with John' (164) for an honest recognition of the contradictions in his past behaviour. Her financial independence, like that of Leonora Frankland in 'For Conscience' Sake', is admirable, but the 'sober pleasure' she derives from tending Clark's grave represents an inability to forsake her 'respectable' (166) widowhood for a second marriage. For this reason, the rather heavy-handed satire of circumstance in the story's closing scene, in which Selina learns that Clark already had a legal wife and child, is an appropriate part of the story's formal irony: the knowledge shatters all illusions Selina or the reader may have had about her 'assumption of a moral relationship to the deceased' (163). The quest for respectability is seen as utterly meaningless. In this late story, Hardy reclaims momentarily the subtlety of his earlier 'life's little ironies' and successfully assimilates, as he had not done in the other narratives written after 1894, simple irony of circumstance with irony of meaning and form.

'A Changed Man', Hardy's last short story,[104] contains some of the techniques found in *Wessex Tales*. It has a traditional basis in the 1854 cholera epidemic in Fordington parish, when the Rev. Henry Moule became a local and indeed national hero through his unflagging efforts to control the spread of the disease.[105] As in 'The Melancholy Hussar', a point is made of explaining the special picturesqueness that military men had in the eyes of Wessex inhabitants 'In those days' (4), and as in 'The Three Strangers', particular details of local life are described: the song 'now nearly disused' (14) that the soldiers sang when leaving a town, the walls that 'formed the field-fences' (17) along the Ridgeway, and the importance of the Sunday sermon to people 'At this point in the nineteenth century' (9). The invalid who witnesses events from his oriel window – the 'person who, next to the actors themselves, chanced to know most of their story' (3) – is an embodiment of the communal point of view, but Hardy found it difficult to sustain this narrative device and dropped it after Laura has moved to Creston, referring to the invalid again only per-functorily in the final sentence: 'What domestic issues super-vened in Vannicock's further story the man in the oriel never knew; but Mrs. Maumbry lived and died a widow.' (23)

Even earlier, however, the invalid's perspective does not constitute the entire narrative point of view, which encompass-es not only the communal vantage point invoked in Hardy's pastoral histories but also the more general philosophical viewpoint common in *Life's Little Ironies*. So Maumbry's charm is associated with his military uniform but also with 'an attractive hint of wickedness in his manner that was sure to make him adorable with good young women' (4), and Laura is presented in self-consciously analytical terms as having 'from the first entered heart and soul into military romance as exhibited in the plots and characters of those living exponents of it who came under her notice' (7). This tendency to see persons as psychological and social types, especially charac-teristic of the *Life's Little Ironies* narrator, is most evident in the explanation for the Maumbry's churchgoing: 'for these light-natured, hit-or-miss, rackety people went to church like others for respectability's sake. None so orthodox as your unmitigated worldling.' (11) In its plot, too, 'A Changed Man' is more like a 'life's little irony' than a 'Wessex tale', despite its traditional content. Of more interest than the attitude of the community is the unexpected change in Maumbry's charac-ter, and the questions about marriage, fidelity, and social responsibility which it implicitly raises.

The complete metamorphosis in Sgt Maumbry is at first treated with a degree of irony. A volatile quality in his character is suggested by the observation that his eyes showed an 'adaptability', allowing one to think 'they might have expressed sadness or seriousness just as readily, if he had had a mind for such' (4–5). His mock solemnity about the ghost raises further doubts about his general credibility and so his sudden turn to the ministry seems at first even more disingenuous – or at least temporary – than one otherwise would suppose. If Alec Durberville is any indication, Hardy was sceptical about conversions by religious enthusiasts like Mr Sainway, and the irony he applied elsewhere to the cliché 'a changed man' – it is used with careful reservation about Captain de Stancy in *A Laodicean* and Michael Henchard in *The Mayor of Casterbridge* – suggests that Hardy was not entirely convinced himself that a person could 'change' as completely and irrevocably as the phrase would suggest.

But when it becomes apparent that Maumbry has really forsaken the secular for the religious way of life, a different question emerges – not the plausibility of so great a transformation, but the difficulty, and even the morality of it when it alters the terms of a marriage. Laura Maumbry had married a man who she presumed would remain essentially a social and worldly being like herself, and has suddenly found her pleasure in life 'considerably diminished' (12) by an unexpected reversal in his personality. Her adulterous relationship with Vannicock is an infidelity, not to the man whom she married, but to the incompatible person into which he suddenly was transformed. This does not justify Laura's taking a lover, but explains in compelling terms her emotional state when doing so. As she phrases her impassioned question to the invalid: 'Do you think . . . that a woman's husband has a right to do such a thing, even if he does feel a certain call to it?' (15) Laura's predicament, and her strategy for coping with it, recall Eustacia Vye's unhappiness after Clym Yeobright has made furze-cutting his whole occupation – dashing at a stroke the social and economic expectations she had when marrying him.

But just as the story begs the question of the plausibility of Maumbry's change of character, so too does it evade the issue of the rightness of his act, by suddenly shifting attention to the cholera epidemic, and to Maumbry's heroism in combatting it. Here questions concerning the morality of Maumbry's transformation, and of Laura's affair, become insignificant in the face of human suffering, and even Laura and Vannicock forsake their elopement plan to join Maumbry in boiling the infectious clothing. In this crisis, if not in his role as preacher, Maumbry is unquestionably 'the man for such an hour' (16), and his death immediately after the completion of his important task (the historical Moule survived the epidemic) establishes him as a hero. On the other hand, it prevents the reader's judging on either of the questions the story has raised: if his change would have been permanent, and if it was fair to his young wife. Laura Maumbry's widowhood after she is finally 'free' to marry constitutes the sort of wry twist found in the conclusion of a 'life's little irony', but the narrative as a whole, despite Hardy's opinion that it is 'the best . . . of the tales' in *A Changed Man*,[106] fails to achieve the sharp satirical quality or the profound poignancy that characterize the best of the *Life's Little Ironies*. The story also fails to portray either the density of social content or the dramatic force of the best of the *Wessex Tales*.

After the publication in 1900 of 'Enter a Dragoon' and 'A Changed Man', Hardy abandoned entirely his career as a writer of prose fiction. But until just before his death he continued to amend and improve his already published works. For the Macmillan Wessex edition in 1912, Hardy made more revisions to the short story volumes, most of them minor,[107] and reorganized the stories of *Wessex Tales* and *Life's Little Ironies* in a way which gave greater coherence and unity to both collections. 'An Imaginative Woman' was moved from *Wessex Tales* to the beginning of *Life's Little Ironies*, while 'A Tradition of Eighteen Hundred and Four' and 'The Melancholy Hussar' were both transferred to *Wessex Tales*. These changes made *Wessex Tales* chiefly a volume of traditional stories, and *Life's Little Ironies* generally more contemporary. The preface printed by Macmillan for *A Group of Noble Dames* was identical to the one Hardy wrote for Osgood, McIlvaine in 1896, but a number of changes were made in the preface to *Wessex Tales*, the most significant of which was the identification of an historical source for 'The Distracted Preacher'. For *Life's Little Ironies*, Hardy produced an entirely new preface, explaining his reasons for shifting the locations of the three stories. The 1896 preface had discussed the sources of 'The Melancholy Hussar' and 'Andrey Satchel and the Parson and Clerk', but Hardy never salvaged this material by adding to the preface of *Wessex Tales* the source of 'The Melancholy

Hussar', or incorporating the information about Parson Toogood of 'A Few Crusted Characters' into his 1912 preface to *Life's Little Ironies*. By failing to retain his account of the traditional material used in his *Life's Little Ironies* volume, Hardy emphasized in his later preface the volume's more consistent unifying principle, the dependence of each of its plots on 'a trick of Nature' (*LLI*, v).

The publication by Macmillan of all of Hardy's works, prose and poetry, prompted the suggestion that he assemble in one final volume of fiction all of his still uncollected stories. The result was *A Changed Man, The Waiting Supper and Other Tales, Concluding with The Romantic Adventures of a Milkmaid*, first printed by Macmillan in October 1913, and simultaneously in America by Harper & Brothers.[108] Hardy told Mrs Henniker as early as 1898 that he did not 'take kindly to publishing [his] stray short stories' because they did not seem 'to be worth reprinting',[109] and he was still disinclined in 1913 to recover what he said in a letter he would gladly have left uncollected.[110] But Hardy none the less agreed to have the stories published 'in order', as he put it in the volume's preface, 'to render them accessible to readers who desire to have them in the complete series issued by my publishers' (vii). A preface which Hardy had earlier sent to Macmillan, but which he rejected before the book's publication, was more specific in its description of his reasons for assembling the stories, saying that they 'would probably never have been collected by me at this time of day if frequent reprints of some of them in America and elsewhere had not set many readers inquiring for them in a volume'.[111] Hardy was referring here to the six stories in *A Changed Man* which were published before the introduction in 1891 of the International Copyright Law.

Hardy's chagrin at the profligate reprinting of his work is evident not only in his original preface to *A Changed Man*, but also in several letters which speak of his being 'almost compelled' to publish the stories in book form, 'There being wretchedly printed copies of some of them in circulation in America'.[112] Of the six stories, 'The Romantic Adventures' in particular was widely printed, and misprinted, in America, and Hardy expressed his annoyance at this fact by refusing to autograph an admirer's copy of a pirated edition.[113] But although Hardy's motives in collecting the stories in *A Changed Man* may at first have had only to do with these early uncopyrighted stories, he also collected, once the project was begun, most of the short fiction he had already published, both before and after the copyright law came into effect. The result was a collection that is miscellaneous in every sense. In his 'Prefatory Note' Hardy referred to *A Changed Man* as 'a dozen minor novels' (vii), while in the title he called it a collection of 'Tales' – a discrepancy of terminology which points to the variance in length, kind, and quality of its contents. Unlike the three previous volumes of short stories, this book is concerned with no single historical period or theme, and employs no consistent narrative technique – it is, as Hardy roughly categorized it in the Wessex edition, a collection of 'Mixed Novels'.

Hardy assembled the twelve stories of *A Changed Man*, many of which he had lost and was forced to solicit from periodicals, during the summer of 1913.[114] He complained repeatedly to publishers and friends that he thought the stories were 'mostly bad',[115] but he never attempted to improve them. Indeed, he could scarcely have had any appetite for such a task at this stage, and put the volume together quite hurriedly.[116] Except in the case of 'The Waiting Supper', few revisions were made to the stories,[117] and Hardy's preface to the volume, which speaks of the narratives 'for what they may be worth' (vii), is defensive in tone. *A Changed Man* was reprinted by Macmillan in 1914 as the eighteenth volume of the Wessex edition, and was given its own exclusive category, 'Mixed Novels'.[118] Hardy had originally placed the collection in the third division of the Wessex edition, 'Novels of Ingenuity',[119] but was forced 'to start a new group of novels' with *A Changed Man*,[120] apparently because of a printer's error which numbered as XVIII–XX the first three volumes of verse. This problem was later ironed out by renumbering the volumes of verse I-III,[121] but Hardy tried to prevent confusion at the time by labelling *A Changed Man* 'IV' for its category and '18' for its place in the sequence of the fiction.[122] It was then necessary to keep the additional classification even though Hardy had had no intention of introducing it when the book was first published. Despite this extraneous and temporary reason for the extra category, however, Hardy was afterwards glad that he had given *A Changed Man* a general heading of its own which described more accurately the miscellaneous quality of its contents and might include any subsequent volume of still uncollected stories.[123]

In speaking of another possible short-story collection, Hardy could only have been referring to those remaining tales which had never been printed in book form: 'How I Built Myself a House', 'Destiny and a Blue Cloak', his two stories for children, 'An Indiscretion in the Life of an Heiress', and two stories from later in his career entitled 'The Doctor's Legend' and 'Old Mrs. Chundle'. It is possible that Hardy never resurrected these pieces because he had lost all track of them, but at least in the case of 'The Doctor's Legend' it appears that he had more specific reasons for leaving it uncollected. Judging from its style, subject matter, and date of composition (early 1890),[124] the story seems to have been written for *A Group of Noble Dames*, but was kept out of the volume and its periodical form published only in America because, as several critics have speculated, it would have offended the living descendants of Joseph Damer, Lord Milton, the eighteenth-century original of the story's cruel and ambitious squire.[125]

As early as 1914, Hardy began discussing with Macmillan the publication of a limited *de luxe* printing of the Wessex novels, but the project did not materialize until after the war, when 'The Mellstock Edition' began to appear in December 1919. The four volumes of short stories were produced for this printing with only minor textual changes,[126] and an addition was made to the *Wessex Tales* preface, noting that although the events of 'A Tradition of Eighteen Hundred and Four' were entirely fabricated by Hardy, he later learned 'that it was a real tradition' (*WT*, x). The few revisions Hardy made for the Mellstock edition were incorporated into later printings of the Wessex edition.[127] Before his death, Hardy probably also did some proofreading for the 1928 Macmillan one-volume *Short Stories of Thomas Hardy*,[128] which included all the narratives assembled for the Wessex edition. The seven stories which had never appeared in any volume have all been printed in some form since Hardy's death, and all but 'How I Built Myself a House' have recently been collected in Macmillan's 'New Wessex Edition'.[129]

Within the broad spectrum of Hardy's experiments in the short story are certain subjects, themes, image patterns, and techniques which are frequently repeated. This fact has led some critics to accuse Hardy of tedious self-duplication,[130] and others to use these similarities as a basis for analysing his work along specific categorical guidelines,[131] yoking together stories from different periods and volumes, and ignoring Hardy's conscious arrangement of them in *Wessex Tales, A Group of Noble Dames*, and *Life's Little Ironies*. Such a method illuminates similarities among all the stories, but arbitrarily removes them both from their chronological context and from the thematic context which Hardy himself chose to give them. A more valuable method of classification has been suggested by Norman Page, who separates them into four general types – 'humorous', 'romantic or supernatural', 'realistic and often ironic or tragic', and 'historical'.[132] Even this method, however, groups together narratives which are dissimilar. Page's historical category includes both the Napoleonic stories from *Wessex Tales*, and those about earlier centuries from *A Group of Noble Dames* – narratives which, though set in the past, are essentially different from each other in tone and narrative technique. Hardy's own organization of the stories, on the other hand, is based not only on subject matter, setting, and theme, but also on an equally important, but less obvious, division – that of narrative voice. The *Noble Dames* stories, filtered through the narrow and distorted perspective of the Antiquarian Club, are different in quite essential ways from the traditional stories in *Wessex Tales*, whose meaning and complexity are based on the clarity and breadth of perspective that characterize the pastoral voice. Even 'A Tradition of Eighteen Hundred and Four', with its unreliable narrator, is intrinsically unlike the stories in *A Group of Noble Dames*: the falseness in Solomon Selby's perception is visual and imaginative, not moral.

The labels I have attached to the three short-story volumes – pastoral histories, ambivalent exempla, and tragedies of circumstance – are merely descriptive of the types of story which emerge from their three different narrative modes. The pastoral perspective draws together the stories of *Wessex Tales*, the subjective perspective of the Antiquarian Club gives the *Noble Dames* stories their two levels of moral interpretation, and the ironic perspective of the voice in *Life's Little Ironies* uncovers the tragedy in conventionally farcical situations. This unity of perspective in each volume serves the double purpose of drawing together disparate kinds of material, and making each book as a whole greater than the sum of its parts. The stories are, of course, self-contained, and most of them are rich enough to merit attention in their own right, but even the greatest of them – 'The Three Strangers', 'The Withered Arm', 'A Tragedy of Two Ambitions', 'On the Western Circuit', and 'The Fiddler of the Reels' – acquire a broader range of meaning when seen in the context of their respective volumes. Because none of the *Noble Dames* stories by itself is superlatively good, the similarities and differences among them are especially important, and the two stories which open the volume add substantially to the value of the rest by setting up the pattern of repetition and contrast which structures the book. Most of the stories in *A Group of Noble Dames*, it must be remembered, were never published separately, and therefore have a special claim to be considered as parts of a single, larger work.

My concern to study Hardy's short stories in terms of the volumes in which he collected them has led me to focus primarily on the differences among the kinds of narrative which he produced during his long and varied fiction-writing career. Something ought to be said, however, about Hardy's general status as a short-story writer. John Berryman has declared that Thomas Hardy 'wrote one thousand pages of the worst short stories that the world has ever seen'.[133] No other critic has spoken quite so disparagingly as this, but the stories have frequently been frowned upon either for failing to treat their themes at greater length,[134] or for not conforming in structure and economy of expression with the qualifications for a 'modern' short story.[135] A common complaint has been, as Elizabeth Bowen puts it, that 'their matter does not dictate their form'.[136] Hardy, however, considered form the most important quality in any piece of writing. As he wrote in 'The Profitable Reading of Fiction',

> to a masterpiece in story there appertains a beauty of shape, no less than to a masterpiece in pictorial or plastic art, capable of giving to the trained mind an equal pleasure. To

recognize this quality clearly when present, the construction of the plot, or fable, as it used to be called, is to be more particularly observed than either in a reading for sentiment and opinions, or in a reading merely to discover the fates of the chief characters. For however real the persons, however profound, witty, or humorous the observations, as soon as the book comes to be regarded as an exemplification of the art of storytelling, the story naturally takes the first place, and the example is not noteworthy as such unless the telling be artistically carried on.[137]

The discrepancy between the allegations of critics who claim that Hardy had no sense of the short story as form, and his own stated concern for 'beauty of shape' in all narratives may be attributed to the rigid definition which the term 'short story' has gradually acquired since Edgar Allan Poe's famous essay on Hawthorne declared the importance of the *single effect*.[138] While Poe's standard can help to illuminate his own work, as well as that of several 'modern' writers, it fails to isolate either the weaknesses or the strengths of an artist such as Hardy, whose sense of form developed from a different tradition altogether, and who was more concerned with 'story' than with 'effect'. It would seem more sensible when speaking of Hardy to think of form in the broader and more flexible sense that Percy Lubbock gives to the word: 'The best form is that which makes the most of its subject.'[139] In his short stories, Hardy invented forms which were eminently suitable for his subjects. This is apparent not only in the excellence of individual stories but, more importantly, in the fact that the form of his stories changed as he altered his material, so that the methods used in *Wessex Tales*, *A Group of Noble Dames*, and *Life's Little Ironies* differ significantly from each other. Hardy's careful arrangement of these volumes is evidence of his own awarness of the distinctiveness of the narrative forms which he created.

Those who have spoken in favour of the short stories have tended, like Irving Howe, to argue that Hardy has 'little to do with the main line of the modern short story' represented by 'Chekhov, Joyce and Hemingway', and that his work ought to be considered as an example of an older form, the tale – 'a more easy-paced and amiable mode of narrative.'[140] Hardy, however, wrote tales that are consciously crafted and uniquely modern. The stories of *Wessex Tales*, through their use of a pastoral voice, are mimetic reworkings of the old traditional tale. While the oral tale, as Howe says, 'stops, starts up again and wanders, seemingly unconcerned with the effects of accumulation or foreshortening',[141] Hardy's pastoral histories, even the longer ones, are tightly controlled narratives, whose digressions are themselves part of the overall pattern of meaning. The *Noble Dames* stories, with their personal narrators, seem to imitate the oral tale more exactly, but their structure and meaning depend upon a concept that is distinctly literary: the discrepancy between the narrator's point of view and that elicited from the reader by the story itself. The narratives in *Life's Little Ironies* are not oral tales at all in Howe's sense, and their clever inversion of sentimental plots suggests an awareness of literary technique frequently associated with, though certainly not unique to, the 'modern' era. In their way, they are as original in form and style as the stories of a Chekhov, a Joyce, or a Hemingway.

All of Hardy's short-story volumes demonstrate a degree of self-consciousness in narrative strategy which makes them distinct from the 'tale' in its simplest sense. Yet Hardy uses this term indiscriminately to describe his stories, perhaps because all of them, including those in *Life's Little Ironies*, are told in a voice that approximates to the spoken word. In the pastoral, the ambivalent, and the ironic voices of each of the volumes is a unique rhetoric which defines the meaning of each story. While being consciously structured literary creations, these narratives fulfil the hope that A. E. Coppard, a writer who was much influenced by Hardy's short stories,[142] expressed for the form: 'The folk tale ministered to an apparently inborn and universal desire to hear tales, and it is my feeling that the closer the modern short story conforms to that ancient tradition of being spoken to you, rather than being read at you, the more acceptable it becomes.'[143] Perhaps the genre of Hardy's short stories can best be described by expanding upon A. F. Cassis's observation that Hardy follows two distinct narrative traditions: 'the tradition of the conscious, artistic literary short story, that of the *écrivain*, and the tradition of the *raconteur*, the narrator who simulates a spoken story in print.'[144] In *Wessex Tales* and the *Noble Dames* stories, the *raconteur* is more visible, while in *Life's Little Ironies* it is the *écrivain* who is more prominent, but in all of the best stories there is a joining of these two roles which produces a quality that is both oral and literary. It is this double dimension in the narrative voice of Hardy's short stories which makes them, like their author, both profoundly traditional and recognizably 'modern'. They are tales of the past and of the present.

Notes

CHAPTER 1   **Wessex Tales:** PASTORAL HISTORIES

1. 'The Profitable Reading of Fiction', in *Thomas Hardy's Personal Writings*, ed. Harold Orel (Kansas University Press, 1966) p. 120.
2. For discussions of the short story in England during the nineteenth century see: T. O. Beachcroft, *The Modest Art* (London: OUP, 1968) p. 120; Wendell V. Harris, 'English Short Fiction in the Nineteenth Century', *Studies in Short Fiction*, 6 (1968) 1–93; Q. D. Leavis, *Fiction and the Reading Public* (London: Chatto & Windus, 1932) pp. 26–32; Brander Matthews, *The Philosophy of the Short Story* (London: Longmans Green, 1912) pp. 56–60; William Somerset Maugham, 'The Short Story', *Transactions of the Royal Society of Literature of the United Kingdom*, NS 25 (1950) 120–34; Frank O'Connor, *The Lonely Voice* (New York: World Publishing Co., 1963) p. 19; Sean O'Faolain, *The Short Story* (New York: Devin-Adair, 1951) pp. 26–32; H. G. Wells, *The Country of the Blind* (London: Thomas Nelson, 1911) pp. iv–v.
3. George Saintsbury, *The English Novel* (London: J. M. Dent, 1913) p. 264.
4. 'The Dorsetshire Labourer', in Orel, p. 169.
5. This is the heading in *The Early Life of Thomas Hardy* for the chapters covering the period between 1887 and 1891.
6. 'The Dorsetshire Labourer', p. 170.
7. 'The Dorsetshire Labourer', pp. 170–1.
8. *Life's Little Ironies* (London: Osgood, McIlvaine, 1896) p. v. Hardy had spoken to two Broadmayne villagers, one of whom witnessed the 1801 execution (*EL*, 153).
9. The description of the execution can be traced to a report in the *Morning Chronicle* noted by Hardy in the 'Trumpet-Major Notebook' (*The Personal Notebooks of Thomas Hardy*, ed. Richard H. Taylor [New York: Columbia University Press, 1979] pp. 124–5). The vicar of Broadwey reported that Hardy came there to examine the Bincombe registers (Carl J. Weber, *Hardy and the Lady from Madison Square* [Waterville, Maine: Colby College Press, 1952] p. 93).
10. Hardy wrote that 'both the women who figure in the story' were 'known' to him (Hardy to William Blackwood, 1 Oct. 1887, in *The Collected Letters of Thomas Hardy*, ed. Richard Little Purdy and Michael Millgate, I [Oxford: Clarendon Press, 1978] p. 168; hereafter cited as *CL*, I).
11. Hardy's grandfather had been involved in smuggling, and 'sometimes had as many as eighty "tubs" in a dark closet' in the cottage at

Bockhampton ('Memoranda I', 22 Mar. 1871, in Taylor, p. 8). Hardy heard more smuggling stories in 1875 from his landlord at Swanage (*EL*, 141–2), while the apple-tree device was described to him by one of his father's employees (*WT*, viii).

12. Taylor, pp. 120, 128–30.
13. 'Facts' notebook, pp. 163–[166]. Hardy may initially have learned of the story elsewhere, since the newspaper extract was not entered in his 'Facts' notebook until at least five years after 'The Distracted Preacher' was published.
14. Helen Cooper, *Pastoral: Medieval into Renaissance* (Totowa, N. J.: Rowman & Littlefield, 1977) p. 2. See also: William Empson, *Some Versions of Pastoral* (London: Chatto & Windus, 1935); Frank Kermode, introd. to *English Pastoral Poetry* (London: Harap Books, 1952) pp. 11–44; John F. Lynen, *The Pastoral Art of Robert Frost* (New Haven, Conn.: Yale University Press, 1960); *Pastoral and Romance*, ed. Eleanor Terry Lincoln (Englewood Cliffs, N. J.: Prentice-Hall, 1969).
15. Empson, p. 23.
16. Lynen, p. 72.
17. Lynen, p. 54.
18. The same process is involved in the reading of Walter Scott's 'The Two Drovers' (note the similar titles), where a proper interpretation of the story depends upon the reader's gradually acquired familiarity with the customs of Scotland.
19. Lynen, p. 126.
20. 'The Dorsetshire Labourer', p. 188.
21. 'The Dorsetshire Labourer', pp. 188–9.
22. 'The Dorsetshire Labourer', p. 168.
23. Ruth A. Firor, *Folkways in Thomas Hardy* (1922; repr. Phila.: University of Pennsylvania Press, 1931) p. 244.
24. See James L. Roberts, 'Legend and Symbol in Hardy's "The Three Strangers" ', *Nineteenth-Century Fiction*, 17 (1962) 192.
25. William Dean Howells to S. L. Clemens, 10 July 1883, in *Mark Twain–Howells Letters*, ed. Henry Nash Smith and William M. Gibson (Cambridge, Mass.: Belknap Press of Harvard University Press, 1960) I, 434.
26. 'Memoranda II', Aug. 1922, in Taylor, p. 60.
27. Richard Little Purdy, *Thomas Hardy: A Bibliographical Study* (1954; rev. edn. Oxford: Clarendon Press, 1968) p. 82.
28. The 'Trumpet-Major Notebook' records that the cocked hat 'was worn by men of every rank & station in the army, & also by a vast number of civilians' (Taylor, p. 142).
29. S. M. Ellis, 'Thomas Hardy: Some Personal Recollections', *Fortnightly Review*, NS 123 (1928) 398.
30. *Life's Little Ironies* (1896) p. v.
31. Mary Caroline Richards, 'Thomas Hardy's Ironic Vision', *The Trollopian*, 3 (1949) 273.
32. *Wessex Tales* (London: Macmillan, 1888) p. 72; *Blackwood's Magazine*, 143 (1888) 34. The assertion that the marks on Gertrude's arm 'were imprinted' in the exact place that Rhoda clutched it in her dream later

read 'she fancied that they were imprinted'; in the sentence 'But she had a good reason to be superstitious now', the word 'good' was changed to 'haunting' (*Blackwood's*, pp. 37, 38; *Wessex Tales* [1888] pp. 83, 87).

33. Stephen to Hardy, 10 Jan. 1888, in *The Life and Letters of Leslie Stephen*, ed. Frederic William Maitland (London: Duckworth, 1906) pp. 393–4.
34. Ellis, p. 397.
35. 'The Uncanny', in *The Standard Edition of the Complete Psychological Works of Sigmund Freud*, trans. and ed. James Strachey, XVII (1919; repr. London: Hogarth Press and the Institute of Psychoanalysis, 1955) 240.
36. See also 'Memoranda I', Dec. 1872, in Taylor, p. 12.
37. 'The Rev. William Barnes, B. D.', in Orel, p. 101; see also *The Mayor of Casterbridge*, in which Henchard consults Conjuror Fall to find out what the weather will be during the harvest, and *Tess*, in which Dairyman Crick considers employing Conjuror Trendle's son to find out why the butter is not turning.
38. Firor reports that 'instances of popular belief in the evil eye until quite recently kept coming up in the Dorset courts' (p. 88).
39. See John Symonds Udal, *Dorsetshire Folk-lore* (Hertford, 1922; repr. St Peter Port, Guernsey: Toucan Press, 1970) pp. 157–8, and Denys Kay-Robinson, *Hardy's Wessex Reappraised* (Newton Abbot: David & Charles, 1972) p. 131. Hardy made a note on the Cerne giant in 1890 ('Memoranda I', 12 Sept. 1890, in Taylor, p. 26).
40. For discussions of the system of renting cows see G. E. Fussell, ' "High Farming" in Southwestern England, 1840–1880', *Economic Geography*, 24 (1948) 57; and Barbara Kerr, 'The Dorset Agricultural Labourer, 1750–1850', *Proc. of the Dorset Natural History and Archaeological Society*, 84 (1962) 176.
41. Rhoda's consistent use of Dorset dialect was an addition to the 1896 Osgood, McIlvaine edition.
42. Firor compares the boy's symbolic position to that of the Greek *pharmakos* and to Odin (p. 111); Hardy may also have intended to invoke the parallel of the crucifixion: the dramatic structure of 'Panthera', his much later dramatic monologue about the Roman governor's officer who discovers that the crucified 'malefactor' whose execution he is overseeing is his own child, bears a resemblance in its climactic recognition scene to the series of disclosures at the hanging in 'The Withered Arm'.
43. *Thomas Hardy* (London, 1941; repr. New York: Haskell House, 1972) p. 18.
44. *Just As It Happened* (London: Cassell, 1950) p. 92. The detail about putting weights on the feet was used in the description of Jack Winter's execution in 'The Winters and the Palmleys'.
45. In an earlier version Lodge committed suicide, but Hardy then sent this 'improvement' to William Blackwood (Hardy to Blackwood, 11 Dec. 1887, in *CL*, I, 170).
46. The railway came to Bridport in 1857 (David St John Thomas, *A Regional History of the Railways of Great Britain*, Vol. I: *The West Country* [1960; rev. edn Bristol: David & Charles, 1966] p. 148).
47. This detail is present even in the *Blackwood's* publication, but Hardy may

already have decided in Jan. 1888 to place the story just before 'Fellow-Townsmen' in the first printing four months later of *Wessex Tales*, and hence to include this link between the two stories.

48. This contrast anticipates the seesawing fates of Henchard and Farfrae in *The Mayor of Casterbridge*.

49. Downe's behaviour recalls Charles Bovary's absurdly extravagant plans for his wife's coffin and tomb.

50. *Thomas Hardy: The Will and the Way* (Kuala Lumpur: University of Malaya Press, 1965) p. 113.

51. *The History of the English Novel*, IX (London: H. F. & G. Witherby, 1938) 54.

52. *Thomas Hardy: The Poetic Structure* (London: Paul Elek, 1971) p. 144.

53. *Thomas Hardy* (New York: Macmillan, 1967) p. 80.

54. For discussions of the historical circumstances see Eric J. Hobsbawm and George Rudé, *Captain Swing* (London: Lawrence & Wishart, 1969), and Cal Winslow, 'Sussex Smugglers', in *Albion's Fatal Tree*, Douglas Hay, et al. (New York: Pantheon Books, 1975) pp. 119–66.

55. Bert G. Hornback, *The Metaphor of Chance* (Ohio University Press, 1971) p. 13. See also William Van O'Connor, 'Cosmic Irony in Hardy's "The Three Strangers"', *English Journal*, 47 (1958) 250.

56. *Real Conversations* (London: Heinemann, 1904) pp. 31–2.

57. 'Memories of Church Restoration', in Orel, pp. 215–16.

58. 'The Dorsetshire Labourer', p. 188.

59. See also 'Maumbry Ring', in which the memory of an eighteenth-century execution interests Hardy because 'it was a definite event' involving 'real flesh and blood, and no longer uncertain visions of possible Romans at their games or barbarians at their sacrifices' (Orel, p. 228).

60. *The Later Life and Letters of Sir Henry Newbolt*, ed. Margaret Newbolt (London: Faber and Faber, 1942) pp. 185–6.

61. See: Donald Davidson, 'The Traditional Basis of Hardy's Fiction', *Southern Review*, 6 (1940) 162–78; Robert Keily, 'Vision and Viewpoint in *The Mayor of Casterbridge*', *Nineteenth-Century Fiction*, 23 (1968) 189–200; David Lodge, *Language of Fiction* (London: Routledge & Kegan Paul, 1966) pp. 164–88.

62. Howe, p. 78.

63. See: Lucille Herbert, 'Thomas Hardy's Views in *Tess of the d'Urbervilles*', *ELH*, 37 (1970) 78; Lodge, 'Thomas Hardy and Cinematographic Form', *Novel*, 7 (1974) 250; J. Hillis Miller, *Thomas Hardy: Distance and Desire* (Cambridge, Mass.: Belknap Press of Harvard University Press, 1970).

64. 'Plots for Five Unpublished Short Stories', ed. Evelyn Hardy, *London Magazine*, 5 (1958) 39–45.

65. 'Fore-say' to Udal, p. 10.

66. 'A Note on the Structure of Hardy's Short Stories', *Colby Library Quarterly*, ser. 10 (1974) p. 290.

67. 'Ellery Queen Builds Collection of Rare Detective Short Stories', *Publishers' Weekly*, 20 Nov. 1943, p. 1946.

68. Freud, p. 220.

Notes

207

69. Freud, p. 237.
70. Freud, p. 243.
71. Freud, p. 244.
72. *The Country and the City* (1973; repr. New York:, OUP, 1975) p. 206.
73. Barnes, p. 1.

CHAPTER 2   **A Group of Noble Dames:** AMBIVALENT
              EXEMPLA

1. Hardy to Harper's, 7 Mar. 1890, quoted in Purdy, p. 66.
2. '"Hodge" As I Know Him: A Talk with Mr. Thomas Hardy', *Pall Mall Gazette*, 2 Jan. 1892, repr. *Thomas Hardy and His Readers*, ed. Laurence Lerner and John Holstrom (London: Bodley Head, 1968) p. 158. See also Kay-Robinson, p. 255, and Hardy to Edward Clodd, 3 June 1891, in *CL*, I, 237.
3. Hardy to Lord Lytton, 15 July 1891, in *CL*, I, 239.
4. Raymond Blathwayt, 'A Chat with the Author of "Tess" ', *Black and White*, 4 (1892) 240.
5. *Hardy the Novelist* (1943; repr. London: Constable, 1965) p. 122.
6. In the periodical publication, Phelipson is a romantic figure killed while trying to elope with Betty after Tupcombe – thinking the person he saw in Betty's room was Reynard – unsettles the ladder under her window (*Harper's New Monthly Magazine*, 80 [1889–90] 36–42).
7. Morrell, p. 162.
8. Betty's secret meetings with Reynard were added for the first edition in 1891.
9. Giles Stephen Holland Fox-Strangways, 6th Earl of Ilchester, *Henry Fox* (London: John Murray, 1920) I, pp. 46–7.
10. Betty's deliberate exposure to smallpox and Phelipson's rejection of her were added in 1891. The use of a contagious disease as a deterrent to and test of love may have been suggested to Hardy by Harrison Ainsworth's *Old St Paul's*, in which Amabel Bloundel's supposed case of the plague momentarily discourages her relentless pursuer, or by Thackeray's *History of Henry Esmond*, where Henry's smallpox produces unexpected anger and panic in Rachel, Lady Castlewood.
11. In the periodical version Uplandtowers resents Barbara's lack of sexual passion for him ('A Group of Noble Dames', *Graphic*, Christmas no. [1890] 8), but changes made for the first edition emphasize that he is angry at her for not engaging in physical intimacy only because it prevents his having a 'lineal successor' (*A Group of Noble Dames* [London: Osgood, McIlvaine, 1891] p. 91).
12. *After Strange Gods* (London: Faber and Faber, 1934) p. 58.
13. A deleted passage in the manuscript places the announcement of Willowes's death before Barbara's marriage to Uplandtowers (f. 34).
14. *A Group of Noble Dames* (1891) p. 103.
15. 'A Group of Noble Dames', *Spectator*, 67 (1891) 164. See also: 'Contemporary Literature', *National Review*, 17 (1891) 845; 'The Merry

Wives of Wessex', *Pall Mall Gazette* (8 July 1891) p. 2; and William Wallace, 'New Novels', *Academy*, 40 (1891) 153.

16. *Conversations in Ebury Street* (New York: Boni & Liveright, 1924) pp. 127–43.
17. Eliot, p. 58.
18. J. I. M. Stewart, *Thomas Hardy* (London: Longman, 1971) p. 37.
19. Brooks, pp. 145–6, and Morrell, p. 114.
20. Brooks, p. 144. Hardy may have got the idea for this sensational turn in his plot from the *Decameron*, where in two successive stories a young lover dies at an inconvenient moment, and the woman is forced to dispose of the body (4th day, stories 6 and 7).
21. 'A Group of Noble Dames', f. 58.
22. 'A Group of Noble Dames', f. 73.
23. 'A Group of Noble Dames', f. 133.
24. Wallace, p. 153.
25. The original title for *Tess* was 'Too Late Beloved' (Purdy, p. 72).
26. 'A Group of Noble Dames', *Graphic*, p. 12.
27. 'A Group of Noble Dames', f. 82.
28. The rhetorical finality of Hill's renunciation, with his appeal to 'God's law' (197), is not unlike Dimmesdale's initial refusal to flee with Hester, and Hawthorne even uses the terms 'passion' and 'principle' (found in the 1884 title of 'The Duchess of Hamptonshire') to describe Dimmesdale's predicament (*The Scarlet Letter* [1850; repr. Ohio State University Press, 1971] p. 200).
29. *Ghosts* was first published in Norwegian three years after the 1878 printing of 'The Duchess of Hamptonshire', and so I do not intend to suggest any influence here.
30. 'Benighted Travellers', *Harper's Weekly*, 25 (1881) 858.
31. 'Benighted Travellers', p. 827.
32. This mid-eighteenth-century Baxby must be a descendant of the seventeenth-century figure in 'Anna, Lady Baxby', as the late eighteenth-century Drenkhard who knows Uplandtowers and the one who also knows the Mottisfonts are of necessity in a later generation than the early seventeenth-century knight who married Lady Penelope. It is possible that Sir John Grebe and Stephen and Betty Fox are contemporary, but in that case, the 'old Duke of Hamptonshire' would have to be an antecedent of Emmeline's mid-nineteenth-century husband.
33. Hardy to Lord Lytton, 15 July 1891, in *CL*, I, 239.
34. Hardy to Alfred Austin, 14 June 1891, in *CL*, I, 238.
35. The burial scene on the *Western Glory* is based on a story about Emma Hardy's brother-in-law who was a curate during the cholera epidemic in Bristol, and who went to visit 'a charming young widow' whom he unknowingly had buried that morning (*EL*, 202).
36. 'Memoranda I', Oct. 1873, in Taylor, p. 14.
37. Ilchester, *Henry Fox*, I, pp. 46–7.
38. Ilchester, *The Home of the Hollands, 1605–1820* (London: John Murray, 1937) p. 35.
39. John Hutchins, *The History and Antiquities of the County of Dorset*, II

(Westminster: J. B. Nicols, 1861; repr. East Ardsley: E P Publishing, 1973) 665. Betty Dornell's epitaph for her husband, 'in which she described him as the best of husbands, fathers, and friends, and called herself his disconsolate widow' (48), constitutes an accurate paraphrasing of the inscription on Stephen Fox's monument (see Hutchins, II, p. 679).

40. Ilchester, *Henry Fox*, I, pp. 46–7.
41. Hutchins, II, p. 665.
42. Ilchester, *Henry Fox*, I, pp. 44–5.
43. Hutchins, II, p. 782.
44. Hutchins, IV (Westminster: J. B. Nichols, 1870; repr. East Ardsley: E P Publishing, 1973) p. 269.
45. Hutchins, IV, p. 271.
46. See: Edward, Earl of Clarendon, *The History of the Rebellion and Civil Wars in England* (Oxford: The Theatre, 1705) I, pp. 343–4; Alexander Chalmers, *The General Biographical Dictionary*, XII (London: J. Nicols, 1813) pp. 79–80; Hutchins, II, p. 789.
47. Hutchins, II, p. 789.
48. Hutchins, III (Westminster, 1868; repr. East Ardsley, 1973) p. 329. The plot also resembles the story of the beautiful Alatiel in the *Decameron* who sleeps with nine men before returning finally to the man who originally was intended to be her spouse (2nd day, 7th story).
49. Hutchins, III, p. 298.
50. Hutchins, III, p. 298.
51. Hutchins, III, pp. 671–2.
52. Hardy to Harper's, 7 Mar. 1890, quoted in Purdy, p. 66.
53. *Thomas Hardy* (London: Martin Secker, 1912; repr. New York: Russell & Russell, 1964) p. 86.
54. Hardy to *Pall Mall Gazette*, 10 July 1891, quoted in Michael Millgate's *Thomas Hardy: His Career as a Novelist* (New York: Random House, 1971) p. 289.
55. *An Essay on Hardy* (CUP, 1978) p. 194.

CHAPTER 3 **Life's Little Ironies:** TRAGEDIES OF CIRCUMSTANCE

1. 'Joseph Conrad and Thomas Hardy', in *The English Novelists*, ed. Derek Verschoyle (New York: Harcourt, Brace, 1936) p. 250.
2. 'The Tree of Knowledge', *New Review*, 10 (1894) 681.
3. Blathwayt, p. 240.
4. Blathwayt, p. 238.
5. Orel, pp. 126–7.
6. The characterization of Ella Marchmill seems to owe something to Hardy's meeting in May 1893 with Mrs Florence Henniker (*One Rare Fair Woman*, ed. Evelyn Hardy and F. B. Pinion [London: Macmillan, 1972] p. 38, n. 116). It is misleading to equate her with the fictional figure, however, and it was perhaps merely wish-fulfilment on Hardy's part to make Ella prefer the poet to her husband.

7. Since the appearance of *Madame Bovary* in 1856, such a character had become almost a convention in the popular literature of the time. Ella resembles the heroine of Mary Elizabeth Braddon's *The Doctor's Wife*, a married woman who falls in love with her own romantic image of a man.

8. Purdy, p. 60.

9. Hardy's treatment of this theme may owe something to Thomas Bailey Aldrich's famous story, 'Marjorie Daw' (1873), in which a young man falls in love, through descriptions of her in letters, with a woman who does not exist. Aldrich was editor of the *Atlantic Monthly* and corresponded occasionally with Hardy (see Millgate, pp. 183, 405).

10. The idea may have been suggested to Hardy by Ibsen's *The Lady from the Sea*, in which a child's eyes uncannily resemble those of his mother's former lover, whom she had seen while she was pregnant. In May 1890, Hardy wrote down in his notebook a summary of Havelock Ellis's account of the play in the *New Spirit* (see Millgate, p. 312).

11. Hardy read August Weismann's *Essays upon Heredity* in 1891 (W. R. Rutland, *Thomas Hardy* [Oxford: Basil Blackwell, 1938] p. 239).

12. This incident may have been suggested by Harrison Ainsworth's *Old St Paul's* (London: George Routledge, 1841), a favourite book of Hardy's youth, in which the heroine and her mother are described as suddenly resembling each other while they are parting, 'for intense emotion, whether of grief or joy, will bring out lines in the features that lie hidden at other times' (p. 229).

13. *Essai de Critique: Thomas Hardy, penseur et artiste* (Paris: Librairie Hachette, 1911) p. 164.

14. This detail is an echo of Mrs Jellyby's misdirected philanthropy in *Bleak House*.

15. 'Hardy's "A Tragedy of Two Ambitions"', *Explicator*, 14 (1956), item 55.

16. 'A Tragedy of Two Ambitions', f.1.

17. *Thomas Hardy* (1949; repr. New York: New Directions, 1964) p. 106.

18. Hardy to Gosse, 1 Aug. 1888, in *CL*, I, 179.

19. Kay-Robinson, p. 59.

20. Cornelius's reference to the Epistle is printed in the *Universal Review* version of the story, but is not present in the manuscript ('A Tragedy of Two Ambitions', *Universal Review*, 2 [1888] 559–60). It was presumably added, therefore, at the proof stage.

21. Edmond Rostand was to use the same letter-writing device in *Cyrano de Bergerac* (1897). In Sheridan's *The Rivals*, the situation is treated as pure farce.

22. *The Quintessence of Ibsenism* (1891; rev. edn London: Constable, 1913) p. xiii.

23. The story was forced to conform to Victorian proprieties for magazine publication (Edith Harnham was made a widow, and all references to Anna's pregnancy were removed). Norman Page has summarized the story's four 'distinct stages' of development (*Thomas Hardy* [London: Routledge & Kegan Paul, 1977] p. 127).

24. Until 1894, the story had read 'chamber' for 'bed-chamber'.

25. 'On the Western Circuit', f. 25; 'On the Western Circuit', *English*

Illustrated Magazine, 9 (1891) 285; *Life's Little Ironies* (1894) p. 115.

26. 'On the Western Circuit', f. 19; 'On the Western Circuit', *English Illustrated Magazine*, 283; *Life's Little Ironies* (1894) p. 107.

27. *Life's Little Ironies* (1894) p. 112.

28. In the manuscript, two alternate titles – 'The Amanuensis' and 'The Writer of the Letters' – were crossed out (f. 1). Hardy's choice of 'On the Western Circuit' widens the story's perspective by admitting into its scope the group of lovers, not just Edith.

29. See Edward C. Sampson, 'Thomas Hardy – Justice of the Peace', *Colby Library Quarterly*, 13 (1977) 263–74.

30. The word 'idle' is used repeatedly to describe Raye's professional and personal life, and was added at two stages of revision: in the sentence describing Raye's letter to Anna, 'which idly requested Anna to send him a tender answer' (123), the adverb 'idly' was added for the periodical version (p. 282), and in 1894, Edith's memory of the 'fascination' of Raye's touch was changed to 'the tenderness of his idle touch' (*Life's Little Ironies* [1894] p. 98).

31. James Joyce to Stanislaus Joyce, 3 Dec. 1906, in *Letters of James Joyce*, ed. Richard Ellmann, II (New York: Viking Press, 1966) p. 199.

32. *Mightier than the Sword* (London: Allen & Unwin, 1938) p. 135.

33. 'Thomas Hardy and Old Poole', *Thomas Hardy Year Book* (St. Peter Port, Guernsey: Toucan Press 1971) p. 86.

34. *OED*.

35. Hutchins, I (Westminster: J. B. Nichols, 1861; repr. East Ardsley: EP Publishing, 1973) pp. 14–15. The surnames of all four characters in 'To Please His Wife' were taken from monuments on the walls of St James's Church in Poole (Hutchins, I, 47–9).

36. The influence of Schopenhauer on Hardy, as he himself indicated in a letter to Helen Garwood (quoted in Walter F. Wright, *The Shaping of the Dynasts* [University of Nebraska Press, 1967] p. 38) must not be overemphasized, but the fact remains that Hardy was acquainted with Schopenhauer's writings as early as 1886 (Wright, pp. 39–40), and marked in his personal copy of *On the Fourfold Root of the Principle of Sufficient Reason* Schopenhauer's claim that the 'fundamental truth' of his doctrine is 'the complete separation between the will and the intellect' (Wright, p. 41), a concept that explains Car'line's uncontrollable urge 'to glide airily in the mazes of an infinite dance' (168) when in the presence of Mop Ollamoor.

37. The phrase 'She's throwed up the sperrits' was added in 1894.

38. In the periodical version Car'line is described as casting her 'questioning eyes upon him' (*Scribner's Magazine*, 13 [1893] 607), but the word 'questioning' was deleted in 1894 (*Life's Little Ironies* [1894] p. 199). It appears, therefore, that Hardy is attempting to make this exchange of glances a single moment of recognition for Car'line.

39. *OED*.

40. Diggory Venn tells Eustacia Vye that Wildeve can be twisted to her will 'like withywind' (*RN*, 105).

41. Under the subtitle 'A New Start', *Early Life* notes that the Great Exhibition of 1862 was Hardy's reason for moving to London (46).

42. This stability does not deny the existence of elements of disharmony in *Under the Greenwood Tree* – the disturbing presences of Grandfather James, Enoch, and the crazed Mrs Day – but the novel's conclusion is an affirmation of marriage and the family as institutions essential to the well-being of the community as a whole, and the sexual act is part there of a wider social ritual.

43. Miller (p. 23) has written the most interesting discussion of the music theme.

44. The same theme is explored in the mesmerizing organ-playing of Aeneas Manston, in the wild frenzy of the wedding supper in *Far from the Madding Crowd*, and in the country dances of *The Return of the Native* and *Tess*. When the image of dancing a reel is invoked by the Spirit of the Years in the forescene of *The Dynasts*, the movements of the dancers are compared to those of puppets animated by a manipulator of strings. In 'The Dance at the Phoenix', music and dancing are emblems of a subconscious and irrational force which can lure 'the single-hearted wife' (*CP*, 47) away from all domestic, maternal, and conjugal responsibilities.

45. 'The Immediate Stages of the Erotic or the Musical Erotic', in *Either/or*, trans. David F. Swenson and Lillian Marvin Swenson (1843; repr. Garden City, N.Y.: Doubleday, 1959) I, p. 72.

46. Hardy to Gosse, 3 Nov. 1907, *Ashley Library*, collected by Thomas James Wise, x (Edinburgh: Dunedin Press, 1930) p. 127.

47. Baker, p. 53.

48. *Thomas Hardy* (London: Longmans Green, 1954) p. 116.

49. 'Introduction: Notes on the Parish Historian', in *Great Short Works of Thomas Hardy* (New York: Harper & Row, 1967) p. xxiv.

50. See Brooks, p. 148, and Hynes, *The Pattern of Hardy's Poetry* (University of North Caroline Press, 1961) p. 81.

51. See Florence Emily Hardy to Sydney Cockerell, in *Friends of a Lifetime*, ed. Viola Meynell (London: Jonathan Cape, 1940) p. 305, where Hardy reported in 1919 that he had seen his grandfather's ghost.

52. *Ashley Library*, x, 123.

53. 'The Uncanny', pp. 238–41.

54. 'Memoranda I', Nov. 1878, in Taylor, p. 19.

55. *Life's Little Ironies* (London: Osgood, McIlvaine, 1896) p. vi. Hutchins notes that he was 'strongly imbued' from childhood 'with a feeling of attachment to the chase, which continued throughout his long life' (II, p. 305).

56. The image comes from details of an execution which Hardy heard about from his father (Flower, p. 92). Other aspects of the same incident are used in 'The Withered Arm'.

57. 'Facts' notebook, p. 97.

58. See also Millgate, p. 312.

59. See, for example, Baker, p. 53.

60. *Thomas Hardy* (London: Hodder & Stoughton, 1894) p. 212.

61. Brooks, p. 12.

62. Richards, p. 277.

63. *A Critical History of English Literature* (London: Secker & Warburg, 1960) II, p. 1073.
64. William Makepeace Thackeray, *Vanity Fair* (1848; repr. Boston: Houghton Mifflin, 1963) p. 5.
65. Thackeray, p. 152.
66. Thackeray, p. 140.
67. Thackeray, p. 5.
68. This situation parallels to some degree Hardy's own. *Early Life* records that Hardy's father, despite urging from his mother, 'had not the tradesman's soul', and refused to take 'more commodious premises nearer to or in the town' for the sake of business (26).

CHAPTER 4 MISCELLANEOUS STORIES: REFLECTIONS ON A CAREER

1. *The Well-Beloved* was published in 1897, but it had been serialized in 1892.
2. Purdy, pp. 301–2.
3. Purdy, p. 268.
4. Purdy, p. 293.
5. Purdy, p. 293.
6. Orel, p. 167.
7. *Young Thomas Hardy* (London: Heinemann, 1975) pp. 76–7.
8. Orel, p. 168.
9. See Millgate, pp. 17–18.
10. Purdy, p. 103.
11. Purdy, p. 103.
12. Robert Graves, *Good-bye to All That* (1929; rev. edn London: Cassell, 1957) p. 271.
13. The original text even contains such phonetic spellings as 'woone' and 'zeed' (printed in Lionel Johnson, *The Art of Thomas Hardy* [London: Elkin Mathews & John Lane, 1894] pp. lix–lxiv).
14. 'Plots for Five Unpublished Short Stories', pp. 35–6.
15. Hardy to William Tinsley, 9 Dec. 1873, in *CL*, I, 25.
16. Purdy, p. 294.
17. William Tinsley, *Random Recollections of an Old Publisher* (London: Simpkin, Marshall, Hamilton, Kent, 1900) I, p. 128.
18. Purdy, p. 294.
19. Purdy, p. 294.
20. Purdy, p. 294.
21. Purdy, p. 294.
22. Purdy, p. 99.
23. Purdy, p. 105.
24. Purdy, p. 294.
25. 'The Thieves Who Couldn't Help Sneezing', *Father Christmas* (1877) p. 3.
26. 'Thieves', p. 1.

27. 'An Indiscretion in the Life of an Heiress', *New Quarterly Magazine*, 10 (1878) 356.
28. Hardy to [Harper and Brothers?], 22 Mar. 1879, in *CL*, I, 63.
29. Purdy, p. 59.
30. Purdy, p. 156.
31. See Guerard, p. 84.
32. Orel, p. 173.
33. See E. T. A. Hoffmann's story, 'The King's Bride', in which a young maiden is lured away from her rural lover by a sinister Baron.
34. Quoted in Millgate, p. 283.
35. 'The Romantic Adventures of a Milkmaid', *Graphic*, summer no. (1883) 24; *A Changed Man* (London: Macmillan, 1913) p. 412.
36. Hardy to John Lane, 16 Sept. 1892, in *CL*, I, 284.
37. Hardy to unknown correspondent, 31 Jan. 1893, in 'Forty Years in an Author's Life: A Dozen Letters (1876–1915) from Thomas Hardy', *Colby Library Quarterly*, ser. 4 (1956) 110.
38. For details about Hardy's negotiations with the *Youth's Companion* and the story's 1892–3 publication in *The Household*, see Purdy, pp. 301–3, and *Our Exploits at West Poley*, ed. Purdy (London: OUP, 1952) pp. vii–xii.
39. Hardy to Perry Mason & Co., 5 Nov. 1883, in *CL*, I, 123.
40. *Our Exploits*, p. 1.
41. *Our Exploits*, p. 10.
42. *Our Exploits*, p. 97.
43. *Our Exploits*, p. 2.
44. *Our Exploits*, p. 98.
45. Purdy, p. 156, n. 2.
46. Taylor, pp. 237–8.
47. Hardy to Henniker, 1 Dec. 1893, in *One Rare Fair Woman*, p. 36.
48. 'Editor's Note' to 'Seven Tales', *The Portable Thomas Hardy* (Harmondsworth: Penguin, 1977) p. 5.
49. Purdy, p. 153.
50. 'The Spectre of the Real', a story which Hardy collaborated on with Florence Henniker in 1893, also contains an accidental drowning.
51. 'Facts' notebook, p. 51. See also p. 66.
52. *Hardy* (1963; repr. Edinburgh: Oliver & Boyd, 1966) p. 21.
53. It is probably one of the stories mentioned by Hardy in a letter to Sir George Douglas, 16 July 1887, in which he declined an invitation to Scotland because he would be 'clearing off some minor sketches which I have long promised to some of the magazines' (*CL*, I, 166).
54. *Dorset County Chronicle* (25 Dec. 1890) 10.
55. It seems dangerous to credit Weber's theory that Hardy wrote the core of 'The Intruder' in the early 1880s and 'added an expanded introduction' to that version in 1887, when *Murray's Magazine* requested a story ('Hardy's Uncollected Tales', in *Revenge Is Sweet* [Waterville, Maine: Colby Chapter of Phi Beta Kappa, 1940] pp. 11–12).
56. Elliott Felkin, 'Days with Thomas Hardy: From a 1918–1919 Diary', *Encounter*, 18 (Apr. 1962) 30.

57. 'Homeston Farm' ('The Waiting Supper', *Murray's Magazine*, 3 [1888] 66) is probably a derivative of 'Bhomston Farm', located close to Hardy's cottage at Higher Bockhampton. The change to 'Elsenford' suggests Nic's ability to 'ford' the meads, but also brings to mind Hamlet's castle at Elsinore – perhaps another reference to the indecisiveness of the lovers.
58. Hardy toned down Nic's language for the 1913 version: the sentence originally had read 'miserly' for 'stingy' and 'flatly' for 'positively' (*Murray's*, p. 52).
59. *The Modern Short Story* (1941; repr. London: Thomas Nelson, 1942) p. 40.
60. 'Facts' notebook, p. [82]. The plot may also be based on a story in the *Decameron* (10th day, story 9) in which a woman's first husband arrives on the scene just as she is marrying the second.
61. Hardy to Macmillan, 29 Feb. 1888, in *CL*, I, 174.
62. Leslie Stephen to Hardy, 19 Nov. 1880 (Dorset County Museum).
63. Hardy to Edward Marston, 1888[?], in *CL*, I, 171.
64. Purdy, pp. 59–60.
65. See Hardy to H. M. Alden, 7 Sept. 1888, in *CL*, I, 180.
66. Hardy to James R. Osgood, 6 Dec. 1888, in *CL*, I, 181.
67. Purdy, p. 62.
68. Purdy, p. 63.
69. Purdy, pp. 65–6.
70. Hardy to Arthur Locker, 28 Mar. 1889, in *CL*, I, 189.
71. Hardy to Locker, 1 Apr. 1889, in *CL*, I, 189.
72. Hardy to Florence Henniker, 22 Oct. 1893, in *One Rare Fair Woman*, pp. 29–30.
73. Hardy to Locker, 28 Mar. 1889, in *CL*, I, 189.
74. Hardy to Locker, 8 Apr. 1889, in *CL*, I, 190.
75. Hardy to Locker, 13 Nov. 1889, in *CL*, I, 201.
76. Hardy to Harper's, 7 Mar. 1890, quoted in Purdy, p. 66.
77. Locker to Hardy, 25 June 1889, quoted in Purdy, p. 66.
78. Hardy to Locker, 30 July 1890, in *CL*, I, 216. See also Hardy to Emma Lavinia Hardy, 24 July 1890, in *CL*, I, 215.
79. Purdy, p. 63.
80. Purdy, p. 67.
81. F. B. Pinion notes that the story 'appears to have been planned for *A Group of Noble Dames*' (*A Hardy Companion* [London: Macmillan, 1968] p. 94).
82. A footnote in Hutchins to the Horsey pedigree mentions the entry in the Poole register in which John Horsey was married to the widow of a Poole merchant, adding that 'no notice is taken of this marriage in the pedigree' (IV, 429, n. i). Hutchins also prints the passage from the Poole register which Hardy quotes in the story (I, 50).
83. 'Facts' notebook, pp. 35–6.
84. Hardy to Henniker, 30 June 1893, in *One Rare Fair Woman*, p. 9.
85. Hutchins, IV, 426–7.
86. Hardy to Harry Quilter, 24 July 1888, in *CL*, I, 178.
87. Purdy, pp. 81–2.
88. Hardy to John Lane, 30 June 1891, in *CL*, I, 239.

89. Purdy, pp. 81–2.
90. Purdy, pp. 94–5.
91. Hardy told Scribner's, 20 Nov. 1892, that he would think about sending them a story (*CL*, I, 289) and mailed the manuscript 13 Jan. 1893 (*LY*, 15).
92. Hardy to Henniker, 1 Dec. 1893, in *One Rare Fair Woman*, pp. 36–7.
93. Purdy, p. 85.
94. Purdy, p. 280.
95. Purdy, p. 281.
96. Purdy, p. 60.
97. Purdy, p. 280.
98. *The Journal of Mary Frampton*, ed. Harriot Georgiana Mundy (London: Sampson Low, Marston, Searle and Rivington, 1885) p. 94. See also Purdy, 'A Source for Hardy's "A Committee-Man of 'The Terror'" ' ', *Modern Language Notes*, 58 (1943) 554–5. There is an excision in the 'Facts' notebook at a point between passages that come before and after this source for the story in *The Journal of Mary Frampton* (p. [160]). It is likely, therefore, that Hardy did copy down this letter and later cut it out either to cover his tracks or simply to make use of the note. The newspaper article which M. B——shows to Mlle V——about British suspicion of Frenchmen in the country is taken almost verbatim from a notice in the 1803 *True Briton* which Hardy had copied down on the first page of the 'Trumpet-Major Notebook' (Taylor, p. 117).
99. Hardy to Henniker, 29 Nov. 1896, in *One Rare Fair Woman*, p. 57.
100. Udal notes that the Monmouth Rebellion is 'an event which never fails to stir the hearts of West Dorset folk' (p. 150).
101. 'The Grave by the Handpost', *Harper's Weekly*, 41 (1897), 1203.
102. Hardy described the custom in a note taken from *The Times* in 1882 ('Memoranda II', 25 May 1882, in Taylor, p. 24). The 'Facts' notebook records an incidence of this practice from J. F. Pennie's autobiography about the interment of a 'Girl who committed suicide' which reminded Hardy of a 'similar burial on Hendford Hill' (p. [4]).
103. The plot recalls Hardy's note about a widow who left five pounds to be buried near her husband but whose daughter 'said the money was not enough to pay for carrying the body . . . out there in the country; so the grave was filled in, and the woman buried where she died' (*LY*, 34).
104. Although 'Enter a Dragoon' was published after 'A Changed Man', its completion date was 1899. Hardy sent 'A Changed Man' to its publisher in early 1900 (Hardy to Clement Shorter, 29 Jan. 1900 [I am grateful to Professor Michael Millgate for bringing this letter to my attention in advance of its publication in the *Collected Letters*]).
105. See Hardy's letters to Handley Moule in *Early Life* (176) and *Later Years* (193–4). Handley Moule's account is in his *Memories of a Vicarage* (London: Religious Tract Society, 1913) pp. 32–3 and 57–9. Henry Moule's descriptions are recorded in his two letters to Prince Albert in *Paupers, Criminals and Cholera at Dorchester in 1854* (St Peter Port, Guernsey: Toucan Press, 1968).
106. Hardy to Sir Frederick Macmillan, 19 Aug. 1913 (British Library).

107. Purdy, p. 286.
108. Purdy, p. 156.
109. Hardy to Henniker, 22 July 1898, *One Rare Fair Woman*, p. 168.
110. Hardy to W. M. Colles, 31 Mar. 1914 (British Library).
111. Cancelled preface to *A Changed Man*, quoted in *TLS* (25 Sept. 1913) 402.
112. Hardy to Sydney Cockerell, 13 Sept. 1913, in *Friends of a Lifetime*, p. 276. See also Hardy to Sir George Douglas, 27 Aug. 1913 (British Library), and Hardy to Colles, 31 Mar. 1914 (British Library).
113. *Hardy and the Lady from Madison Square*, p. 236.
114. In his preface to *A Changed Man*, Hardy thanks all 'the proprietors and editors of the newspapers and magazines' (vii) who had sent him copies of stories. One of these was 'What the Shepherd Saw', which Hardy had lost, and which was supplied by Macmillan (Hardy to Maurice Macmillan, 6 Aug. 1913 [British Library]).
115. Hardy to Henniker, 2 Nov. 1913, in *One Rare Fair Woman*, p. 156. See also: Hardy to Maurice Macmillan, 6 Aug. 1913 (British Library); Hardy to Douglas, 27 Aug. 1913 (British Library); Hardy to Cockerell, 3 Sept. 1913, in *Friends of a Lifetime*, p. 276; Hardy to Colles, 31 Mar. 1914 (British Library).
116. Most of the work must have been done between 6 Aug. 1913, when Hardy said he was not sure about having the stories ready in time (Hardy to Maurice Macmillan [British Library]), and 19 Aug. 1913, when he sent *A Changed Man* to Macmillan (Hardy to Sir Frederick Macmillan [British Library]).
117. Purdy, p. 154.
118. Purdy, p. 284.
119. Hardy to Sir Frederick Macmillan, 19 Aug. 1913 (British Library).
120. Hardy to Sir Frederick Macmillan, 14 Dec. 1913 (British Library).
121. Purdy, p. 284.
122. Hardy to Sir Frederick Macmillan, 14 Dec. 1913 (British Library).
123. Hardy to Sir Frederick Macmillan, 14 Dec. 1913 (British Library).
124. Purdy, p. 299.
125. See: Purdy, p. 299; Pinion, p. 81; Weber, 'Hardy's Uncollected Tales', p. 14. For discussions of the historical circumstances on which the story is based, see Rev. Canon Herbert Pentin, 'The Old Town of Milton Abbey', *Proc. of the Dorset Field and Antiquarian Club*, 25 (1904) 1–7, and his 'Thomas Hardy and Milton Abbey', *Colby Library Quarterly*, ser. 3 (1954) 262–4.
126. Purdy, pp. 287–8.
127. Purdy, p. 286. Millgate suggests, however, that 'it is possible that some corrections sent for the re-set Mellstock were deemed insufficiently important to justify shifting the existing type of the Wessex edition' ('The Making and Unmaking of Hardy's Wessex Edition', in *Editing Nineteenth-Century Fiction*, ed. Jane Millgate [New York: Garland, 1978] p. 73).
128. 'The Making and Unmaking of the Wessex Edition', p. 72.
129. *Old Mrs. Chundle and Other Stories*, ed. F. B. Pinion (London: Macmillan, 1977).

130. See Wilfred Gibson, 'Hardy's Short Stories', *Bookman*, 74 (1928) 149, and Wing, p. 17.
131. See Janice Stewart Bohi, 'Thomas Hardy's Short Stories: A Critical Approach', Diss. Case Western Reserve 1973, and Alexander Fischler, 'Thomas Hardy's Short Stories: Their Relation to Major Trends and Interests in the Criticism of His Works', Diss. Washington 1961.
132. Page, p. 123.
133. 'Hardy and His Thrush', in *The Freedom of the Poet* (New York: Farrar, Straus & Giroux, 1976) p. 243.
134. See: Abercrombie, p. 78; Bayley, pp. 223–5; Edmund Blunden, *Thomas Hardy* (1942; repr. London: Macmillan, 1951) pp. 204–5; Cecil, p. 53, n. 1; Evelyn Hardy, *Thomas Hardy* (London, 1954; repr. New York: Russell & Russell, 1970) pp. 183–4; Harris, p. 48; Arthur S. McDowall, *Thomas Hardy* (London: Faber and Faber, 1931) pp. 59–60; and William Minto, 'The Work of Thomas Hardy', *Bookman*, I (1891) 101.
135. See Henry Seidel Canby and Alfred Dashiell, *A Study of the Short Story* (1913; rev. edn New York: Henry Holt, 1935) p. 46; Bates, *The Modern Short Story*, p. 41; and Beachcroft, pp. 113–14.
136. 'Introduction: The Short Story', in *Faber Book of Modern Stories* (London: Faber and Faber, 1937) p. 8. See also: Hynes, 'Introduction: Notes on the Parish Historian', p. xxiii; Frederick Wedmore, 'The Short Story', *Nineteenth Century*, 43 (1898) 407; and Cornelius Weygandt, 'The Mastery of Thomas Hardy', in *A Century of the English Novel* (New York: Century, 1925) p. 227.
137. Orel, p. 120.
138. Rev. of *Twice-Told Tales* and *Mosses from an Old Manse*, in *Complete Works of Edgar Allan Poe*, ed. James A. Harrison (1847; repr. New York: AMS Press 1965) XIII, 153.
139. *The Craft of Fiction* (1921; repr. London: Jonathan Cape 1960) p. 40.
140. Howe, p. 76. See also: Walter E. Allen, *Some Aspects of the American Short Story* (London: OUP, 1973) p. 4; Richard C. Carpenter, *Thomas Hardy* (New York: Twayne, 1964) pp. 69–70; and Frank O'Connor, p. 174.
141. Howe, p. 79.
142. Coppard reports that after he read *Life's Little Ironies*, 'it was clear to me that my real mission in life was to write not poetry any more but short stories' ('On First Getting into Print', *Colophon*, Part 6 [1931] n. pag.).
143. Foreword to *The Collected Tales of A. E. Coppard* (New York: Alfred A. Knopf 1948) p. viii.
144. Cassis, p. 287.

A Selected Bibliography

Abercrombie, Lascelles, *Thomas Hardy: A Critical Study* (London: Martin Secker, 1912; repr. New York: Russell & Russell, 1964).

Allen, Walter E., *Some Aspects of the American Short Story* (London: OUP, 1973).

Baker, Ernest A., *The History of the English Novel*, vol. IX (London: H. F. & G. Witherby, 1938).

Bartlett, Phyllis, 'Hardy's Shelley', *Keats-Shelley Journal*, 4 (1955) 15–29.

——, '"Seraph of Heaven": A Shelleyan Dream in Hardy's Fiction', *PMLA*, 70 (1955) 624–35.

Bates, H. E., *The Modern Short Story: A Critical Survey* (1941; repr. London: Thomas Nelson, 1942).

Bayley, John, *An Essay on Hardy* (Cambridge University Press, 1978).

Beach, Joseph Warren, 'The Short Story', in *A History of English Literature*, ed. Hardin Craig (New York: Oxford University Press, 1950) pp. 604–8.

Beachcroft, T. O., *The English Short Story*, 2 vols (London: Longmans Green, 1964).

——, *The Modest Art: A Survey of the Short Story in English* (London: OUP, 1968).

Benazon, Michael, '"The Romantic Adventures of a Milkmaid": Hardy's Modern Romance', *English Studies in Canada*, 5 (1979) 56–65.

Blathwayt, Raymond, 'A Chat with the Author of "Tess"', *Black and White*, 4 (1892) 238–40.

Blunden, Edmund, *Thomas Hardy* (1942; repr. London: Macmillan, 1951).

Bowen, Elizabeth, 'Introduction: The Short Story', in *Faber Book of Modern Stories* (London: Faber and Faber, 1937) pp. 7–19.

Brooks, Jean R., *Thomas Hardy: The Poetic Structure* (London: Paul Elek, 1971).

Brooks, Philip, 'Notes on Rare Books', rev. of 'The Thieves Who Couldn't Help Sneezing', *New York Times Book Review*, 13 Dec. 1942, p. 34.

Brown, Douglas, *Thomas Hardy* (London: Longman, 1954).

Canby, Henry Seidel, *The Short Story in English* (New York: Henry Holt, 1909).

Canby, Henry Seidel and Alfred Dashiell, *A Study of the Short Story* (1913; rev. edn New York: Henry Holt, 1935).

Carpenter, Richard C., 'How to Read *A Few Crusted Characters*', in *Critical Approaches to the Fiction of Thomas Hardy*, ed. Dale Kramer (London: Macmillan, 1979) pp. 155–71.

——, *Thomas Hardy* (New York: Twayne Publishers, 1964).

Carter, Angela, 'The Heroines of Hardy: Women Struggling to Love', *Radio Times*, 22 Nov. 1973, pp. 54–59.

Cassis, A. F., 'A Note on the Structure of Hardy's Short Stories', *Colby Library Quarterly*, 10th ser. (1974) pp. 287–96.

Cecil, Lord David, *Hardy the Novelist: An Essay in Criticism* (1943; repr. London: Constable 1965).

Cockerell, Sydney, 'Early Hardy Stories', *TLS*, 14 Mar. 1935, p. 160.

'Contemporary Literature', rev. of *A Group of Noble Dames*, *National Review*, 17 (1891) 838–48.

Cotterel, George, rev. of *Three Notable Stories* in *Academy*, 38 (1890) 88.

Cramer, Jeffrey S., 'Hardy, Henniker, and "The Spectre of the Real"', *Thomas Hardy Society Review*, 1 (1977) 89–91.

'Editor's Study', rev. of *A Group of Noble Dames* in *Harper's New Monthly Magazine*, 83 (1891) 641–2.

Ellis, S. M., 'Thomas Hardy: Some Personal Recollections', *Fortnightly Review*, NS 123 (1928) 393–406.

Felkin, Elliott, 'Days with Thomas Hardy: From a 1918–1919 Diary', *Encounter*, 18 (Apr. 1962) 27–33.

'Fiction', rev. of *A Group of Noble Dames* in *Speaker*, 3 (1891) 683.

'Fiction', rev. of *A Group of Noble Dames* and *The Well-Beloved* in *Athenaeum*, no. 4437, 9 Nov. 1912, p. 553.

'Fiction', rev. of *Wessex Tales* and *A Pair of Blue Eyes* in *Athenaeum*, no. 4424, 7 Sept. 1912, p. 244.

Firor, Ruth A., *Folkways in Thomas Hardy* (1922; repr. Phila.: University of Pennsylvania Press, 1931).

Fischler, Alexander, 'Theatrical Techniques in Thomas Hardy's Short Stories', *Studies in Short Fiction*, 3 (1966) 435–45.

Gatrell, Simon, 'Thomas Hardy and the Dance', *Thomas Hardy Year Book 1975* (St Peter Port, Guernsey: Toucan Press) pp. 42–7.

Gerber, Helmut E., 'Hardy's "A Tragedy of Two Ambitions"', *Explicator*, 14 (1956) item 55.

Gibson, Wilfred, 'Hardy's Short Stories', *Bookman*, 74 (1928) 148–9.

Giordano, Frank R., Jr, 'Characterization and Conflict in Hardy's "The Fiddler of the Reels"', *Texas Studies in Literature and Language*, 17 (1975) 617–33.

Gittings, Robert, *Thomas Hardy's Later Years* (Boston: Little, Brown & Co., 1978).

——, *Young Thomas Hardy* (London: Heinemann, 1975).

Gosse, Edmund. 'Thomas Hardy's Lost Novel', *Sunday Times*, 22 Jan. 1928, p. 8.

Green, David Bonnell, 'The First Publication of "The Spectre of the Real"', *Library*, 15 (1960) 60–1.

'A Group of Noble Dames', *Literary World*, 43 (1891) 556–8.

'A Group of Noble Dames', *Spectator*, 67 (1891) 163–4.

Guerard, Albert J., *Thomas Hardy* (1949; repr. New York: New Directions, 1964).

Hardy, Evelyn, *Thomas Hardy* (London: Hogarth Press, 1954; repr. New York: Russell & Russell, 1970).

Hardy, Florence Emily, *The Early Life of Thomas Hardy, 1840–1891* (London: Macmillan, 1928).

——, *The Later Years of Thomas Hardy, 1892–1928* (London: Macmillan, 1930).

Hardy, Thomas, *The Collected Letters of Thomas Hardy*, ed. Richard Little Purdy and Michael Millgate, 2 vols (I, Oxford: Clarendon Press, 1978; vol. II, Oxford: Clarendon Press, 1980). See also forthcoming volumes.

——, *The Literary Notes of Thomas Hardy*, ed. Lennart A. Björk, vol. I, Göteborg, Sweden: Acta Universitatis Gothoburgensis, 1974).

——, *One Rare Fair Woman: Thomas Hardy's Letters to Florence Henniker, 1893–1922*, ed. Evelyn Hardy and F. B. Pinion (London: Macmillan, 1972).

——, *The Personal Notebooks of Thomas Hardy*, ed. Richard H. Taylor (London: Macmillan, 1979).

——, 'Plots for Five Unpublished Stories', ed. Evelyn Hardy, *London Magazine*, 5 (1958) 33–45.

——, *Thomas Hardy's Notebooks and Some Letters from Julia*

Augusta Martin, ed. Evelyn Hardy (London: Hogarth Press, 1955).

——, *Thomas Hardy's Personal Writings*, ed. Harold Orel (Lawrence: Kansas University Press, 1966; London: Macmillan 1963).

'Hardy's and Black's Latest', rev. of *A Group of Noble Dames* in *Literary Opinion*, 7 (July 1891) 17–18.

Harris, Wendell V., 'English Short Fiction in the Nineteenth Century', *Studies in Short Fiction*, 6 (1968) 1–93.

Hedgcock, F. A., *Essai de Critique: Thomas Hardy penseur et artiste* (Paris: Librairie Hachette, 1911).

Hornback, Bert G., *The Metaphor of Chance: Vision and Technique in the Works of Thomas Hardy* (Ohio University Press, 1971).

Howe, Irving, 'A Note on Hardy's Stories', *Hudson Review*, 19 (1966) 259–66.

——, *Thomas Hardy* (New York: Macmillan, 1967).

Hynes, Samuel, 'Introduction: Notes on the Parish Historian', in *Great Short Works of Thomas Hardy* (New York: Harper & Row, 1967) pp. vii–xxvii.

——, *The Pattern of Hardy's Poetry* (University of North Carolina Press, 1961).

Johnstone, F. V., 'Thomas Hardy and Old Poole', *Thomas Hardy Year Book 1971* (St Peter Port, Guernsey: Toucan Press) pp. 84–7.

Jones, Lawrence, 'The Music Scenes in *The Poor Man and the Lady*, *Desperate Remedies*, and *An Indiscretion in the Life of an Heiress*', *Notes and Queries*, n.s. 24 (1977) 32–4.

Kay-Robinson, Denys, *Hardy's Wessex Re-appraised* (Newton Abbot: David & Charles, 1972).

——, 'The Lower Longpuddle Mystery', *Thomas Hardy Year Book 1973–74* (St Peter Port, Guernsey: Toucan Press) pp. 77–80.

Larkin, Peter, 'Irony and Fulfillment in Hardy's "A Mere Interlude"', *Journal of the Eighteen Nineties Society*, no. 9 (1978) pp. 16–21.

Lea, Hermann, *Thomas Hardy's Wessex* (London: Macmillan, 1913).

'Literature of the Day', rev. of 'The Romantic Adventures of a Milkmaid' in *Lippincott's Magazine*, 32 (Sept. 1883) 334–6.

Macdonnell, Annie, *Thomas Hardy* (London: Hodder & Stoughton, 1894).

McDowall, Arthur S., *Thomas Hardy: A Critical Study* (London: Faber and Faber, 1931).

McGrath, Fergal, rev. of *The Short Stories of Thomas Hardy* in *Studies: An Irish Quarterly Review of Letters, Philosophy and Science*, 17 (1928) 504–5.

Matthews, Brander, *The Philosophy of the Short-story* (1884; rev. edn 1888; repr. London: Longmans Green, 1912).

Maugham, William Somerset, 'The Short Story', *Essays by Divers Hands: Transactions of the Royal Society of Literature of the United Kingdom*, ed. Edward Marsh, NS 25 (1950) 120–34.

May, Charles E., 'Hardy's Diabolical *Dames*: A Generic Consideration', *Genre*, 7 (1974) 307–21.

'The Merry Wives of Wessex', *Pall Mall Gazette*, 10 July 1891, p. 2.

Miller, J. Hillis, *Thomas Hardy: Distance and Desire* (Cambridge, Mass: Belknap Press of Harvard University Press, 1970).

Millgate, Michael, 'Hardy's Fiction: Some Comments on the Present State of Criticism', *English Literature in Transition*, 14 (1971) 230–6.

——, 'The Making and Unmaking of Hardy's Wessex Edition', *Editing Nineteenth-Century Fiction*, ed. Jane Millgate (New York: Garland, 1978) pp. 61–82.

——, *Thomas Hardy: His Career as a Novelist* (New York: Random House, 1971).

Minto, William, 'The Work of Thomas Hardy', *Bookman*, 1 (1891) 99–101.

'The Modern Short Story', *TLS*, 29 Jan. 1925, pp. 61–2.

Morley, Christopher, 'An Indiscretion', *Saturday Review*, 11 (1934–35) 551.

Morrell, Roy, *Thomas Hardy: The Will and the Way* (Kuala Lumpur: University of Malaya Press, 1965).

Moynahan, Julian, 'Editor's Introduction', in *The Portable Thomas Hardy* (Harmondsworth: Penguin, 1977) pp. xiii–xxxii.

——, 'Editor's Note' to 'Seven Tales', in *The Portable Thomas Hardy* (Harmondsworth: Penguin, 1977) pp. 3–6.

'New Books and Reprints', rev. of *A Group of Noble Dames* in *Saturday Review*, 71 (1891) 757–8.

'Novels of the Week', rev. of *A Group of Noble Dames* in *Athenaeum*, no. 3323 (1891) 35–6.

O'Connor, Frank, *The Lonely Voice: A Study of the Short Story* (New York: World Publishing Co., 1963; London: Macmillan 1963).

O'Connor, William Van, 'Cosmic Irony in Hardy's "The Three Strangers"', *English Journal*, 47 (1958) 248–54, 262.

O'Faolain, Sean, *The Short Story* (New York: Devin-Adair Co., 1951).

Page, Norman, 'Hardy's Short Stories: A Reconsideration', *Studies in Short Fiction*, 11 (1974) 75–84.

——, *Thomas Hardy* (London: Routledge & Kegan Paul, 1977).

Pain, Barry, *The Short Story* (London: Martin Secker, 1916).

Pentin, Herbert, 'The Old Town of Milton Abbey', *Proceedings of the Dorset Natural History and Antiquarian Field Club*, 25 (1904) 1–7.

——, 'Thomas Hardy and Milton Abbey', *Colby Library Quarterly*, 3rd ser. (1954) pp. 262–4.

Pinion, F. B., *A Hardy Companion: A Guide to the Works of Thomas Hardy and Their Background* (London: Macmillan, 1968).

——, (ed.), *'Life's Little Ironies' and 'A Changed Man'* (London: Macmillan, 1977).

——, (ed.), *Old Mrs. Chundle and Other Stories, with the Famous Tragedy of the Queen of Cornwall* (London: Macmillan, 1977).

——, *Thomas Hardy: Art and Thought* (London: Macmillan, 1977).

——, (ed.), *'Wessex Tales' and 'A Group of Noble Dames'* (London: Macmillan, 1977).

Purdy, Richard Little, introd. to *Our Exploits at West Poley*, ed. Richard Little Purdy (London: OUP, 1952).

——, 'A Source for Hardy's "A Committee-Man of 'The Terror'"', *Modern Language Notes*, 58 (1943) 554–5.

——, *Thomas Hardy: A Bibliographical Study* (1954; rev. edn Oxford: Clarendon Press, 1968).

——, 'Thomas Hardy and Florence Henniker: The Writing of "The Spectre of the Real"', *Colby Library Quarterly*, 1st ser. (1944) pp. 122–6.

Quinn, Maire A., 'Thomas Hardy and the Short Story', in *Budmouth Essays on Thomas Hardy: Papers Presented at the 1975 Summer School*, ed. F. B. Pinion (Dorchester: Thomas Hardy Society, 1976) pp. 74–85.

'Recent Fiction', rev. of *A Group of Noble Dames* in *Critic*, 16 (1891) 128.

'Recent Novels', rev. of *A Group of Noble Dames* in *Nation*, 53 (1891) 72.

Reilley, J. J., 'Short Stories of Thomas Hardy', *Catholic World*, 128 (1929) 407–15.

Richards, Mary Caroline, 'Thomas Hardy's Ironic Vision', *The Trollopian*, 3 (1949) 265–79, and *Nineteenth-Century Fiction*, 4 (1949) 21–35.

Roberts, James L., 'Legend and Symbol in Hardy's "The Three Strangers"', *Nineteenth-Century Fiction*, 17 (1962) 191–4.

Rutland, William, *Thomas Hardy: A Study of His Writings and Their Background* (Oxford: Basil Blackwell, 1938).

Ryan, Michael, 'One Name of Many Shapes: *The Well-Beloved*', in *Critical Approaches to the Fiction of Thomas Hardy*, ed. Dale Kramer (London: Macmillan, 1979) pp. 172–92.

Sandison, Helen E., 'An Elizabethan Basis for a Hardy Tale?', *PMLA*, 54 (1939) 610–12.

Scott, James F., 'Thomas Hardy's Use of the Gothic: An Examination of Five Representative Works', *Nineteenth-Century Fiction*, 17 (1963) 363–80.

Shanks, Edward, 'Reviews: Thomas Hardy', rev. of *The Short Stories of Thomas Hardy* in *Saturday Review*, 145 (1928) 495.

Short, Clarice, 'Thomas Hardy and the Military Man', *Nineteenth-Century Fiction*, 4 (1949) 129–35.

'Six Volumes of Short Stories', rev. of *A Group of Noble Dames* in *Book Buyer*, 8 (1891) 261–2.

'The Soldiers of Thomas Hardy', *TLS*, 27 Aug. 1914, p. 401.

Stewart, J. I. M., *Thomas Hardy: A Critical Biography* (London: Longman, 1971).

Thomas Hardy and His Readers: A Selection of Contemporary Reviews, ed. Laurence Lerner and John Holstrom (London: Bodley Head, 1968).

Thomas Hardy: The Critical Heritage, ed. R. J. Cox (London: Routledge & Kegan Paul, 1970).

Wallace, William, 'New Novels', rev. of *A Group of Noble Dames* in *Academy*, 40 (1891) 152–3.

Weber, Carl J., 'An Elizabethan Basis for a Hardy Tale? – An Addendum', *PMLA*, 56 (1941) 598–600.

——, 'Hardy's Uncollected Tales', in *Revenge Is Sweet: Two Short Stories by Thomas Hardy* (Waterville, Maine: Colby

Chapter of Phi Beta Kappa, 1940) pp. 7–16.
——, introd. to Thomas Hardy, *An Indiscretion in the Life of an Heiress* (1935; repr. New York: Russell & Russell, 1965) pp. 1–20.
——, 'A Masquerade of Noble Dames', *PMLA*, 58 (1943) 558–63.
Wedmore, Frederick, 'The Short-story', *Nineteenth Century*, 43 (1898) 406–16.
Wells, Herbert George, introd. to *The Country of the Blind and Other Stories* (London: Thomas Nelson, 1911) pp. iii–ix.
Weygandt, Cornelius, 'The Mastery of Thomas Hardy', in *A Century of the English Novel, Being a Consideration of the Place in English Literature of the Long Story; Together with an Estimate of its Writers from the Heyday of Scott to the Death of Conrad* (New York: Century, 1925) pp. 211–28.
Wing, George, *Hardy* (1963; repr. Edinburgh: Oliver & Boyd, 1966).
——, 'Tess and the Romantic Milkmaid', *Review of English Literature*, 3 (1962) 22–30.

Index

Abercrombie, Lascelles, 89, 209n.53, 218n.134
'Absent-Mindedness in a Parish Choir', 142, 146, *148*, 150
Academy, The, 67–8; 208nn.15, 24
Ainsworth, Harrison, 207n.10, 210n.12
'Alarm, The', 162
Albert, Prince, 216n.105
Alden, H. M., 215n.65
Aldrich, Thomas Bailey, 210n.9
'Alicia's Diary', 157, *173–5*
Allen, Walter E., 218n.140
'Alonzo the Brave and Fair Imogine', 112
'Amabel', 159
'Amanuensis, The', 211n.28; *see also* 'On the Western Circuit'
'Ancient Earthworks and What Two Enthusiastic Scientists Found Therein', 171; *see also* 'Tryst at an Ancient Earthwork, A'
'Ancient Earthworks at Casterbridge', 171; *see also* 'Tryst at an Ancient Earthwork'
'Andrey Satchel and the Parson and Clerk', 143, *146–7*, 150, 151, 193–4, 212n.55
'Anna, Lady Baxby', *76–8*, 80, 84, 86–7 (historical sources), 91, 92, 183, 208n.32
Archer, William, 43–4, 206n.56
Ashley Library, The, 212nn.46, 52
'At Shag's Heath', 188
Atlantic Monthly, 210n.9
Austin, Alfred, 208n.34

Baker, Ernest, 32, 141, 206n.51; 212nn.47, 59

'Barbara (Daughter of Sir John Grebe)', 183; *see also* 'Barbara of the House of Grebe'
'Barbara of the House of Grebe', *57–62*, 64, 69, 74, 76, 78, 80–1, 84, 88 (historical sources), 91–2, 136, 175, 183, 198; 207nn.11, 13; 208n.32
Barnes, William, 47, 49, 160, 206n.65, 207n.73
Bates, H. E., 95, 179, 209n.1, 215n.59, 218n.135
Bayley, John, 93, 209n.55, 218n.134
Beachcroft, T. O., 203n.2, 218n.135
'Beauty and the Beast', 62
Bedford, 5th Earl of (William Russell; later 1st Duke of Bedford), 86–7
Beethoven, Ludwig van, 110
'Benighted Travellers', 165, 183; 208nn.30, 31; *see also* 'Honourable Laura, The'
Berryman, John, 198, 218n.133
Bible, references to, 34, 36, 39, 43, 65, 94, 100, 101, 116, 118, 130
Black and White, 207n.4; 209nn.3, 4
Blackwood, William, 203n.10, 205n.45
Blackwood's Edinburgh Magazine, 22, 204–5n.32, 205–6n.47
Blathwayt, Raymond, 207n.4; 209nn.3, 4
Blomfield, Arthur, 158
Blunden, Edmund, 218n.134
Boccaccio, Giovanni, 84, 90, 208n.20, 215n.60
Bohi, Janice Stewart, 218n.131
Bookman, The, 218nn.130, 134
Bowen, Elizabeth, 198, 218n.136

Braddon, Mary Elizabeth, 210n.7
'Bride-Night Fire, The', 159–60,
    162, 213n.13
Bristol, 2nd Earl of (George Digby),
    86–7
British   Library,   216n.106;
    217nn.110, 112, 114, 115, 116,
    119, 120, 122, 123
British Museum, *see* British Library
Brontë, Emily, 42
Brooks, Jean R., 35, 153, 206n.52;
    208nn.19, 20; 212nn.50, 61
Brown, Douglas, 141, 212n.48
Browning, Robert, 33, 174, 176
Bunyan, John, 33, 143
Bürger, Gottfried Augustus, 112
Butler, Rev. William, 146, 212n.55
Byron, Lord (George Gordon), 70,
    166

Canby, Henry Seidel, 218n.135
'Candour in English Fiction', 97,
    209n.5
Carlyle, Jane Welsh, 184
Carpenter, Richard C., 218n.140
Cassis, A. F., 47–8, 200, 206n.66,
    218n.144
Cecil, Lord David, 52–3, 207n.5,
    218n.134
Chalmers, Alexander, 209n.46
Chambers's Journal, 158
'Changed Man, A', 157, *190–3*;
    216nn.104, 105
Changed Man, A, xii, 157, 158, 164,
    168–9, 176, 187, 193, 194–6
    (publishing history), 214n.35;
    217nn.111, 114, 116
Charles   Scribner's   Sons,   *see*
    Scribner's Sons, Charles
Chaucer, Geoffrey, 64, 90, 93
Chekhov, Anton, 199–200
'Christmas Reminiscence, A', 189;
    see also 'Grave by the Handpost,
    The'
'Cinderella', 167
Clarendon, 1st Earl of (Edward
    Hyde), 209n.46
Clemens, Samuel Langhorne, *see*
    Twain, Mark

Clodd, Edward, 145, 207n.2, 212n.
    52
Cockerell, Sydney Sir, 212n.51;
    217nn.112, 115
*Collected Letters of Thomas Hardy,
    The* (eds Richard Little Purdy
    and Michael Millgate), 203–16
    passim
Colles, W. M., 217nn.110, 115
'Committee-Man of "The Terror",
    A', 157, *186–7*, 216n.98
Complete Poems of Thomas Hardy, The,
    ed. James Gibson, xii, 114
Cooper, Anthony Ashley, *see* Shaf-
    tesbury, 5th Earl of
Cooper, Helen, 4, 204n.14
Coppard, A. E., 200; 218nn.142,
    143
Cornhill Magazine, 161
Crabbe, George, 180

Daiches, David, 154, 213n.63
Damer, Joseph, *see* Milton, Lord
'Dance at the Phoenix, The', 162,
    212n.44
Dante Alighieri, 127, 135
Darcy, Lady Penelope, 87–8
Dashiell, Alfred, 218n.135
Davidson, Donald, 206n.61
Defoe, Daniel, 13
'Demon Lover, The', 136, 166, 167,
    168
Desperate Remedies, 106, 160, 161,
    212n.44
'Destiny and a Blue Cloak', 157,
    160–2, 163, 165, 196
Dickens, Charles, 138, 148, 158,
    189, 210n.14
Digby, George, *see* Bristol, 2nd Earl
    of
'Distracted   Preacher,   The',   3,
    37–40, 40–1, 82, 164, 181, 189,
    193,   203–4n.11,   204n.13,
    206n.54
'Distracted Young Preacher, The',
    164; *see also* 'Distracted Preacher,
    The'
'Doctor's Legend, The', 158, 196,
    217n.125

Dorset County Chronicle, 175, 176, 179, 214n.54
Dorset County Museum, 215n.62
'Dorsetshire Labourer, The', 2, 10, 45, 60, 166; 203nn.4, 6, 7; 204nn. 20, 21; 206n.58, 214n.32
Douglas, Sir George, 217nn.112, 115
'Duchess of Hamptonshire, The', *80–3*, 84, 85, 92, 163, 183; 208nn.28, 29, 32, 35
'Duke's Reappearance, The', 157, *187–8*
Dynasts, The, 162, 212n.44

Early Life of Thomas Hardy, The, xii, 32–216 *passim*
Eliot, George, 105, 117, 137, 145
Eliot, T. S., 60, 62, 207n.12, 208n.17
Ellis, Havelock, 210n.10
Ellis, S. M., 204n.29, 205n.34
'Emmeline; or Passion versus Principle', 163; *see also* 'Duchess of Hamptonshire, The'
Empson, William, 4; 204nn.14, 15
English Illustrated Magazine, 171, 210–11n.25, 211n.26
'Enter a Dragoon', 157, 186, *189–90*, 193, 216n.104
Erskine, Lord (Thomas Erskine, 1750–1823), 184

'Facts' notebook, 149, 172, 179–80, 184, 204n.13, 212n.57, 214n.51; 215nn.60, 83; 216nn.98, 102
Far from the Madding Crowd, xii, 36, 136–7, 160–1, 175, 181, 212n.44
Father Christmas, 163; 213nn.25, 26
Faulkner, William, 19
Felkin, Elliott, 214n.56
'Fellow-Townsmen', 2–3, *28–33*, 35, 37, 40, 41, 43, 47, 79, 161, 164, 172, 181; 205nn.46, 47; 206nn.48, 49
'Few Crusted Characters, A', 91, 95, *141–52*, 176, 181, 186, 194
'Fiddler of the Reels, The', 95, 118, *132–41*, 151–2, 162, 166, 169, 185, 198; 211nn.36, 37, 38, 40,

41; 212nn.42, 43, 44; 216n.91
'Fire at Tranter Sweatley's, The', 159; *see also* 'Bride-Night Fire, The'
Firor, Ruth, 11, 204n.23; 205nn.38, 42
'First Countess of Wessex, The', 51, 53, *54–7*, 58, 62, 76, 78, 80–1, 83, 84, 85–6 (historical sources), 90, 91, 182, 183, 198; 207nn.6, 8, 10; 208nn.32, 39
Fischler, Alexander, 218n.131
'Fisherman and His Wife, The', 131
Flaubert, Gustave, 121, 206n.49, 210n.7
Flower, Newman, 28, 205n.44, 212n.56
'For Conscience' Sake', 38, *109–13*, 120, 128, 152, 154, 185, 190; 210nn.12, 14
Ford, Ford Madox, 127–8, 211n.32
Fortnightly Review, 204n.29
'Forty Years in an Author's Life: A Dozen Letters (1876–1915) from Thomas Hardy', 214n.37
Fox, Charles James, 85
Fox, Stephen, *see* Ilchester, 1st Earl of
Fox-Strangways, Giles Stephen Holland, *see* Ilchester, 6th Earl of
Freud, Sigmund, 23, 48–9, 145, 205n.35, 206n.68; 207nn.69, 70, 71; 212n.53
Fussell, G. E., 205n.40

Gage, John, 87–8
Garwood, Helen, 211n.36
Gerber, Helmut E., 114, 210n.15
Gibson, James, *see Complete Poems of Thomas Hardy, The*
Gibson, Wilfred, 218n.130
Gittings, Robert, 158, 213n.7
Godwin, William, 165
Gosse, Edmund, 117, 141, 210n.18, 212n.46
Graphic, The, 76, 84, 169, 182, 183, 207n.11, 208n.26, 214n.35
'Grave by the Handpost, The', 157, *189*; 216nn.101, 102, 103

Graves, Robert, 213n.12
Grimm, J. L. K. and W. K., *see*
  'Fisherman and His Wife, The'
Group of Noble Dames, A, xii, *51–94*,
  95, 129, 157, 163, 164, 165, 171,
  175, 181–3 (publishing history),
  184, 193, 196–201 *passim*;
  207nn.8, 11, 14; 208nn.21, 22, 23,
  26, 27; 215n.81
Guerard, Albert J., 117, 210n.17,
  214n.31

Haggard, Rider, 45
Hand of Ethelberta, The, 155, 161, 162
Hardy, Emma Lavinia (1st wife),
  183, 208n.35, 215n.78
Hardy, Evelyn, 218n.134; *see also*
  One Rare Fair Woman and 'Plots
  for Five Unpublished Short
  Stories'
Hardy, Florence Emily (2nd wife),
  xii, 212n.51; *see also Early Life of
  Thomas Hardy, The* and *Later Years
  of Thomas Hardy, The*
Hardy, Jemima (mother), 139, 188,
  213n.68
Hardy, Thomas (father), 28, 139,
  148, 212n.56, 213n.68
Hardy, Thomas (grandfather), 139,
  148
Harper & Brothers, 51, 164, 181,
  183, 186, 194, 207n.1, 209n.52,
  214n.28, 215n.76
Harper's (New Monthly) Magazine,
  182, 207n.6
Harper's Weekly, 164; 208nn.30, 31;
  216n.101
Harris, Wendell V., 203n.2,
  218n.134
Hawthorne, Nathaniel, 19, 82, 116,
  133, 165, 170, 199, 208n.28,
  218n.138
Hay, Douglas, 206n.54
Hedgcock, F. A., 112, 210n.13
Hemingway, Ernest, 199–200
Henniker, Florence (Mrs Arthur),
  171, 182, 184, 185, 187, 194,
  209n.6; 214nn.47, 50; 215nn.72,
  84; 216nn.92, 99; 217nn.109, 115

'Her Death and After', 162
'Her Dilemma', 159
Herbert, Lucille, 206n.63
Hertford, Marquis of (William
  Seymour), 86
Hervey, William, 87–8
*History and Antiquities of the County of
  Dorset, The*, 51, 85, 86, 87–8, 130,
  184, 208–15 *passim*
'History of the Hardcomes, The',
  142, *144–5*, 150, 151–2, 172
Hobsbawm, Eric J., 206n.54
Hoffmann, E. T. A., 214n.33
Holder, Rev. Caddell, 208n.35
Holstrom, John, *see Thomas Hardy
  and His Readers*
Homer, 34, 78–9
'Honourable Laura, The', *83–4*, 85,
  90, 91, 129, 165, 183
Hornback, Bert G., 206n.55
Horner, Thomas, *see* Strangways-
  Horner, Thomas
Horsey, John, 215n.82
Household, The, 214n.38
'How I Built Myself a House', 157,
  158–9, 160, 173–4, 196
Howe, Irving, 38, 46, 199–200;
  206nn.53, 62; 218nn.140, 141
Howells, William Dean, 204n.25
Hutchins, John, *see History and An-
  tiquities of the County of Dorset, The*
Hyde, Edward, *see* Clarendon, 1st
  Earl of
Hynes, Samuel, 142; 212nn.49, 50;
  218n.136

Ibsen, Henrik, 82, 98, 120, 152–3,
  208n.29, 210n.10
Ilchester, 1st Earl of (Stephen Fox),
  85–6
Ilchester, 6th Earl of (Giles Stephen
  Holland   Fox-Strangways),
  207n.9; 208nn.37, 38; 209nn.40,
  42
'Imaginative Woman, An', *98–104*,
  108, 109, 120, 121, 152, 153, 154,
  162, 172, 174–5, 186, 193,
  209n.6; 210nn.7, 9, 10, 11
'Impulsive Lady of Croome Castle,

The', 163, 183; *see also* 'Duchess of Hamptonshire, The'

'Incident in the Life of Mr. George Crookhill', 142, *149*, 150

'Indiscretion in the Life of an Heiress, An', 157, *163–4*, 196, 214n.27

'Interlopers at the Knap', 2, 3, *33–7*, 40, 42, 47, 170, 181

'Intruder: A Legend of the Chronicle Office, The', 176, 214n.55; *see also* 'Waiting Supper, The'

'Jack and the Beanstalk', 163

'Jack the Giant Killer', 131, 163

James, Henry, 169

Johnson, Lionel, 213n.13

Johnstone, H. F. V., 128, 211n.33

Jolliffe, Captain Peter, 130

Journal of Mary Frampton, The, 186, 216n.98

Joyce, James, 127–8, 199–200, 211n.31

Joyce, Stanislaus, 211n.31

Jude the Obscure, xii, 57, 96, 106, 108, 113, 114, 157, 160, 185, 186

Kay-Robinson, Denys, 205n.39, 207n.2, 210n.19

Keily, Robert, 206n.61

Kermode, Frank, 204n.14

Kerr, Barbara, 205n.40

Kierkegaard, Soren, 139–40, 212n.45

'Lady Caroline (Afterwards Marchioness of Stonehenge), The', 183; *see also* 'Marchioness of Stonehenge, The',

'Lady Icenway, The', *69–74*, 84, 85, 90, 91, 92

'Lady Mottisfont', *66–9*, 78, 84, 85, 91, 183, 208n.32

'Lady Penelope, The', *78–80*, 84, 87–8 (historical sources), 90, 91, 92, 182, 183, 208n.32, 209n.48

Lane, John, 214n.36, 215n.88

Laodicean, A, 74, 89–90, 164, 168, 192

Later Years of Thomas Hardy, The, xii, 1–216 *passim*

Leavis, Q. D., 203n.2

'Legend of the Year Eighteen Hundred and Four, A', 14; *see also* 'Tradition of the Year Eighteen Hundred and Four, A'

'Leipzig', 162

Lerner, Laurence, *see Thomas Hardy and His Readers*

Life's Little Ironies, xii, 17, 20, 32, 82, *95–156*, 157, 159, 169, 171, 173, 174, 175, 180, 181, 184–6 (publishing history), 189, 190, 191, 193–4, 197–201 *passim*, 203n.8, 204n.30, 210n.25; 211nn.26, 27, 30, 38; 212n.55, 218n.142

Lincoln, Eleanor Terry, 204n.14

'Little Red Riding Hood', 167

Locker, Arthur, 183; 215nn.70, 71, 73, 74, 75, 77, 78

Lodge, David, 206nn.61, 63

Londonderry, Lady (Theresa, née Chetwynd-Talbott), 96

Longman's Magazine, 182

Lubbock, Percy, 199, 218n.139

Lynen, John F., 5, 7; 204nn.14, 16, 17, 19

Lytton, 1st Earl of (Edward Robert Lytton-Bulwer-Lytton), 51, 84, 207n.3, 208n.33

Macdonnell, Annie, 153, 212n.60

Macmillan, Sir Frederick, 216n.106; 217nn.116, 119, 120, 122, 123

Macmillan, Maurice, 217nn.114, 115, 116

Macmillan & Co., 180, 181, 194, 195, 196, 215n.61; 217nn.114, 116; *see also* Mellstock Edition, New Wessex Edition, and Wessex Edition

'Marchioness of Stonehenge, The', *62–6*, 67, 69, 84, 85, 91, 92, 183, 208n.20

Marston, Edward, 215n.63

Martin, Julia Augusta, 52

'Master John Horseleigh, Knight', 157, *184*; 215nn.81, 82

Matthews, Brander, 203n.2
Maugham, William Somerset, 203n.2
'Maumbry Ring', 206n.59
Mayor of Casterbridge, The, xii, 3, 28–9, 36, 45, 55, 113, 170, 171, 173, 181, 192, 205n.37, 206n.48
McDowall, Arthur S., 218n.134
'Melancholy Hussar of the German Legion, The', 2, 3, *16–21*, 27, 29, 40, 41–2, 45, 47, 175, 184–5, 190, 193–4; 203nn.8, 9
Mellstock Edition (Macmillan), 196
'Memoranda I' (notebook), 203n.11; 205nn.36, 39; 208n.36, 212n.54
'Memoranda II' (notebook), 204n.26, 216n.102
'Memories of Church Restoration', 45, 206n.57
'Mere Interlude, A', 157, *171–3*, 215n.60
Meredith, George, 159
Miller, J. Hillis, 206n.63, 212n.43
Millgate, Michael, 209n.54; 210nn.9, 10; 212n.58, 213n.9, 214n.34, 216n.104; 217nn.127, 128; *see also Collected Letters of Thomas Hardy, The*
Milton, John, 53, 119
Milton, Lord (Joseph Damer; later 1st Earl of Dorchester), 196
Minto, William, 218n.134
Moore, George, 62, 208n.16
Morning Chronicle, 203n.9
Morrell, Roy, 30–1, 56, 206n.50, 207n.7, 208n.19
Moule, Handley, 216n.105
Moule, Rev. Henry, 190, 193, 216n.105
Moynahan, Julian, 171, 214n.48
Mozart, Wolfgang Amadeus, 139–40
Murray's Magazine, 214n.55; 215nn.57, 58

National Review, 207n.15
'Netty Sargent's Copyhold', 142, *149–50*

'Neutral Tones', 159
Nevinson, Henry, 27, 205n.43
New Quarterly Magazine, 164, 214n.27
New Review, 96, 209n.2
New Spirit, 210n.10
New Wessex Edition (Macmillan), 196, 217n.129
New York Times, 161
Newbolt, Margaret, 45–6, 206n.60
Notebooks, 23, 85, 96, 97, 107, 113–14; *see also* 'Facts', 'Memoranda', 'Trumpet-Major Notebook', and *Personal Notebooks of Thomas Hardy, The*

O'Brien, Lady Susan, 52, 85
O'Connor, Frank, 203n.2, 218n.140
O'Connor, William Van, 206n.55
O'Faolain, Sean, 203n.2
'Old Andrey's Experiences as a Musician', 142, 143, *147–8*, 150
'Old Mrs. Chundle', 157–8, 196
'On the Application of Coloured Bricks and Terra Cotta to Modern Architecture', 158
'On the Western Circuit', *120–8*, 151, 154, 155–6, 169, 172, 174–5, 185, 198; 210nn.21, 23, 24, 25; 211nn.26, 28, 30
One Rare Fair Woman (eds Evelyn Hardy and F. B. Pinion), 209n.6, 214n.47; 215nn.72, 84; 216nn.92, 99; 217nn.109, 115
Orel, Harold, *see Thomas Hardy's Personal Writings*
Osgood, James R., 215n.66
Osgood, McIlvaine & Co., 183, 186; Wessex Novels Edition, 186, 193, 203n.8, 205n.41, 212n.55
'Our Exploits at West Poley', 157, *169–70*, 196; 214nn.38, 40, 41, 42, 43, 44

Page, Norman, 197, 210n.23, 218n.132
Pair of Blue Eyes, A, 148, 175
Pall Mall Gazette, 93; 207nn.2, 15; 209n.54

'Panthera', 205n.42
Pennie, J. F., 216n.102
Pentin, Rev. Canon Herbert, 217n.125
Perry Mason & Co., 214n.39
Personal Notebooks of Thomas Hardy, The (ed. Richard H. Taylor), 203nn.9, 11; 204nn.12, 26, 28; 205nn.36, 39; 208n.36, 212n.54, 214n.46; 216nn.98, 102
'Pied Piper, The', 135
Pinion, F. B., 215n.81; 217nn.125, 129; *see also One Rare Fair Woman*
'Plots for Five Unpublished Short Stories' (ed. Evelyn Hardy), 206n.64, 213n.14
Poe, Edgar Allan, 199, 218n.138
Poems of the Past and the Present, xii, 54
Poor Man and the Lady, The, 52, 159, 163
Portsmouth, 5th Earl of (Isaac Newton Wallop), 146
Procter, Mrs Anne Benson, 32
'Profitable Reading of Fiction, The', 1, 198–9, 203n.1, 218n.137
Prose Edda of Snorri Sturluson, The, 34, 42
Purdy, Richard Little, 162–217 *passim*
Pursuit of the Well-Beloved, The, see Well-Beloved, The

Queen, Ellery, 48, 206n.67
Quilter, Harry, 215n.86

Radcliffe, Mrs Ann, 22, 81
'Rapunzel', 105
Return of the Native, The, xii, 19, 63, 82, 148, 181, 192, 211n.40, 212n.44
'Rev. William Barnes, B. D., The', 205n.37
Richards, Mary Caroline, 20, 153, 204n.31, 212n.62
Richardson, Samuel, 174
Rivers, Mary, Countess of (née Kitson), 87
Roberts, James L., 204n.24

'Romantic Adventures of a Milkmaid, The', 157, 158, *166–9*, 182, 194; 214nn.33, 35
Rostand, Edmond, 210n.21
Rudé, George, 206n.54
Russell, Lady Anne, 86–7
Russell, William, *see* Bedford, 5th Earl of
Rutland, W. R., 210n.11

Saintsbury, George, 1, 203n.3
Sampson, Edward C., 211n.29
'San Sebastian', 103, 162
'Satires of Circumstance', 78, 98, 153, 189, 190
Schopenhauer, Arthur, 132, 211n.36
Scott, Sir Walter, 55, 57, 90, 112, 163, 174–5, 204n.18
Scribner's Magazine, 211n.38
Scribner's Sons, Charles, 216n.91
Second Shepherd's Play, The, 11
'Sergeant's Song, The', 162
Seymour, William, *see* Hertford, Marquis of
Shaftesbury, 5th Earl of (Anthony Ashley Cooper), 88
Shakespeare, William, 5, 23, 35, 37, 65, 81, 89, 97, 120, 166, 167, 177–8, 179, 215n.57
'Shame of the Halboroughs, The', 116; *see also* 'Tragedy of Two Ambitions, A'
Shaw, George Bernard, 110, 120, 152, 210n.22
Shelley, Percy Bysshe, 100–1
Sheridan, Richard Brinsley, 210n.21
Short Stories of Thomas Hardy, The (Macmillan), 196
Shorter, Clement K., 171, 216n.104
Snorri Sturluson, *see Prose Edda of Snorri Sturluson, The*
'Son's Veto, The', 38, 82, *104–9*, 113, 128, 151, 152, 154, 156, 172, 185
Spectator, The, 62, 207n.15
'Spectre of the Real, The', 214n.50
'Squire Petrick's Lady', *74–6*, 78, 84,

'Squire Petrick's Lady' (*Contd.*)
88–9 (historical sources), 91, 92, 102–3, 162
Stephen, Leslie, 22, 180–1, 205n.33, 215n.62
Stewart, J. I. M., 208n.18
Strafford, 1st Earl of (Thomas Wentworth), 87
Strangways-Horner, Elizabeth (later 1st Countess of Ilchester), 85–6
Strangways-Horner, Susannah, 57, 85–6
Strangways-Horner, Thomas, 85–6
'Superstitious Man's Story, The', 142, *145–6*, 150

Talbot, Lady Elizabeth, 186
Taylor, Richard H., *see Personal Notebooks of Thomas Hardy, The*
Tess of the d'Urbervilles, xii, 24, 52, 73, 74, 82, 84, 96, 106, 108, 113, 122, 163, 166, 171, 181, 183, 192, 205n.37, 208n.25, 212n.44
Thackeray, William Makepeace, 154–5, 158, 207n.10; 213nn.64, 65, 66, 67
'Thieves Who Couldn't Help Sneezing, The', 157, *163*, 169, 196; 213nn.25, 26
Thomas, David St John, 205n.46
Thomas Hardy and His Readers (eds). Laurence Lerner and John Holstrom, 207n.2
Thomas Hardy's Personal Writings (ed. Harold Orel), 203nn.1, 4, 6, 7; 204nn.20, 21, 22; 205n.37; 206nn.57, 58, 59; 209n.5; 213nn.6, 8; 214n.32, 218n.137
'Three Strangers, The', 2, 3, *6–12*, 21, 37, 40–1, 42–3, 47, 89, 165, 166, 181, 190–1, 198, 204n.18
Times, The, 216n.102
Times Literary Supplement, 217n.111
Tinsley, William, 160, 161; 213nn.15, 17
'To Please His Wife', 95, *128–32*, 148, 151, 156, 185, 211n.35
'Tony Kytes, the Arch-Deceiver',
142, *143–4*, 145, 150, 151
'Too Late Beloved', 208n.25; *see also Tess of the d'Urbervilles*
'Tradition of Eighteen Hundred and Four, A', 2, 3, *12–16*, 21, 43, 46, 48, 165, 185, 188, 193, 196, 197, 204n.28
'Tragedy of Two Ambitions, A', 82, 106, *113–20*, 128, 129, 151, 152, 154, 156, 172, 175, 176, 184–5, 198; 210nn.15, 16, 20
'Tree of Knowledge, The', 209n.2
Trenchard, George, 87–8
True Briton, 216n.98
Trumpet-Major, The, xii, 3, 162, 163, 186
'Trumpet-Major Notebook, The', 3, 203n.9; 204nn.12, 28; 216n.98
'Tryst at an Ancient Earthwork, A', 157, *170–1*, 173
Twain, Mark, 12, 169–70, 204n.25
'Two Men, The', 159
Two on a Tower, xii, 173, 175–6

Udal, John Symonds, 205n.39, 206n.65, 216n.100
Under the Greenwood Tree, xii, 8, 138–9, 141, 148, 149, 212n.42
Universal Review, 184–5, 210n.20

'Valenciennes', 162
Voltaire, F. M. Arouet de, 94

'Waiting Supper, The', 157, 158, 172, *175–80*, 195; 214nn.53, 55; 215nn.57, 58
Wallace, William, 67–8, 207–8n.15, 208n.24
Wallop, Isaac Newton, *see* Portsmouth, 5th Earl of
Walpole, Robert (later 1st Earl of Orford), 85–6
Walters, Peter, 88–9
Webb, Barbara, 88
Weber, Carl J., 203n.9, 214n.55; 217nn.113, 125
Wedmore, Frederick, 218n.136
Weismann, August, 210n.11
Well-Beloved, The, 180, 185, 213n.1

Wells, H. G., 203n.2

Wentworth, Thomas, *see* Strafford, 1st Earl of

Wessex Edition (Macmillan), xii, 51, 193–4, 195, 196

'Wessex Folk', 151, 186; *see also* 'Few Crusted Characters, A'

Wessex Novels Edition, *see* Osgood, McIlvaine

Wessex Tales, xii, *1–50*, 51, 52, 54, 95, 133, 143, 157, 159, 160, 164, 172, 175, 180–1 (publishing history), 184, 186, 188–201 *passim*, 203–4n.11, 204–5n.32; 205nn.41, 47

Weygandt, Cornelius, 218n.136

'What the Shepherd Saw', 157, *164–6*, 217n.114

Williams, Raymond, 49, 207n.72

Wing, George, 173, 214n.52, 218n.130

Winslow, Cal, 206n.54

'Winters and the Palmleys, The', 141–2, 143, *148–9*, 150, 151, 205n.44, 212n.56

Wise, Thomas James, *see Ashley Library, The*

'Withered Arm, The', 2, 3, *21–8*, 29, 40, 42, 43, 45, 47, 48, 49, 89, 161, 175, 181, 198, 203n.10, 204–5n.32; 205nn.37, 38, 39, 40, 41, 42, 44, 45; 205–6n.47, 212n.56

'Woman of Imagination, A', 98; *see also* 'Imaginative Woman, An'

Woodlanders, The, xii, 19, 78, 96, 113, 136, 149, 152, 160, 176, 181

Wright, Walter F., 211n.36

'Writer of the Letters, The', 211n.28; *see also* 'On the Western Circuit'

Youth's Companion, The, 169, 214n.38